The Snowden Files

Luke Harding is a journalist, writer and award-winning foreign correspondent with the *Guardian*. Between 2007 and 2011 he was the *Guardian*'s bureau chief in Moscow. The Kremlin expelled him from the country in the first case of its kind since the cold war, in part because of his ⁀rting on Alexander Litvinenko's murder.

He ıs the author of five non-fiction books: *The Snowden Files: The Inside Story of the World's Most Wanted Man*; *Mafia State: How One Reporter Became an Enemy of the Brutal New Russia*; *WikiLeaks: Inside Julian Assange's War on Secrecy*; *The Liar: The Fall of Jonathan Aitken* (the last two co-written with David Leigh) and *A Very Expensive Poison: The Definitive Story of the Murder of Litvinenko and Russia's War with the West*.

Two have been made into Hollywood movies. Dreamworks' *The Fifth Estate*, based on *WikiLeaks*, was released in 2013. Director Oliver Stone's biopic *Snowden*, adapted from *The Snowden Files*, appeared in 2016. In 2014, Luke was awarded the James Cameron prize. His books have been ⁀⁀⁀⁀⁀⁀ five languages. Luke lives near ⁀⁀⁀⁀⁀ elance journalist Phoebe ⁀⁀⁀

Further praise for *The Snowden* ⁀⁀⁀

'This is the stuff ⁀⁀⁀⁀⁀⁀⁀⁀⁀⁀ novels are made.' *L*⁀

'Without ⁀⁀⁀⁀⁀⁀⁀ on,

THE SNOWDEN FILES

The Inside Story of the World's Most Wanted Man

LUKE HARDING

First published in 2014
by Faber & Faber, Bloomsbury House, 74–77 Great Russell Street,
London WC1B 3DA

Published with Guardian Books
Guardian Books is an imprint of Guardian Newspapers Ltd
www.guardianbooks.co.uk

This paperback edition published in 2016

Typeset by seagulls.net
Printed in England by CPI Group (UK) Ltd, Croydon, CR0 4YY

A CIP record for this book is available from the British Library

978–1783–35104–6

Contents

Foreword

Edward Snowden is one of the most extraordinary whistleblowers in history. Never before has anyone scooped up en masse the top-secret files of the world's most powerful intelligence organisations, in order to make them public. But that was what he did.

His skills are unprecedented. Until the present generation of computer nerds came along, no one realised it was possible to make off with the electronic equivalent of whole libraries full of triple-locked filing cabinets and safes – thousands of documents and millions of words.

His motives are remarkable. Snowden set out to expose the true behaviour of the US National Security Agency and its allies. On present evidence, he has no interest in money – although he could have sold his documents to foreign intelligence services for many, many millions. Nor does he have the kind of left-wing or Marxist sentiments which could lead to him being depicted as unAmerican. On the contrary, he is an enthusiast for the American constitution, and, like other fellow 'hacktivists', is a devotee of libertarian politician Ron Paul, whose views are well to the right of many Republicans.

What Snowden has revealed is important. His files show that the methods of the intelligence agencies that carry out electronic eavesdropping have spiralled out of control, largely thanks to the political panic in the US which followed the terrorist attacks of 9/11.

Let off the legal leash and urged to make America safe, the NSA and its British junior partner, the Government Communications Headquarters, GCHQ (secretly allied with the internet and telecommunications giants who control the hardware), have used all their technical skills to 'master the internet'. That is their phrase, not ours. Democratic control has been vague, smothered in secrecy and plainly inadequate.

The result has been a world that is spied on. The technologies that the west has trumpeted as forces for individual freedom and democracy – Google, Skype, mobile phones, GPS, YouTube, Tor, e-commerce, internet banking and all the rest – are turning into machines for surveillance that would have astonished George Orwell, the author of *1984*.

The *Guardian* was, I am glad to say, first among the free press to publish Snowden's revelations. We saw it as our duty to break the taboos of secrecy, with due regard, as Snowden himself wanted, to the safety of individuals and the protection of genuinely sensitive intelligence material.

I am proud we did so: fierce debate and demands for reform have been now launched across the world – in the US itself, in Germany, France, Brazil, Indonesia, Canada, Australia, even in deferential Britain. The *Guardian* was eventually forced to publish from the safety of its New York division, because of British legal harassment. I think that readers of this book might well see the value of introducing a UK equivalent to the first amendment of the US constitution, which protects the freedom of the press. It is a freedom that can protect us all.

Alan Rusbridger
Editor-in-chief, *Guardian*
London, February 2014

Prologue: The Rendezvous

Mira Hotel, Nathan Road, Hong Kong
Monday 3 June 2013

'I don't want to live in a world where everything
that I say, everything I do, everyone I talk to,
every expression of creativity or love or
friendship is recorded ...'
EDWARD SNOWDEN

It began with an email.

'I am a senior member of the intelligence community ...'

No name, no job title, no details. The *Guardian* columnist Glenn Greenwald, who was based in Brazil, started to correspond with this mysterious source. Who was he? The source said nothing about himself. He was an intangible presence, an online ghost. Possibly even a fiction.

After all, how could it be real? There had never before been a big leak out of the National Security Agency. Everybody knew that America's foremost intelligence-gathering organisation, based at Fort Meade near Washington DC, was impregnable. What the NSA did was a secret. Nothing got out. 'NSA, No Such Agency', as the Beltway wits had it.

Yet this strange person did appear to have access to some remarkable top-secret documents. The source was sending Greenwald a sample of highly classified NSA files, dangling them in front of his nose. How the ghost purloined them with such apparent ease was a mystery. Assuming they were genuine, they appeared to blow the lid off a story of global importance. They suggested the White House wasn't just spying on its enemies (bad guys, al-Qaida, terrorists, the Russians), or even on its supposed allies (Germany, France), but on the communications of millions of private US citizens.

Joined with the US in this mass snooping exercise was the UK. The NSA's British counterpart, GCHQ, was based deep in the English countryside. The UK and USA had a close intelligence-sharing relationship dating back to the second world war. To the uncharitable, Britain was the US's reliable poodle. Alarmingly, the documents revealed that the NSA was stumping up millions of dollars for British surveillance activities.

And now Greenwald was about to meet his Deep Throat. Promising further disclosures, the source was summoning him to fly from his home in Rio de Janeiro to Hong Kong, run by communist China and thousands of miles away. Greenwald felt the location was 'bizarre' and confusing: did he have a senior foreign posting there?

The rendezvous was to be in Kowloon's Mira Hotel, a chic, modern edifice in the heart of the tourist district, and a short cab ride away from the Star Ferry to Hong Kong Island. Accompanying Greenwald was

Laura Poitras, also an American citizen, documentary film-maker and notable thorn in the side of the US military. She had been a matchmaker, the first to point Greenwald in the ghost's direction.

The two journalists were given meticulous instructions. They were to meet in a less-trafficked, but not entirely obscure, part of the hotel, next to a large plastic alligator. They would swap pre-agreed phrases. The source would carry a Rubik's cube. Oh, and his name was Edward Snowden.

It appeared the mystery interlocutor was an experienced spy. Perhaps one with a flair for the dramatic. Everything Greenwald knew about him pointed in one direction: that he was a grizzled veteran of the intelligence community. 'I thought he must be a pretty senior bureaucrat,' Greenwald says. Probably 60-odd, wearing a blue blazer with shiny gold buttons, receding grey hair, sensible black shoes, spectacles, a club tie ... Greenwald could visualise him already. Perhaps he was the CIA's station chief in Hong Kong; the mission was down the road.

This theory, mistaken as it was, was based on two clues: the very privileged level of top-secret access the source appeared to enjoy, and the sophistication of his political analysis. With the very first batch of secrets the source had sent a personal manifesto. It offered his motive – to reveal the extent of what he regarded as the 'suspicion-less' surveillance state. It claimed the technology to spy on people had run way beyond the law. Meaningful oversight had become impossible.

The scale of the NSA's ambition was extraordinary, the source said. Over the past decade the volume of digital information coursing between continents had increased. Exploded, even. Against this backdrop the agency had drifted from its original mission of foreign intelligence gathering. Now, it was collecting data on everybody. And storing it. This included data from both the US and abroad. The NSA was secretly engaged in nothing less than electronic mass observation. Or so the source had said.

The pair reached the alligator ahead of schedule. They sat down. They waited. Greenwald briefly pondered whether the alligator had some significance in Chinese culture. He wasn't sure. Nothing happened. The source didn't show. Strange.

If the initial meeting failed, the plan was to return later the same morning to the same anonymous corridor, running between the Mira's glitzy internal shopping mall and one of its restaurants. Greenwald and Poitras came back. They waited for a second time.

And then they saw him – a pale, spindle-limbed, nervous, preposterously young man. In Greenwald's shocked view, he was barely old enough to shave. He was dressed in a white T-shirt and jeans. In his right hand he was carrying a scrambled Rubik's cube. Had there been a mistake? 'He looked like he was 23. I was completely discombobulated. None of it made sense,' Greenwald says.

The young man – if indeed he were the source – had sent encrypted instructions as to how the initial verification would proceed:

POITRAS: What time does the restaurant open?

THE SOURCE: At noon. But don't go there, the food sucks ...

The exchange was faintly comic. Greenwald – nervous – said his lines, struggling to keep a straight face.

Snowden then said simply: 'Follow me.' The three walked silently towards the lift. No one else was around – or, at least, nobody they could see. They rode to the first floor, and followed the cube-man to room 1014. He opened the door with his swipe card, and they entered. 'I went with it,' Greenwald says.

It was already a weird mission. But now it had acquired the feel of a wild-goose chase. This thin-framed student type was surely too callow to have access to super-sensitive material? Optimistically, Greenwald speculated that possibly he was the son of the source, or his personal assistant. If not, then the encounter was a waste of time, a hoax of Jules Verne proportions.

Poitras, too, had been secretly communicating with the source for four months. She felt she knew him – or at least the online version of him. She was also struggling to adjust. 'I nearly fainted when I saw how old he was. It took me 24 hours to rewire my brain.'

Over the course of the day, however, Snowden told his story. He was, he said, a 29-year-old contractor with the National Security Agency. He had been based at the NSA's regional operations centre in Kunia on the Pacific island of Hawaii. Two weeks ago he had quit his job, effectively abandoned and bid farewell to his girlfriend, and secretly boarded a flight to Hong Kong. He had taken with him four laptops.

The laptops were heavily encrypted. But from them Snowden had access to documents taken from NSA and GCHQ's internal servers. Tens of thousands of documents, in fact. Most were stamped 'Top Secret'. Some were marked 'Top Secret Strap 1' – the British higher tier of super-classification for intercept material – or even 'Strap 2', which was almost as secret as you could get. No one – apart from a restricted circle of security officials – had ever seen documents of this kind before. What he was carrying, Snowden indicated, was the biggest intelligence leak in history.

Greenwald noticed the accumulated debris of many days of room service – trays, abandoned bowls of noodles, dirty cutlery. Snowden said he had ventured out just three times since checking into the Mira under his own name a fortnight earlier. He sat on the bed as Greenwald bombarded him with questions: where did you work, who was your boss in the CIA, why? Greenwald's credibility was on the line. So was that of his editors at the *Guardian*. Yet if Snowden were genuine, at any moment a CIA SWAT team could burst into the room, confiscate his laptops, and drag him away.

Snowden, they began to feel certain, was no fake. His information could well be real. And his reasons for becoming a whistleblower were cogent, too. His job as a systems administrator meant – he explained lucidly, persuasively, coolly – that he had a rare overview of the

NSA's extraordinary surveillance capacities, that he could see the dark places where the agency was going.

The NSA could bug 'anyone', from the president downwards, he said. In theory the spy agency was supposed to collect only signals intelligence on foreign targets, known as SIGINT. In practice this was a joke, Snowden told Greenwald: it was already hoovering up metadata from millions of Americans. Phone records, email headers, subject lines, seized without acknowledgement or consent. From this you could construct a complete electronic narrative of an individual's life – their friends, their lovers, their joys, their sorrows.

Together with GCHQ, the NSA had secretly attached intercepts to the undersea fibre-optic cables that ringed the world. This allowed the US and UK to read much of the globe's communications. Secret courts were compelling telecoms providers to hand over data. What's more, pretty much all of Silicon Valley was involved with the NSA, Snowden said – Google, Microsoft, Facebook, even Steve Jobs's Apple. The NSA claimed it had 'direct access' to the tech giants' servers.

While giving themselves unprecedented surveillance powers, the US intelligence community was concealing the truth about its activities, Snowden said. If James Clapper, the director of national intelligence, had deliberately lied to Congress about the NSA's programs, he had committed a felony. The NSA was flagrantly violating the US constitution and the right to privacy. It had even put secret back doors into online encryption software – used to make secure bank payments – weakening the system for everybody.

As Snowden told the story, the NSA's behaviour seemed culled from 20th-century dystopian fiction. It was recognisable from the writings of Aldous Huxley or George Orwell. But the NSA's ultimate goal seemed to go even further: to collect everything from everybody, everywhere and to store it indefinitely. It signalled a turning point. It looked like the extirpation of privacy. The spy agencies had hijacked the internet – once a platform for individuality and self-expression. Snowden used the word 'panopticon'. This was a significant coinage by the 18th-century British philosopher and codifier Jeremy Bentham. It described an ingenious circular jail where the warders could see the prisoners at all times, without their knowing if they were being observed.

And this, Snowden asserted, was why he had decided to go public. To throw away his life and career. He told Greenwald he didn't want to live in a world 'where everything that I say, everything that I do, everyone I talk to, every expression of love or friendship is recorded'.

Over the coming weeks, Snowden's claims would ignite an epochal debate. They would enrage the White House and Downing Street. And they would cause international havoc, as Snowden slipped out of Hong Kong, attempted to gain asylum in Latin America, and got stuck in Vladimir Putin's Moscow.

In America and Europe (though not at first in the Britain of James Bond), there was a spirited argument about the right balance between security and civil liberties, between freedom of speech and privacy. Despite the febrile polarisation of US politics, right-wing libertarians and left-wing Democrats joined together to support Snowden. Even President Obama conceded the debate was overdue and reform was required. Though this didn't stop US authorities from cancelling Snowden's passport, charging him with espionage and demanding his return from Russia.

The fight to publish Snowden's story was to present the journalists themselves with dramatic problems – legal, logistical, editorial. It pitted a famous newspaper, its global website and a few media allies against some of the most powerful people on the planet. And it would lead to the destruction of the *Guardian*'s computer hard drives in an underground basement, watched over by two British GCHQ boffins. The machine-smashing was to be a particularly surreal episode in the history of western journalism and its battles against the state.

As he sat in his Hong Kong hotel room, throwing the switch to launch all this, Snowden was calm. According to Greenwald, he was convinced of the rightness of his actions, intellectually, emotionally and psychologically. In the aftermath of his leaks, Snowden recognised imprisonment would surely follow. But during that momentous summer he radiated a sense of tranquility and equanimity. He had reached a rock-like place of inner certainty. Here, nothing could touch him.

1

TheTrueHOOHA

Ellicott City, near Baltimore
December 2001

'Nothing at last is sacred but the integrity
of one's own mind.'
RALPH WALDO EMERSON,
'Self-Reliance', *Essays: First Series*

In late December 2001, someone calling themselves
'TheTrueHOOHA' had a question. TheTrueHOOHA
was an 18-year-old American male, an avid gamer, with
impressive IT skills and a sharp intelligence. His real
identity was unknown. But then everyone who posted
on Ars Technica, a popular technology website, did so
anonymously. Most contributors were young men. All
were passionately attached to the internet.

TheTrueHOOHA wanted tips on how to set up
his own web server. It was a Saturday morning, a little
after 11am local time. He posted: 'It's my first time. Be
gentle. Here's my dilemma: I want to be my own host.
What do I need?'

Soon Ars's regular users were piling in with helpful
suggestions. Hosting your own web server wasn't a
big deal, but did require a Pentium 200 computer,
at least, plenty of memory and decent bandwidth.

TheTrueHOOHA liked these answers. He replied: 'Ah, the vast treasury of geek knowledge that is Ars.' At 2am he was still online (albeit rather tired: 'Yawn. Bedtime, gotta rise up early for more geek stuff tomorrow, ya know,' he wrote).

TheTrueHOOHA may have been an Ars novice. But his replies were fluent and self-assured. 'If I sound like a belligerent, self-important, 18-year-old upstart with no respect for his elders, you are probably onto something,' he typed. He took a dim view of his teachers, apparently, writing: 'Community colleges don't have the brightest professors, you know.'

TheTrueHOOHA would become a prolific Ars contributor. Over the next eight years he authored nearly 800 comments. He chatted frequently on other forums, too, especially #arsificial. Who was he? He appeared to do a wide variety of jobs; he described himself variously as 'unemployed', a failed soldier, a 'systems editor', and someone who had US State Department security clearance.

Was there a touch of Walter Mitty? His home was on the east coast of America in the state of Maryland, near Washington DC. But by his mid-twenties he was already an international man of mystery. He popped up in Europe – in Geneva, London, Ireland (a nice place, apparently, apart from the 'socialism problem'), Italy and Bosnia. He travelled to India.

TheTrueHOOHA kept mum about what exactly he did. But there were clues. Despite having no degree, he knew an astonishing amount about computers, and seemed to spend most of his life online. Something of an autodidact, then. His politics appeared staunchly Republican. He believed strongly in personal liberty, defending, for example, Australians who farmed cannabis plants.

At times he could be rather obnoxious. He told one fellow-Arsian, for example, that he was a 'cock'; others who disagreed with his sink-or-swim views on social security were 'fucking retards'. Even by the free-for-all standards of chat rooms – much like a bar where anybody could pull up a stool – TheTrueHOOHA was an opinionated kind of guy.

Other users never learned TheTrueHOOHA's off-screen name. They did glimpse what he looked like, though. In April 2006, a couple of months shy of his 23rd birthday, TheTrueHOOHA posted photos of himself, taken at an amateur modelling shoot. They show a handsome young man, with pale skin and delicately bruised eyes, somewhat vampiric in appearance, staring moodily into the camera. In one shot, he wears a strange leather bracelet.

'Cute,' one user posted. 'No love for the wristband eh?' TheTrueHOOHA queried, when someone said he looked gay. He insisted he was heterosexual. And added casually: 'My girlfriend is a photographer.'

TheTrueHOOHA's chat logs cover a colourful array of themes: gaming, girls, sex, Japan, the stock market, his disastrous stint in the US army, his impressions of multi-racial Britain, the joys of gun ownership. ('I have a Walther P22. It's my only gun but I love it to death,' he wrote in 2006.) In their own way, the logs form a *Bildungsroman*, a novel of youthful experience, written by someone from the first generation that grew up with the internet.

Then in 2009 the entries fizzle away. Something happens. The early exuberance disappears; the few last posts are dark and brooding. An edge of bitterness creeps in. In February 2010 he makes one of his final posts. TheTrueHOOHA mentions a thing that troubles him: pervasive government surveillance. He writes:

Society really seems to have developed an unquestioning obedience towards spooky types.

I wonder how well would envelopes that became transparent under magical federal candlelight have sold in 1750? 1800? 1850? 1900? 1950? Did we get to where we are today via a slippery slope that was entirely within our control to stop? Or was it a relatively instantaneous sea change that sneaked in undetected because of pervasive government secrecy?

TheTrueHOOHA's last post is on 21 May 2012. After that he disappears, a lost electronic signature amid the vastness of cyberspace. But a year later, as we now know, TheTrueHOOHA, aka Edward Snowden, travels to Hong Kong.

Edward Joseph Snowden was born on 21 June 1983. Friends know him as 'Ed'. His father Lonnie Snowden and mother Elizabeth – known as Wendy – were high-school sweethearts who married at 18. Lon was an officer in the US coast guard; Snowden spent his early years in Elizabeth City, along North Carolina's coast, where the coast guard has its biggest air and naval base. He has an older sister, Jessica. Like other members of the US forces, Snowden Snr has strong patriotic views. He is a conservative. And a libertarian.

But he is also a thoughtful conservative. Snowden's father is articulate, well-read and quotes the works of the poet Ralph Waldo Emerson, who advocated a man adhering to his own principles against the dictates of a corrupt state. On joining the coast guard, Lon Snowden swore an oath to uphold the US constitution and the Bill of Rights. He meant it. For him the oath was not just a series of empty phrases: it underpinned the solemn American contract between a citizen and the state.

When Snowden was small – a boy with thick blond hair and a toothy smile – he and his family moved to Maryland, within DC's commuter belt. Snowden went to primary and middle schools in Crofton, Anne Arundel County, a town of pleasant villas between DC and Baltimore. Neither of Snowden's former schools is visually alluring; both look like windowless brick bunkers. (The first, at least, has a garden with shrubs, butterflies and a stand-alone plane tree next to the car park.) In his mid-teens, Snowden moved on to nearby Arundel High, which he attended for one and a half years.

As his father recalls, Snowden's education went wrong when he fell ill, probably with glandular fever. He missed 'four or five months' of class. Another factor hurt his studies: his parents were drifting apart. Their troubled marriage was on its last legs, and he failed to finish high school. In 1999, aged 16, Snowden enrolled at Anne Arundel Community College. The college's sprawling campus boasts baseball and football stadiums and the sporting motto: 'You can't hide that wildcat pride.'

Snowden took computer courses, and later earned his GED (General Educational Development), a high-school diploma equivalent. But his failure to complete high school would be a source of lingering embarrassment and defensiveness. In February 2001, Snowden's mother filed for divorce. It came through three months later.

In the aftermath of this messy break-up, Snowden lived with a room-mate, and then with his mother, in Ellicott City, just west of Baltimore. His mother's home is situated in a self-contained housing development named Woodland Village, with its own swimming pool and tennis court. Her grey two-storey town house is next to a grassy slope. There is a children's playground; geraniums and hostas grow in the yards; middle-aged ladies can be seen walking large, glossy dogs. It is a friendly place. Neighbours recall seeing Snowden through the open curtains, usually at work on his computer.

The town in which they lived was named after Andrew Ellicott, a Quaker who emigrated from England in 1730. In the late 18th century, Ellicott City was a prosperous place, with flour mills on the east bank of the river, and sturdy houses of dark local granite. There was even a British cannon. Baltimore, with its port, was nearby. By the 21st century, the mills were long gone, or turned into heritage sites. In some cases they had been literally washed away. The main local employer in Maryland now was the federal government. Washington DC was a short commute away.

Snowden grew up under the giant shadow of one government agency in particular. From his mother's front door it takes 15 minutes to drive there. Half way between Washington and Baltimore, the agency is strictly off limits. It clearly has a secret function. Half-hidden by trees is a giant green cube-shaped building. Curious antennae dot the roof. There is an enormous car park, a vast power station and a white, golf ball-like radome. Inside are satellite dishes. There are electrified fences and an atmosphere of heavy-duty security. An entrance sign off the Baltimore–Washington Parkway reads: 'NSA next right. Employees only.'

This discreet metropolis is the headquarters of the National Security Agency (NSA), the US's foreign signals spying organisation since 1952. As a teenager, Snowden knew all about the NSA. His college was practically next door. Many of his mother's neighbours worked there. They set off by car every morning, through rolling green Maryland countryside, returning from the 1,000-acre complex at Fort Meade every evening. The Puzzle Palace, or SIGINT city, as it is known, employs 40,000 people. It is the largest hirer of mathematicians in the United States.

For Snowden, however, the likelihood of joining this crepuscular government world was remote. In his early twenties, his focus was on computers more generally. To him, the internet was 'the most important invention in all human history'. He chatted online to people 'with all sorts of views that I would never have encountered on my own'. He spent days surfing the net and playing Tekken, a Japanese role-play game. He wasn't only a nerd: he kept fit, practised kung fu and, according to one entry on Ars, 'dated Asian girls'.

But he recognised that this didn't really add up to much of a career. In 2003, he posts: 'I'm an MCSE [Microsoft Certified Solutions Expert] without degree or clearance who lives in Maryland. Read that as unemployed.'

Snowden's father, meanwhile, had moved to Pennsylvania. He was about to re-marry.

The 2003 US-led invasion of Iraq prompted Snowden to think seriously about a career in the military. Like his father – who ended up spending three decades in the US coast guard – Snowden says he had the urge to serve his country. 'I wanted to fight in the Iraq war because I felt like I had an obligation as a human being to help free people from oppression.' His motives seem idealistic, and in line with President George W Bush's then-stated goals for the overthrow of Saddam Hussein.

Snowden thought about joining the US special forces. The military offered what seemed, on the face of it, an attractive scheme, whereby recruits with no prior experience could try out to become elite soldiers. In May 2004 he took the plunge and enlisted. He reported to Fort Benning in Georgia, a large US military camp. The scheme meant eight to 10 weeks' basic training, then an advanced infantry course. Finally there was an assessment of suitability for special forces.

His spell in the US military was a disaster. Snowden was in good physical shape but an improbable soldier. He was short-sighted, with -6.50/-6.25 vision. ('My visual acuity ends at about four inches from my eyes, and my optometrist always has a good laugh at me,' he posted.) He also had unusually narrow feet. 'It took 45 minutes for the civilians in Ft. Benning to find combat boots that would fit me,' he tells Ars – an episode that ended in an unpleasant reprimand from his drill sergeant.

Few of his new army colleagues, he maintained, shared his sense of noble purpose, or his desire to help oppressed citizens throw off their chains. Instead, his superiors merely wanted to shoot people. Preferably Muslims. 'Most of the people training us seemed pumped up about killing Arabs, not helping anyone,' he says.

Then during infantry training he broke both his legs. After more than a month's uncertainty, the army finally discharged him.

Back in Maryland, he got a job as a 'security specialist' at the University for Maryland's Center for Advanced Study of Language. It was 2005. (He appears to have begun as a security guard, but then moved back into IT.) Snowden was working at a covert NSA facility on the university's campus. Thanks perhaps to his brief military history, he had broken into the world of US intelligence, albeit on a low rung. The Center worked closely with the US intelligence community – or IC as it styled itself – providing advanced language training.

Snowden may have lacked a degree, but in mid-2006 he landed a job in information technology at the CIA. He was rapidly learning that his exceptional IT skills opened all kinds of interesting government doors. 'First off, the degree thing is crap, at least domestically. If you "really" have 10 years of solid, provable IT experience … you CAN get a very well-paying IT job,' he writes in July 2006. 'I have no degree, nor even a high school diploma, but I'm making much more than what they're paying you even though I'm only claiming six years of experience. It's tough to "break in", but once you land a "real" position, you're made.'

Snowden had figured out that US government service offered exciting possibilities including foreign travel and generous perks. You didn't need to be James Bond – merely apply for a 'standard IT specialist position'. He describes the State Department as 'the place to be right now'.

One of the perks was access to classified information: 'Yeah, working in IT for the State Department guarantees you'll have to have Top Secret clearance.' He also offers tips on career strategy. State was 'understaffed right now'. He goes on: 'Europe posts are competitive, but you can get in the door much easier if you express an interest in going to near-east hellholes. Once you're in, tough out the crappy tour and you should be able to pick from a list of preferred posts.' Later he remarks, 'Thank god for wars.'

Snowden's job-hopping worked for him personally. In 2007 the CIA sent him to Geneva in Switzerland on his first foreign tour. He was 24. His new job was to maintain security for the CIA's computer network and look after computer security for US diplomats based at the Geneva mission (the diplomats may have been high-powered but many had only a basic understanding of the internet). He was a telecommunications information systems officer. He also had to maintain the heating and air-conditioning.

Switzerland was an awakening and an adventure. It was the first time Snowden had lived abroad. Geneva was a hub for all sorts of spies – American, Russian and others. It hid commercial and diplomatic secrets. The city was home to a large community of bankers, as well as several UN secretariats and the HQs of multinational companies; about a third of its residents were foreigners. It was genteel, sedate and organised. Most of its residents were wealthy but a migrant underclass lived here too. (Snowden expressed amazement at how down-at-heel Nigerians swiftly mastered Switzerland's numerous languages.)

The US mission where Snowden had diplomatic cover was in the centre of town – a 1970s glass and concrete block, accessed via a wrought-iron gate and protected by a hedge and wall. The Russian mission was close by. Snowden lived in a comfortable four-bedroom US government flat directly overlooking the River Rhône, at 16 Quai du Seujet, in the Saint-Jean Falaises part of town. In terms of lifestyle, the posting was hard to beat. A few blocks east was Lake Geneva, where the US ambassador had his residence. Not far away were the Alps and the challenges of climbing, skiing and hiking.

The Ars Technica logs paint a portrait of a young man who, initially at least, still viewed the world through a provincial US prism. To begin with, Snowden had mixed feelings about the Swiss. In one chat he complains of high prices ('you guys wouldn't believe how expensive shit is here'), the lack of tap water in restaurants, and the exorbitant cost of hamburgers – $15.

There were other moments of culture shock, over the metric system and Swiss affluence ('Jesus Christ are the Swiss rich. The fucking McDonald's workers make more money than I do,' he exclaims). But in general he warms to his new picturesque surroundings. In one exchange he writes:

\<TheTrueHOOHA\>   the roads are 35 inches wide

\<TheTrueHOOHA\>   with 9000 cars on them, two tram tracks, and a bus lane

\<TheTrueHOOHA\>   and a bike lane

\<TheTrueHOOHA\>   i imagine mirrors get clipped off all the time

\<TheTrueHOOHA\>   I'm afraid I'd bump into someone and have to pay for it.

\<User3\>   do they have a large immigrant population doing the lower-class work?

<TheTrueHOOHA>   Yeah. Lots of unidentifiable southeast asian people and eastern europeans who don't speak french or english

<TheTrueHOOHA>   but don't get me wrong -- this place is amazing

<TheTrueHOOHA>   it's like living in a postcard

<TheTrueHOOHA>   it's just nightmarishly expensive and horrifically classist

<User4>   TheTrueHOOHA: where are you? .ch?

<TheTrueHOOHA>   Yeah. Geneva, Switzerland

<User4>   wicked!

<TheTrueHOOHA>   Yeah… it's pretty cool so far

In Geneva Snowden was exposed to an eclectic range of influences. He took part in Chinese New Year celebrations with his martial arts club. According to *Der Spiegel* Snowden participated in similar celebrations in Washington. At his flat in Geneva he hung a bar from the roof and kept fit by doing pull-ups. 'He once gave me a one-on-one martial arts lesson, and I was surprised by his abilities – and very amused that he seemed unable to go very easy on a newbie,' Mavanee Anderson, a friend in Geneva, wrote in Tennessee's *Chattanooga Times Free Press*.

Snowden worked in a protected part of the US mission. His real job was CIA field officer. For public purposes, however, he was an American diplomat; during his time in Geneva he used the cover-name Dave M Churchyard, personnel number 2339176. *Der Spiegel* reported that many of his colleagues were unaware of Snowden's job, including a group of marines who were stationed at the building to provide security. In July 2007, one Saturday evening, Snowden went out with around 15 embassy personnel for dinner in the old city. The American party included several soldiers with top secret clearance.

They were aware of Snowden's true role. 'I know what you do,' one of them told Snowden teasingly. 'I admire you.' Other colleagues took up the theme. Snowden suggested a change of venue, but the speculation spilled over into another bar. It was a tricky moment for Snowden, *Spiegel* reported, citing one person who was there. The incident demonstrated how perilous undercover work could be. Afterwards Snowden avoided large groups and ventured out with one friend at a time. On another occasion, the magazine said, he was invited to a birthday party. The host clicked a photo of her guests and posted it on Facebook; a horrified Snowden demanded it be removed. It was.

Snowden took spycraft seriously. And soon his superiors noticed his talents. According to Greenwald, in April 2008 Snowden was part of a team from the US Geneva mission that travelled to Romania. Its task was to prepare for a visit by President George W Bush to the NATO summit in Bucharest. The CIA appears to have selected Snowden because of his impressive technical and cyber-security skills; the travelling White House delegation an obvious target for espionage.

During his Europe trip Bush expressed strong support for NATO membership for Georgia and Ukraine. This infuriated Vladimir Putin. (For Putin, NATO's eastward expansion amounted to unacceptable encroachment in Russia's post-Soviet backyard. Putin would go on to invade both countries, in 2008 and 2014 respectively.) The secret service took care of Bush's personal security, while Snowden and other CIA officers did reconnaissance.

Snowden's had been a comparatively insular upbringing on the US east coast. But now he was living in the heart of Europe, thanks to the US government, and helping the White House with trusted assignments. His CIA job brought other privileges, too. When he got parking tickets he didn't pay them. He cited diplomatic immunity. He was also sent on assignment to other European CIA stations, where he installed computer software. According to Ars Technica, Snowden travelled to Sarajevo, where he listened to the Muslim call to prayer from his hotel room. He visited Bosnia and Spain – giving opinions on their food and women. He raced motorbikes in Italy.

Back at base Snowden sometimes wondered whether Switzerland was a 'bit racist'. At the same time he was impressed by Swiss attitudes towards individual liberty, and the fact that prostitution was legal. During this period he was also a fervent believer in capitalism and free markets.

His faith was practical as well as doctrinal. For much of his Swiss period he was playing the stock market, unapologetically shorting stocks and watching with a fascinated horror as the 2008 global crash unfolded, sucking the US and Europe into a vortex. Sometimes he made money; quite often he lost it.

He chats online about his exploits. He defends the gold standard. He is dismissive of high unemployment – seeing it, according to Ars, as 'necessary' and a 'correction to capitalism'. When one user asks how 'do you deal with 12 per cent unemployment?', Snowden hits back: 'Almost everyone was self-employed prior to 1900. Why is 12 per cent unemployment so terrifying?'

The figure who most closely embodied Snowden's maverick right-wing views was Ron Paul, the most famous exponent of American libertarianism, who enjoyed an enthusiastic grassroots following, especially among the young. Paul spent 30 years in Congress, on and off, defying both the Republican establishment and the political consensus. He was a bitter opponent of socialism, Keynesian economics and the Federal Reserve. He was against US intervention abroad. He loathed government surveillance.

Snowden supported Paul's 2008 bid for the US presidency. He was also impressed with the Republican candidate John McCain, describing him as an 'excellent leader' and 'a guy with real values'. He wasn't an Obama supporter as such. But he didn't object to him either. During the election, Snowden said he might back Obama if he could somehow team up with McCain – an unlikely prospect. TheTrueHOOHA posts on Ars: 'We need an idealist first and foremost. Hillary Clinton, I think, would be a pox on the country.'

Once Obama won and became president, Snowden came to dislike him intensely. He criticised the White House's attempts to ban assault weapons. The lodestar in Snowden's thinking, at this time and later, was the US constitution; in this case the second amendment and the right to bear arms. Snowden was unimpressed by affirmative action. He was also against social security, believing that individuals shouldn't go running to the state for help, even in times of trouble.

A couple of users called him out on this, one posting: 'Yeah! Fuck old people!'

TheTrueHOOA responded with fury. He wrote: 'You fucking retards ... my grandmother is eighty fucking three this year and, you know what, she still supports herself as a goddamned hairdresser ... maybe when you grow up and actually pay taxes, you'll understand.'

Another topic made him even angrier. The Snowden of 2009 inveighed against government officials who leaked classified information to newspapers – the worst crime conceivable, in Snowden's apoplectic view. In January of that year the *New York Times* published a report on a secret Israeli plan to attack Iran. It said that President Bush had 'deflected' a request from Israel for specialised bunker-busting bombs to carry out the risky mission. Instead Bush had told the Israelis he had authorised 'new covert action' to sabotage Iran's suspected nuclear-weapons programme.

The *Times* said its story was based on 15 months' worth of interviews with current and former US officials, European and Israeli officials, other experts and international nuclear inspectors.

TheTrueHOOHA's response, published by Ars Technica, is worth quoting in full:

<TheTrueHOOHA>   HOLY SHIT
                     http://www.nytimes.com/2009/01/11/
                     washington/11iran.html?_r=1&hp

<TheTrueHOOHA>   WTF NYTIMES

<TheTrueHOOHA>   Are they TRYING to start a war?
                     Jesus christ
                     they're like wikileaks

<User19>   they're just reporting, dude.

<TheTrueHOOHA>   They're reporting classified shit

<User19>   Shrugs

<TheTrueHOOHA>   about an unpopular country surrounded by
                     enemies already engaged in a war
                     and about our interactions with said country
                     regarding planning sovereignty violations of
                     another country
                     you don't put that shit in the NEWSPAPER

<User19>   Meh

<TheTrueHOOHA>   moreover, who the fuck are the anonymous
                     sources telling them this?

<TheTrueHOOHA> those people should be shot in the balls.

<TheTrueHOOHA> 'But the tense exchanges also prompted the White House to step up intelligence-sharing with Israel and brief Israeli officials on new American efforts to subtly sabotage Iran's nuclear infrastructure, a major covert program that Mr. Bush is about to hand off to President-elect Barack Obama.'

<TheTrueHOOHA> HELLO? HOW COVERT IS IT NOW? THANK YOU

<User19> Meh

<TheTrueHOOHA> I wonder how many hundreds of millions of dollars they just completely blew.

<User19> You're over-reacting. It's fine.

<TheTrueHOOHA> It's not an overreaction. They have a HISTORY of this shit

<User19> with flowers and cake.

<TheTrueHOOHA> these are the same people who blew the whole 'we could listen to osama's cell phone' thing the same people who screwed us on wiretapping over and over and over again. Thank God they're going out of business.

<User19>   the NYT?

<TheTrueHOOHA> Hopefully they'll finally go bankrupt this year.
                yeah.

A few minutes later the chat continues:

<User19>   It's nice they report on stuff.

<TheTrueHOOHA> I enjoy it when it's ethical reporting.

<TheTrueHOOHA> political corruption, sure

<TheTrueHOOHA> scandal, yes

<User19>   is it unethical to report on the government's
              intrigue?

<TheTrueHOOHA> VIOLATING NATIONAL SECURITY? no

<User19>   meh.

<User19>   national security.

<TheTrueHOOHA> Um, YEEEEEEEEEEEES.

<TheTrueHOOHA> that shit is classified for a reason

<TheTrueHOOHA> it's not because 'oh we hope our citizens don't
                find out'

<TheTrueHOOHA>   it's because 'this shit won't work if iran knows what we're doing.'

<User19>   Shrugs

<TheTrueHOOHA>   'None would speak on the record because of the great secrecy surrounding the intelligence developed on Iran.'

<TheTrueHOOHA>   direct. quote.

<TheTrueHOOHA>   THEN WHY ARE YOU TALKING TO REPORTERS?!

<TheTrueHOOHA>   'Those covert operations, and the question of whether Israel will settle for something less than a conventional attack on Iran, pose immediate and wrenching decisions for Mr. Obama.'

<TheTrueHOOHA>   THEY'RE NOT COVERT ANYMORE

<TheTrueHOOHA>   Oh you've got to be fucking kidding me. Now the NYTimes is going to determine our foreign policy?

<TheTrueHOOHA>   And Obama?

<TheTrueHOOHA>   Obama just appointed a fucking POLITICIAN to run the CIA!

<User11>   yes unlike every other director of CIA ever

<User11>   oh wait, no

<TheTrueHOOHA> I am so angry right now. This is completely unbelievable.

The 'fucking politician' was Leon Panetta, appointed by Obama in 2009 despite his evident lack of intelligence background. The appointment was supposed to draw a line under the intelligence scandals of the Bush years – the renditions, the secret CIA prisons and the illegal wiretapping.

Snowden evidently knew of WikiLeaks, a niche transparency website whose story would later intersect with his own. But he didn't like it. At this point, Snowden's antipathy towards the *New York Times* was based on his opinion that 'they are worse than Wikileaks'. Later, however, he would go on to accuse the paper of not publishing quickly enough and of sitting on unambiguous evidence of White House illegality. These are somewhat contradictory views.

Certainly Snowden's anti-leaking invective seems stunningly at odds with his own later behaviour. But there is a difference between what the *Times* arguably did – reveal details of sensitive covert operations – and what Snowden would do in 2013. Snowden nowadays explains: 'Most of the secrets the CIA has are about people, not machines and systems, so I didn't feel comfortable with disclosures that I thought could endanger anyone.'

In fact, Snowden would trace the beginning of his own disillusionment with government spying to this time in

Switzerland, and to the near-three years he spent around CIA officers. His friend Mavanee Anderson, a legal intern working for the US mission to the UN in Geneva at that time, describes him as quiet, thoughtful, introspective, and someone who carefully weighed up the consequences of any action. By the end of his Geneva stint, she claims Snowden was experiencing a 'crisis of conscience'.

Snowden later spoke of a formative incident. He told Greenwald that CIA operatives tried to recruit a Swiss banker in order to get hold of secret financial information. Snowden said they pulled this off by getting the banker drunk and then encouraging him to drive home, which he foolishly did. The Swiss police arrested him. The undercover agent offered to help, and exploited the incident successfully to befriend and then recruit the banker.

'Much of what I saw in Geneva really disillusioned me about how my government functions and what its impact is in the world. I realised that I was part of something that was doing far more harm than good,' he said.

Any decision to spill US government secrets as a result was inchoate, an idea slowly forming in Snowden's head. Nor, it appears, had he yet seen the most contentious documents he was later to leak. Snowden says that he was ready to give President Obama the benefit of the doubt, and was waiting for him to reverse the most egregious civil liberties abuses of the Bush era. They included Guantanamo Bay, a US military dumping ground for fighters rounded up on the battlefield, some of whom had no connection with extremism or al-Qaida, and yet who languished for years without trial.

Snowden wanted Obama to bring to account those from Team Bush who were responsible: 'Obama's campaign promises and election gave me faith that he would lead us toward fixing the problems he outlined in his quest for votes. Many Americans felt similarly. Unfortunately, shortly after assuming power, he closed the door on investigating systemic violations of law, deepened and expanded several abusive programmes, and refused to spend the political capital to end the kind of human rights violations we see in Guantanamo, where men still sit without charge.'

What did Snowden's bosses know of his unhappy state of mind? In 2009 Snowden fell out with one of his Geneva colleagues. He gave an account of the incident to the *New York Times*'s James Risen. According to Risen, Snowden was keen to get promoted but got embroiled in a 'petty email spat' with a superior, whose judgement he challenged. Months later, Snowden was filling in his annual CIA self-evaluation form. He detected flaws in the personnel web application and pointed those out to his boss. His boss told him to drop it but eventually agreed to allow Snowden to test the system's susceptibility to hacking.

Snowden added some code and text 'in a non-malicious manner', proving his point. His immediate boss signed off on it. But then the more senior manager with whom Snowden had clashed previously discovered what he had done and was furious. The manager entered a derogatory report – known as a 'derog' in spy parlance – into Snowden's file.

This relatively trivial episode was important in one respect: it may have demonstrated to Snowden the futility of raising grievances via internal channels. Complaining upwards only led to punishment, he could have concluded. But for now there were new horizons to explore.

In February 2009 Snowden resigned from the CIA. His personnel file, whatever it contained, was never forwarded to his next employer – the NSA. Now Snowden was to work as a contractor at an NSA facility on a US military base, out in Japan.

The opportunities for contractors had boomed in the years since 9/11, as the burgeoning US security state outsourced intelligence tasks to private companies. Top officials such as the NSA's former director Michael Hayden moved effortlessly between government and corporations. This was a revolving door – a lucrative one. Snowden was now on the payroll of Dell, the computer firm. The early lacunae in his CV were by this stage pretty much irrelevant. He had top-secret clearance and outstanding computer skills. Whatever misgivings his former CIA colleagues may have had were lost in the system.

Snowden felt passionately about Japan from his early teens. He had spent a year and a half studying Japanese; he dropped '*Arigatou gozaimasu*!' and other phrases into his first Ars chat. Snowden sometimes used the Japanese pronunciation of his name. He dubbed himself: 'E-do-waa-do' and wrote in 2001: 'I've always dreamed of being able to "make it" in Japan. I'd love a cushy .gov job over there.' He played Tekken obsessively; playing an everyman-warrior battling evil against the odds shaped his moral outlook, he later said. Between 2002 and 2004 he worked as the webmaster for Ryuhana Press, a Japanese anime website.

Snowden was keen to improve his language and technical skills. In 2009 he signed up for summer school at a Tokyo-based campus affiliated to the University of Maryland's University College.

During Japan, Snowden's online activity dries up, however. He pretty much stops posting on Ars Technica. Japan marks a turning point. It is the period when Snowden goes from disillusioned technician to proto-whistleblower. As Snowden had sight of more top-secret material, showing the scale of NSA data mining, his antipathy towards the Obama administration grew. 'I watched as Obama advanced the very policies that I thought would be reined in,' Snowden says, adding of his Japan period: 'I got hardened.'

Between 2009 and 2012 Snowden says he found out just how all-consuming the NSA's surveillance activities are: 'They are intent on making every conversation and every form of behaviour in the world known to them.' He also realised another uncomfortable truth: that the congressional oversight mechanisms built into the US system and designed to keep the NSA in check had failed. 'You can't wait around for someone else to act. I had been looking for leaders, but I realised that leadership is about being the first to act.'

By the time he left Japan in 2012, Snowden was a whistleblower-in-waiting.

2

CIVIL DISOBEDIENCE

The NSA's Regional Cryptologic Center,
Kunia, Hawaii

'The authority of government, even such as I
am willing to submit to ... is still an impure one:
to be strictly just, it must have the sanction
and consent of the governed.'

HENRY DAVID THOREAU,
'Civil Disobedience'

In March 2012, Snowden left Japan and moved across
the Pacific to Hawaii. At the same time, it seems he
donated to his libertarian political hero Ron Paul. An
'Edward Snowden' contributed $250 to Paul's presiden-
tial campaign from an address in Columbia, Maryland.
The record describes the donor as an employee of Dell.
In May, Snowden donated a second $250, this time from
his new home at Waipahu, describing himself as a 'senior
adviser' for an unstated employer.

Snowden's new job was at the NSA's regional cryptological centre (the 'Central Security Service') on the
main island of Oahu, in Honolulu. He was still a Dell
contractor. The centre is one of 13 NSA hubs outside
Fort Meade devoted to SIGINT, and in particular to
spying on the Chinese. The logo of 'NSA/CSS Hawaii'

features two green palm trees set on either side of a tantalising archipelago of islands. The main colour is a deep oceanic blue. At the top are the words: 'NSA/CSS Hawaii'; at the bottom, 'Kunia'. It looks an attractive place to work.

He arrived on the volcanic island in the middle of the Pacific with a plan. The plan now looks insane. It was audacious, but – viewed dispassionately – almost certainly going to result in Snowden's incarceration for a very long time and possibly for the rest of his life.

The plan was to make contact anonymously with journalists interested in civil liberties. Proven journalists whose credentials and integrity could not be doubted. And – though quite how this would happen was a little hazy – to leak to them stolen top-secret documents. The documents would show evidence of the NSA's illegality. They would prove that the agency was running programs that violated the US constitution. To judge by what he later said, Snowden's aim was not to spill state secrets wholesale. Rather, he wanted to turn over a selection of material to reporters and let them exercise their own editorial judgement.

To corroborate his claims about the NSA to a sceptical Fourth Estate would not only require lots of documents, Snowden realised. It would also take a preternatural degree of cunning. And a cool head. And some extraordinary good fortune.

Snowden's new post was NSA systems administrator. This gave him access to a wealth of secret material. Most analysts saw much less. But how was he supposed to reach out to reporters? Sending a regular email was unthinkable. And meeting them in person was difficult, too: any trip had to be cleared with his NSA superiors 30 days in advance. Also, Snowden didn't 'know' any reporters. Or at least not personally.

His girlfriend of eight years, Lindsay Mills, joined him in June on Oahu, which means 'the gathering place'. Mills grew up in Baltimore, graduated from Maryland Institute College of Art, and had had a long-distance relationship with Snowden in Japan. Aged 28, she had worked in a number of jobs – ballet dancer, dance teacher, fitness instructor and pole-dance specialist. Her biggest passion was photography. Mills took a regular photograph of herself – often wearing not much – and posted it on her blog. It was titled: 'L's journey. Adventures of a world-travelling, pole-dancing superhero.'

Snowden and Mills rented a three-bedroom, two-bathroom bungalow at 94-1044 Eleu Street, a sleepy, tree-lined neighbourhood in Waipahu, which was a former sugar plantation 15 miles west of Honolulu. It was a blue wooden property, comfortable but not luxurious, with no view of sea or mountains. The front yard had a small lawn, a Dwarf Bottlebrush shrub, some palm trees and a neighbour's avocado leaning in. The rear had more palm trees, concealing it from the street and a knoll where teenagers furtively smoked.

A sticker on the front door – 'Freedom isn't free', adorned with a Stars and Stripes – hinted at Snowden's convictions. Neighbours seldom, if ever, spoke to him. 'A couple of times I'd see him across the street and he nodded and that was it. My impression was that he was a very private person. He did his own thing,' said Rod Uyehara, who lived directly opposite. A retired army veteran, like many in the neighbourhood, he assumed the young man with short hair was also military.

The island's surroundings would have given Snowden plenty to brood about during his daily commute up Kunia Road. To the west of his bungalow cocoon lie the Wai'anae Mountains, the remains of an ancient volcano. The peaks are inhabited by menacing, bruised clouds: they have a tendency to suddenly replicate, blacken the sky and hammer the valley with torrential rain.

Behind him, to the south, was Pearl Harbor, the target of Japan's surprise attack on 7 December 1941. A day of 'infamy', as Franklin Roosevelt put it, which caught America's spymasters with their pants down and brought the US into the second world war.

At the time, ramping up intelligence capabilities, the chastened spooks built a vast tunnel complex in the middle of Oahu, and called it 'the hole'. Originally intended as an underground aircraft assembly and storage plant, it was turned into a chamber to make charts, maps and models of Japanese islands for invading US forces. After the war it became a navy command centre and was reinforced to withstand chemical, biological and radiological attack.

Today it is known as the Kunia Regional Security Operations Center (RSOC) and hosts the US Cryptological System Group, an agency staffed by specialists from each branch of the military as well as civilian contractors. At some point the facility's nickname changed to 'the tunnel'.

Snowden's bungalow was seven miles away, on the nearest housing estate – just 13 minutes, door to door. Largely deserted countryside stretches in between. It is not a beautiful drive. The two-lane highway dips and rises, flanked by high mounds of earth and tangles of weeds, which obscure the landscape. It is easy to feel boxed in. Occasionally you glimpse corn seed plantations and yellowing fields.

'The tunnel' had two main spying targets: the People's Republic of China and its unpredictable, troublesome Stalinist satellite, North Korea. It was clear to everyone – not just NSA analysts – that China was a rising military and economic power. The NSA's mission in the Pacific was to keep a watchful eye on the Chinese navy, its frigates, support vessels and destroyers, as well as the troops and military capabilities of the People's Liberation Army (PLA). Plus the PLA's computer networks. If penetrated, these were a rich source of data.

By this point Snowden was a China specialist. He had targeted Chinese networks. He had also taught a course on Chinese cyber-counterintelligence, instructing senior officials from the Department of Defense how to protect their data from Beijing and its avid hackers. He was intimately familiar with the NSA's active operations against the Chinese, later saying he had 'access to every target'.

The Japanese were no longer the enemy. Rather, they were among several prosperous East Asian nations whom the US considered as valuable intelligence partners. The NSA co-ordinated its SIGINT work with other allies in the region. Visitors to the subterranean complex included the new defence chief of South Korea's security agency, the incoming boss of Thailand's national security bureau and delegations from Tokyo. 'The tunnel' also tracked Thailand and the Philippines, supporting counter-terrorism operations there, as well as in Pakistan.

According to an NSA staffer who spoke to *Forbes* magazine, Snowden was a principled and ultra-competent, if somewhat eccentric, colleague. Inside 'the tunnel' he wore a hoodie featuring a parody NSA logo. Instead of a key in an eagle's claws it had a pair of eavesdropping headphones covering the bird's ears. His co-workers assumed the sweatshirt, sold by the Electronic Frontier Foundation, was a joke.

There were further hints of a non-conformist personality. Snowden kept a copy of the constitution on his desk. He flourished it when he wanted to argue against NSA activities he felt violated it. He wandered the halls carrying a Rubik's cube. He also cared about his colleagues, leaving small gifts on their desks. He almost lost his job sticking up for one co-worker who was being disciplined.

The RSOC where Snowden worked is just one of several military installations in the area. Displays of US power abound. A giant satellite dish peeks from a hillside. CH-47 Chinook helicopters whump overhead. Camouflage trucks trundle by. Young men and women in uniform drive SUVs, sports cars and motorbikes. They go fast. As one Dodge Convertible's bumper sticker put it: 'Get in. Sit down. Shut up. Hold on.'

The RSOC is almost invisible from the road, the complex set back behind dogwood trees and a 10-foot-high metal fence topped with barbed wire. There is just one small, generic sign – 'Government property. No trespassing' – to indicate this is an official facility. Take the turn off and you roll down a hill to a guardhouse containing two navy guards in blue camouflage with pistols strapped to their thighs. Beyond the security barrier is a car park with more than a hundred vehicles, as well as several billboards warning against drunk driving. '006 days since the last accident,' says one.

Given the number of vehicles, the dearth of people or buildings – just a few cabins – is puzzling, until you realise everyone is underground. They enter via a long, curious-looking, rectangular structure with an orange roof built into a steep hillside of brown earth. The gradient is so steep it's a wonder the structure doesn't slide down. Steps lead up the dark mouth. 'The doors inside are huge. It's like something out of *King Kong*. It takes ages just to get in,' said a former air force officer who worked here.

Exfiltrating secret material from here would be a high-risk undertaking. It would require quite remarkable nerve.

In the regular blog written by Snowden's partner, Lindsay Mills, Snowden makes the odd oblique appearance. She calls him E. He is very much an off-stage presence – a loyal boyfriend, certainly, but one who is prone to myste-rious absences and disappearances. As in Switzerland, Hawaii Snowden is a man with a mask.

On just a couple of occasions, E poses with Mills in her weekly portraits, posted to Instagram. You don't see his face. In one shot Snowden is on a beach, bent over, trousers rolled up to his knees. A flapping black winter coat hides his face. Probably he's laughing, but it's difficult to tell, and he reminds one of a Richard III impersonator. 'A world where people move like ravens,' Mills writes on her blog, noting: 'a rare shot of E'. Someone points out that Snowden looks a bit like Quasimodo. Mills shoots back: 'Don't mess with E!'

Mills described the motivation for her blog: 'Been shooting daily self portraits for several years now. They're not just for mothers. 😉😃 I find it helps me work out my emotions and document my life. Not that anyone would be interested in it, but someday I may thank myself for these shots. Or hate myself 😃 – either way I'll feel something. 😉' The portraits are done in bright colours – a sort of artist's diary – with Mills dressing up to capture a mood or an emotion. Many are coquettish. She meditates, hangs from trees or watches the Hawaii sunset.

Snowden kept himself apart from other staff during the 13 months he spent in Hawaii. He was by nature reserved but he had special reason to be guarded. If it came off, his leak would be the most significant since the Pentagon Papers, eclipsing the 2010 release of US diplomatic cables and warlogs by a disaffected US army private, Chelsea (formerly Bradley) Manning. It would lift the lid on mass surveillance, not just of millions of Americans but the entire world. But it was a big if. A slip on his part, a careless word, an unusual work request, a rogue flash drive, could arouse questions, with potentially catastrophic consequences.

Snowden was surrounded by spies dedicated to detecting hidden codes and patterns, to discovering secrets. If they discovered his, he would likely be quietly tried, convicted and jailed for decades, an anonymous geek who tried and failed to steal data from his employers. Little wonder Snowden appeared buttoned up.

Friends likened him teasingly to Edward Cullen, the vampire played by Robert Pattinson from the *Twilight* saga. Snowden was pale, enigmatic, solemn and seldom seen by day. He hardly ever appeared at social gatherings. 'He would barely say anything and hang out on the side, sort of hovering. So it became a sort of game to involve him, like "Go Team Edward!"' recalls one. 'At a birthday party one night we prodded him into making an actual speech. It was about five words.'

Snowden did describe his life in Hawaii as 'paradise'. This, certainly, was how the *Honolulu Star-Advertiser* also tells it, declaring on its masthead: 'The pulse of paradise.' What passed for news headlines – 'Officials contemplate weekend harbor hours', 'Pacific aviation museum honors daredevil', 'Bush blaze doused on Maui' – tended to boost the image of a tropical idyll.

But for Snowden there were few outward signs of fun. No surfing, no golf, no lounging on the beach. 'He was pale, pale, pale, pale, as if he never got out in the sun,' the friend says. (In contrast, Barack Obama, who has a sister on Oahu, gives every impression of savouring the beaches, the surf and the shave ice, the local version of a snow cone.)

Compared to Snowden, glued to his laptops, his partner Lindsay Mills was a social butterfly. After arriving in Hawaii she joined Pamela and the Pole Kats, a group that trained and performed using poles. It was not stripping – they did athletic performances at the Mercury, a hipster bar in downtown Honolulu, once a month. Mills also participated in street performances on the first Friday of each month.

Despite her outward sociability, though, Mills remained a puzzle to some acquaintances in Hawaii. She half-hid behind huge sunglasses. She did not volunteer much personal information. Many were unaware she even had a boyfriend. She didn't appear to have a job – that is, beyond her photography and dancing – yet drove a new SUV. The source of her prosperity was another riddle.

Pam Parkinson, who founded the pole group, introduced Mills to the Waikiki Acrobatic Troupe, a dozen or so dancers, jugglers, tightrope walkers, fire-breathers and hula-hoopers who gathered a few times a week.

On Sundays they practised till sunset at a park overlooking the beach in Waikiki. Mills thrived among this bohemian bunch, though by the standards of her new friends she was straight-laced. 'She wouldn't laugh at a sex joke,' one recalled. Terryl Leon, co-ordinator of the troupe, said Mills was new to acrobatics but determined to improve. 'She was working a short acrobatic sequence. I'd give her tips on form and technique. She was a bit reserved. Very pretty, attentive, alert, focused and co-operative.'

Snowden on occasion collected Mills from practice but seldom got out of the car or spoke to her friends. 'She didn't really talk about him,' one said. One exception was when Snowden was away for a prolonged spell and Mills lamented the difficulty of long-distance relationships. The troupe gossiped about her friendship with her 'acro-partner', a young muscular man named Bow. But, as Mills's blog made clear, she remained devoted to E.

E himself, meanwhile, was still biding his time at the NSA. Behind his quiet, unassuming surface, his disenchantment and anger with his employers was growing.

Ed Snowden was not the first person from inside the NSA to be disillusioned by what he discovered there, and by the dark trajectory of US security policy after 9/11. Snowden had watched closely the case of Thomas Drake. Drake, a US air force and navy veteran, was an executive at the NSA. After the 11 September attacks, he became unhappy with the agency's secret counter-terrorism programs – in particular, an intelligence-collecting tool called TRAILBLAZER. Drake felt it violated the fourth amendment against arbitrary searches and seizures.

Drake decided to raise his concerns through all the right channels. He complained to his NSA bosses. Using a prescribed framework for whistleblowers, he also testified to the NSA's inspector general, the Pentagon and before the House and Senate congressional oversight committees. Finally, in frustration, he went to the *Baltimore Sun*. This ingenuous approach didn't work. In 2007 the FBI raided his home. Drake faced 35 years in jail. Only in 2011, after four years of anxiety, did the government drop the major charges, with Drake pleading guilty to a minor misdemeanour. He was put on probation.

For Snowden, Drake was an inspiration (the two would later meet). The punitive way the authorities hounded Drake convinced Snowden, moreover, that there was no point in going down the same path. He knew others who had suffered in similar circumstances. They included an NSA employee who jokingly included a line in an email that said: 'Is this the PLA or the NSA?' Snowden told James Risen that inside the NSA 'there's a lot of dissent – palpable with some even.' But that most people toed the line through 'fear and a false image of patriotism', construed as 'obedience to authority'.

As an outside contractor, working for Dell, Snowden wasn't entitled to the same whistleblower protections as Drake. Even if he had reported his concerns over NSA surveillance nothing would have happened, he later told Risen. He believed his efforts 'would have been buried forever', and that he would have been discredited and ruined. 'The system does not work. You have to report wrongdoing to those most responsible for it.'

Snowden had lost faith in meaningful congressional oversight of the intelligence community. Instead, Congress was part of the problem, he felt. In particular he was critical of the 'Gang of Eight', the group of congressional officials who are notified about the most sensitive US intelligence operations.

By December 2012, he had made up his mind to contact journalists. Asked at what moment he had decided to blow the whistle, Snowden says: 'I imagine everyone's experience is different, but for me, there was no single moment. It was seeing a continuing litany of lies from senior officials to Congress – and therefore the American people – and the realisation that that Congress, specifically the Gang of Eight, wholly supported the lies that compelled me to act. Seeing someone in the position of James Clapper – the director of national intelligence – baldly lying to the public without repercussion is the evidence of a subverted democracy. The consent of the governed is not consent if it is not informed.'

In March 2013, Clapper told the Senate intelligence committee that the US government does 'not wittingly' collect data on millions of Americans. The statement was untrue, as Snowden would reveal and Clapper would himself later admit. It was also perhaps a felony.

By his account, one document in particular pushed Snowden over the edge. He stumbled upon a classified 2009 report by the NSA's inspector general – the same person to whom Drake had complained. Snowden had been carrying out a 'dirty word search': he was spring-cleaning the system to remove material that shouldn't have been there. When he opened the document he couldn't stop himself from reading it.

The report was a detailed 51-page account of how the Bush administration had carried out its illegal wiretapping program following 9/11. The program, codenamed STELLAR WIND, involved the collection of content and metadata from millions of Americans without a warrant. Some of the facts about the wiretapping scandal had emerged a few years earlier, but nothing like the whole story. For Snowden this was incontrovertible proof that senior US officials were breaking the law. Without, he learned, any repercussions at all. 'You can't read something like that and not realise what it means for all of the systems we have,' he told the *New York Times*.

In Hawaii, by early 2013, Snowden's sense of outrage was still growing. But his plan to leak appeared to have stalled. He faced too many obstacles. To get access to a final tranche of documents Snowden required greater security privileges than he enjoyed in his position at Dell. Clapper made his ill-fated appearance before the Senate in March. The same month Snowden took a new job with the private contractor Booz Allen Hamilton, yielding him access to a fresh trove of information. According to the NSA staffer who spoke to *Forbes*, Snowden turned down an offer to join the agency's Tailored Access Operations, a group of elite hackers. He had entered the final tense weeks of his double life.

Snowden's last workplace was in downtown Honolulu. It is a shiny, corporate contrast to the RSOC bunker. It occupies the 30th floor of Makai Tower, on Bishop Street, in the financial district. The reception has beige furnishings, framed vintage maps and a television, volume low, tuned to Fox News. Instead of a windowless canteen filled with buzz-cut soldiers, Booz Allen Hamilton staff in suits and Hawaiian shirts stroll through a sunlit courtyard of fountains and choose from dozens of restaurants. The nearest pub, Ferguson's, isn't exactly rowdy: it offers bacon-wrapped dates, baked Brie and red pepper tzatziki.

Booz Allen Hamilton's chairman and president, Ralph Shrader, made complacent assurances about security on the company blog: 'In all walks of life, our most trusted colleagues and friends have this in common. We can count on them. No matter what the situation or challenge, they will be there for us. Booz Allen Hamilton is trusted in that way. You can count on that.'

Snowden may have allowed himself a wry smile. He was counting on his new employer not to suspect anything. Snowden was reaching the point of no return. Elements in the US government, he knew, would see his actions as a cyber version of Pearl Harbor, a sneak attack. For it to come from within, from a supposed 'traitor', would make the wrath all the worse. That Snowden saw it as an act of patriotism, a defence of American values, would soften Washington's vengeance not a bit.

Snowden's own name was an apposite one for a man engaged in such risky enterprises. In the 1590s in Britain, John Snowden, a Catholic priest, became a double agent working for Lord Burghley, Queen Elizabeth's lord treasurer. The historian Stephen Alford describes this Snowden as 'subtle, intelligent and self-assured'. His job was to spy on Catholic emigrés on the continent who were consorting with the Spanish and plotting against Elizabeth. Snowden used ciphers, secret letters and other tricks. The Elizabethans called such men 'intelligencers' or 'espials'; what they got up to was espiery. (The French term *espionage* only came into use from the 18th century onwards.)

But Edward Snowden, the modern-day espial, could not use his true name if he was to reach out to the US reporters who worked on national security, and who so far had no clue that Snowden existed. To make contact with them he would need a codename. Given the gravity of what he was undertaking, TheTrueHOOHA seemed jejune. Snowden came up with something new. He chose the handle 'Verax', a classical Latin adjective meaning 'truth-telling'. The word *verax* is rather rare. It crops up in Plautus, Cicero and Horace. It is used particularly of oracles and supernatural sources.

Snowden intended to become just such a prophetic voice from deep inside the intelligence community. As with his real surname, his codename had a history: two obscure British dissenters also called themselves 'Verax'. One was Henry Dunckley, a 19th-century Baptist social critic who used the nom de plume in the *Manchester Examiner*. The other was Clement Walker, a 17th-century Somerset parliamentarian during the English civil war who was eventually locked up and died in the Tower of London. Significantly, *verax* is also an antonym of *mendax*. Mendax means 'deceiving' and was the handle used by Julian Assange of WikiLeaks when he was a young Australian hacker. WikiLeaks, with their electronic mass-leaking of US army files from Afghanistan, and of State Department diplomatic cables from all over the world, had recently plunged the US administration into uproar. Perhaps Snowden's allusion was deliberate.

Outwardly, his life continued as before. Read with hindsight, his girlfriend's blog entries seem poignant. On 1 March, Mills writes that she will be an 'international woman of mystery' and that her Friday show later the same evening has a '007' theme.

The performance goes well. Three days later she writes: 'When I was a child most of my friends would play dress up and fantasize about being a princess, superman or pickle rancher (I have some weird friends). I would imagine being a spy. Running down sewer tunnels to escape treacherous enemies, eavesdropping on important adult conversations, and giving a full report to General Meow. So getting the opportunity to play a Bond and a babe for even a few minutes during my performance on Friday was very fulfilling. And the spy high of Friday night must have subconsciously stuck in my brain, for the following evening E and I randomly pick *Skyfall* for our date night movie.'

Eleven days later, on 15 March, there is news: 'We received word that we have to move out of our house by May 1. E is transferring jobs. And I am looking to take a mini trip back East. Do I move with E, on my own, to Antarctica? ... For now I'll spin my magic ball and see where I land.'

On 30 March, in the evening, Snowden flies off to the US mainland. Over the next couple of weeks he attends training sessions at Booz Allen Hamilton's office near Fort Meade; various intelligence agency contractors have offices next door to SIGINT city. His new salary is $122,000 a year plus a housing allowance. On 4 April he has dinner with his father. Lon Snowden says his son seemed preoccupied and nursing a burden. 'We hugged as we always do. He said: "I love you, Dad." I said: "I love you, Ed."'

In mid-April, Mills and Snowden get the keys to their new Hawaii home. It's two streets away from their old one.

Mills writes: 'My favourite part of moving is the pre-unpacking stage where I can roll around big empty rooms in soft window light (I may have been a cat in my former life). We took time to envision what each room could look like once we crammed our things in them. And even discussed hanging silks in the two-story main room.'

Snowden makes a valedictory appearance in her photo-blog. The pair arrange themselves on the bare floor of their home. Mills, in a striking blue dress, lies on her back and smiles at him; as ever, Snowden's thoughts are inscrutable since the camera only records the back of his head. His glasses are abandoned several feet away. What is going through his mind?

In the second half of April, Mills travels home to the east coast of the US herself. She cruises antique shops with her mother, helps redecorate her family house and sees old friends. In early May she returns to Honolulu. She blogs about feeling torn between two different worlds. Snowden, meanwhile, is settling into his new job at Booz.

Or so it appears. In reality, Snowden is probably scraping the NSA's servers. 'My position with Booz Allen Hamilton granted me access to lists of machines all over the world [that] the NSA hacked,' Snowden told the *Washington Post*, adding that that was exactly why he'd accepted it.

Months later, the NSA was still trying to puzzle out what exactly happened; Snowden hasn't fully explained how he carried out the leak. But as a systems administrator Snowden could access the NSA's intranet system, NSAnet.

This was set up following 9/11 to improve liaison between different parts of the US's intelligence community.

Snowden was one of around 1,000 NSA 'sysadmins' allowed to look at many parts of this system. (Other users with top-secret clearance weren't allowed to see all classified files.) He could open a file without leaving an electronic trace. He was, in the words of one intelligence source, a 'ghost user', able to haunt the agency's hallowed places. He may also have used his administrator status to persuade others to entrust their login details to him. GCHQ trustingly shares its top-secret British material with the NSA, which in turn makes it available to an army of outside contractors. This meant Snowden had access to British secrets, too, through GCHQ's parallel intranet, GCWiki.

Although we don't know exactly how he harvested the material, it appears Snowden downloaded NSA documents onto thumbnail drives. The method is the same as that used by Manning, who downloaded and sent to WikiLeaks a quarter of a million US diplomatic cables on a CD marked 'Lady Gaga' while working in a steamy field station outside Baghdad.

Thumb drives are forbidden to most staff. But a 'sysadmin' could argue that he or she was repairing a corrupted user profile, and needed a backup. The thumb drive could then be carried away to bridge the 'airgap' that existed between the NSA system and the regular internet.

Why did nobody raise the alarm? Was the NSA asleep? Sitting in Hawaii, Snowden could remotely reach into the NSA's servers, some 5,000 miles away in Fort Meade, through what was known as a 'thin client' system. Most staff had already gone home for the night when Snowden logged on, six time zones away. His activities took place while the NSA napped. Plus Snowden was extremely good at what he did – he was an 'IT genius' in the words of Anderson, his friend from Geneva – so he was able to move undetected through a vast internal system.

After four weeks in his new job, Snowden tells his bosses at Booz he is feeling unwell. He wants some time off and requests unpaid leave. When they check back with him he tells them he has epilepsy. It is the same condition that affects his mother Wendy, who uses a guide dog.

And then, on 20 May, he vanishes.

Mills's blog reflects some of the pain and anguish she felt on discovering that E had walked out of her life. By 2 June it becomes clear something has gone very wrong.

She writes: 'While I have been patiently asking the universe for a livelier schedule I'm not sure I meant for it to dump half a year's worth of experience in my lap in two weeks' time. We're talking biblical stuff – floods, deceit, loss … I feel alone, lost, overwhelmed, and desperate for a reprieve from the bipolar nature of my current situation.'

Five days later Mills removes her blog. She also wonders publicly about deleting her Twitter account. A creative body of work stretching back over several years, it includes dozens of photos of herself, and some of her E.

'To delete or not to delete?' she tweets. She doesn't delete.

3

THE SOURCE

Gavea, Rio de Janeiro, Brazil
December 2012

'Whoso would be a man must be a nonconformist.'
RALPH WALDO EMERSON,
Self-reliance and Other Essays

From the top of Sugar Loaf Mountain, the city of Rio de Janeiro appears as a precipitous swirl of greens and browns. In the sky, black vultures turn in slow spirals. Below – far below – is downtown and a shimmer of skyscrapers. Fringing it are beaches and breakers frothing endlessly on a turquoise sea. Standing above, arms outstretched, is the art deco statue of Christ the Redeemer.

Rio's famous beaches, Copacabana and Ipanema, lie at either side of a claw-shaped stretch of coast. Copacabana has long enjoyed a louche reputation. And yes, there are lewd sand sculptures of skimpily dressed women with big buttocks, next to green-yellow-blue-white Brazilian flags. But these days Copacabana is more of a hangout for the geriatric rich. Few others can afford to live in the luxury flats overlooking this dreamy Atlantic coast.

On weekday mornings, residents emerge, stretch, and walk their pampered pooches. Skateboarders trundle along a cycle lane; there are juice bars, restaurants, pavement cafes. Over on the beach tanned locals play football – Brazil's national obsession – or volleyball. Much of human life is here, sitting in the balmy days of winter under the rubber trees. But the girl from Ipanema is a rare sight. You are more likely to encounter her granny.

From Rio's south-western district of Gávea, the road twists sharply up into Floresta da Tijuca, the world's biggest urban forest, home to capuchin monkeys and toucans. It's usually several degrees cooler than the sea-level beaches. Keep going and you eventually arrive at a secluded mountain home. Is it some sort of dog sanctuary? A sign on the metal gate proclaims 'Cuidado Com O Cão': beware of the dog. The warning is superfluous: from the house comes a wild yapping and yowling. The dogs – small ones, big ones, black ones, dun ones – greet visitors by pawing at their legs; dog droppings litter a tropical yard; a mountain stream gurgles alongside. If there is mutt heaven, this is surely it.

The house's non-dog denizen is Glenn Greenwald. Greenwald, aged 46, is one of the more prominent US political commentators of his generation. Well before the Snowden story made him a household name, Greenwald had built up a following. A litigator by profession, he spent a decade working in the federal and state court system. The son of Jewish parents, truculent, gay, radical and passionate about civil liberties, Greenwald found his voice in the Bush era. In 2005 he gave up his practice to concentrate on writing full time. His online blog attracted a wide readership. From 2007 he contributed to Salon.com as a columnist.

From his home in Rio, Greenwald frequently appears as a pundit on US TV networks. This means driving down the mountain in his red Kia (which smells of dog) to a studio in the city's hippodrome. Security staff greet him warmly in Portuguese – he speaks it fluently. The studio has a camera, a chair and a desk. Seated at the desk, the camera depicts him in the uniform of a killer lawyer: clean shirt, smart jacket, tie. Under the table, and unseen by his audience in New York or Seattle, Greenwald will wear flip-flops and a pair of beach shorts.

This hybrid outfit bespeaks a wider duality, between private and professional. In his private life, Greenwald is soft-hearted. He is obviously a sucker for distressed beasts; he and his partner David Miranda have scooped up 10 strays. They also dog-sit other people's and keep an additional cat. Greenwald and Miranda met when the journalist came to Rio for a two-month holiday in 2005; it was Greenwald's second day in town, and he was lying on the beach. They quickly fell in love; Greenwald says he lives in Miranda's Brazilian coastal home city because US federal law refused to recognise same-sex marriages. (It does now). Miranda works as Greenwald's journalist-assistant. And when you meet him, Greenwald is mild, easy to get along with, chatty and kind.

Professionally, though, Greenwald is a different creature: adversarial, remorseless, sardonic and forensic. He is a relentless pricker of what he regards as official US hypocrisy. Greenwald has been a waspish critic of the George W Bush administration, and of Obama. He is scathing of Washington's record. Citizens' rights, drone strikes, foreign wars, the US's disastrous engagement with the Muslim world, Guantanamo Bay, America's 'global torture regime' – all have been subjects for Greenwald's Swiftian pen. In long, sometimes torrential posts, he has chronicled the US government's alleged crimes around the world. Greenwald's outspoken views on privacy make him arguably America's best-known critic of government surveillance.

Fans view him as a radical hero in the revolutionary tradition of Thomas Paine, a courageous journalist-pamphleteer. Enemies regard him as an irritant, an 'activist', even a traitor. Two of his books cover the foreign policy and executive abuses of the Bush era. A third, *With Liberty and Justice for Some* (2011), examines the double standards in America's criminal justice system. Greenwald argues persuasively that there is one rule for the powerless and another for those in high office who break the law, and invariably get away with it. The book delves into a theme important to both Greenwald and Snowden: the illegal wiretapping scandal in the Bush White House, and the fact that nobody was ever punished for it.

In August 2012, Greenwald left Salon.com and joined the *Guardian* as a freelance columnist. It was a nice fit. The paper's editor, Alan Rusbridger, sees the *Guardian* as inhabiting an editorial space distinct from most American newspapers – with less reverence for the notions of professional demarcation and detachment that, rightly or wrongly, shape much US journalism. More than most media outlets, the *Guardian* has embraced new digital technologies that have radically disrupted the old order.

Rusbridger observes: 'We have, I think, been more receptive to the argument that newspapers can give a better account of the world by bringing together the multiple voices – by no means all of them conventional journalists – who now publish on many different platforms and in a great variety of styles. That's how Greenwald ended up on the *Guardian*.'

Greenwald thus personifies a debate over what it means to be a journalist in the 21st century, in a new and noisy world of digital self-publishing, teeming with bloggers, citizen reporters and Twitter. Some have called this digital ecosystem outside mainstream publishing 'the Fifth Estate', in contrast to the establishment Fourth. Hollywood even used the name for a movie about WikiLeaks.

However, Rusbridger adds: 'Greenwald does not much like being described as a member of the Fifth Estate – largely because there's a persistent attempt by people in politics and the law as well as journalism to limit protections (for example, over sources or secrets) to people they regard (but struggle to define) as bona fide journalists. But he recognisably does have a foot in both camps, old and new.'

For sure, Greenwald believes in a partisan approach to journalism – but one, he says, that is grounded in facts, evidence and verifiable data. Typically he uses detail to smite his opponents, prising corrections from temples of US fact-checking, such as the *Washington Post* and the *New York Times*.

In an illuminating conversation with Bill Keller, a former editor of the *New York Times*, Greenwald acknowledges that 'establishment media venues' have done some 'superb reporting' in recent decades. But he argues that the default model in US journalism – that the reporter sets aside his subjective opinions in the interests of a higher truth – has led to some 'atrocious journalism' and toxic habits. These include too much deference to the US government of the day, and falsely equating a view that is true with one that isn't, in the interests of 'balance'.

The idea that journalists can have no opinions is 'mythical', Greenwald says. He reserves special contempt for one particular class: journalists who in his view act as White House stooges. He calls them sleazeballs. He asserts that instead of taking the powerful to task, the DC press corps frequently perform the role of courtier.

Keller, meanwhile, along with other thoughtful editors, have their own critique of 'advocacy journalism'. Keller says: 'The thing is, once you have publicly declared your "subjective assumptions and political values", it's human nature to want to defend them, and it becomes tempting to minimise facts, or frame the argument, in ways that support your declared viewpoint.'

In the months to come, Greenwald's own brand of advocacy journalism was going to be subjected to more public scrutiny than he could ever have imagined.

In December 2012, one of Greenwald's readers pinged him an email. The email didn't stand out; he gets dozens of similar ones every day. The sender didn't identify himself. He (or it could have been a she) wrote: 'I have some stuff you might be interested in.'

'He was very vague,' Greenwald recalls.

This mystery correspondent had an unusual request: he asked Greenwald to install PGP encryption software on to his laptop. Once up and running, it allows two parties to carry out an encrypted online chat. If used correctly, PGP guarantees privacy (the initials stand for 'Pretty Good Privacy'); it prevents a man-in-the-middle attack by a third party. The source didn't explain why this curious measure was needed.

Greenwald had no objections – he had been meaning for some time to set up a tool widely employed by investigative journalists, by WikiLeaks and by others suspicious of government snooping. But there were two problems. 'I'm basically technically illiterate,' he admits. Greenwald also had a lingering sense that the kind of person who insisted on encryption might turn out to be slightly crazy.

A few days later, his correspondent emailed again.

He asked: 'Have you done it?'

Greenwald replied that he hadn't. The journalist asked for more time. Several more days passed.

Another email arrived. It persisted: 'Have you done it?'

Frustrated, Greenwald's unknown correspondent now tried a different strategy. He made a private YouTube tutorial showing step by step how to download the correct encryption software – a 'how to' guide for dummies. This video had little in common with the Khan Academy: its author remained anonymous, an off-screen presence. It merely contained a set of instructions. 'I saw a computer screen and graphics. I didn't see any hands. He was very cautious,' Greenwald says.

The freelance journalist watched. But – stretched by other demands – didn't quite get round to following its strictures. He forgot about it. 'I wanted to do it. I work a lot with hacker types,' Greenwald says. But ultimately: 'He didn't do enough to get himself up my priority list.'

Five months later, during their encounter in Hong Kong, Greenwald realised his would-be source back in late 2012 had been none other than Edward Snowden. Snowden was among Greenwald's community of readers. Liking Greenwald's world view, his brio and his uncompromising approach to government, Snowden had reached out to him, but unsuccessfully. 'Snowden told me: "I can't believe you didn't do it. It was like: 'Hey, idiot!'"'

Snowden in Hawaii was thousands of miles away from Brazil. There was little prospect of a physical meeting. Online contact was essential. Yet Greenwald had been too distracted even to follow Snowden's simple encryption guide. The whistleblower's frustration must have been considerable. Greenwald says: 'He must have been thinking: "I'm just about to take this enormous fucking risk, to throw my life away, get killed, do the biggest security leak ever, and he [Greenwald] can't even be bothered to get an encryption code."'

As a consequence of this PGP debacle, several weeks passed uselessly. Snowden seemed to have no safe route through to Greenwald. The columnist carried on unaware, penning polemics in his remote mountain home. Marauding jungle monkeys would often invade, picking fights with the dogs, sometimes pelting them with branches, or retreating into dense thickets of bamboo.

At other times Greenwald rolled around with his animals; he says this is a welcome distraction from politics and the remorseless stream of Twitter.

At the end of January 2013, Snowden tried a different way to get to him. He sent an email to Laura Poitras. He was hoping to open an anonymous channel to the documentary film-maker, who was Greenwald's friend and a close collaborator. Poitras was another leading critic of the US security state – and one of its more prominent victims.

For nearly a decade, Poitras had been working on a trilogy of feature-length films about America in the years following 9/11. The first, *My Country, My Country* (2006), was an acclaimed portrait of Iraq in the aftermath of US invasion, told through the story of a Sunni Iraqi doctor who stood as a candidate in the 2005 post-Saddam election. The film was intimate, moving, compelling and brave – a luminous piece of work, nominated in 2007 for an Academy Award.

Poitras's next film, *The Oath* (2010), was shot in Yemen and Guantanamo Bay. It features two Yemenis swept up in President Bush's war on terror. One, Salim Hamdan, was accused of being Osama bin Laden's driver and detained in Guantanamo; the other, Hamdan's brother-in-law, was a former bin Laden bodyguard. Through them, Poitras created a powerful and human-scale critique of the dark Bush–Cheney years.

The response from US officials was astounding. For six years, between 2006 and 2012, agents from the Department of Homeland Security detained Poitras each time she entered the US. This happened around 40 times, she says. On each occasion, the agents would interrogate her, confiscate laptops and mobile phones, and demand to know whom she had met. They would seize her camera and notebooks. Sometimes she was held for three or four hours. Nothing incriminating was ever discovered.

Once, in 2011, when she was stopped at John F Kennedy international airport in New York, she refused to answer questions about her work, citing the first amendment. The border agent told her: 'If you don't answer our questions, we'll find our answers on your electronics.'

In response to this harassment, Poitras adopted new strategies. She became an expert in encryption. She learned how to protect her source material and sensitive information. She understood why, given the NSA's pervasive spying capabilities, this was sometimes very important. She no longer travelled with electronic gear. Sensibly, Poitras decided to edit her next film from outside America. She moved temporarily to the German capital, Berlin.

In 2012, Poitras was working on the concluding part of the trilogy. Its theme this time was America, and the alarming rise of domestic surveillance. One of her interviewees was William Binney, an NSA whistleblower. Binney was a mathematician who had spent nearly 40 years at the agency, and helped automate its foreign eavesdropping. He left in 2001 and blew the whistle on domestic spying.

That summer Poitras made an 'op-doc' for the *New York Times* website: a short film that was part of her work-in-progress. In the accompanying *Times* article, Poitras described what it was like being an NSA 'target'.

From afar, Snowden observed Poitras's harsh treatment. He knew who she was and what she had been through. Asked later by the *Times* journalist Peter Maass why he had approached Greenwald and Poitras, rather than his own paper, Snowden replied: 'After 9/11, many of the most important news outlets in America abdicated their role as a check to power – the journalistic responsibility to challenge the excesses of government – for fear of being seen as unpatriotic and punished in the market during a period of heightened nationalism. From a business perspective, this was the obvious strategy, but what benefited the institutions, ended up costing the public dearly. The major outlets are still only beginning to recover from this cold period.'

He continued: 'Laura and Glenn are among the few who reported fearlessly on controversial topics throughout this period, even in the face of withering personal criticism, and resulted in Laura specifically becoming targeted … She had demonstrated the courage, personal experience and skill needed to handle what is probably the most dangerous assignment any journalist can be given – reporting on the secret misdeeds of the most powerful government in the world – making her an obvious choice.'

In Berlin, Poitras brooded over the email that now came in from Snowden: 'I am a senior member of the intelligence community. This won't be a waste of your time …' (The claim was something of an exaggeration. Not in terms of Snowden's access to secret material but job title – he was a relatively junior infrastructure analyst.) Snowden asked for her encryption key. She gave it. She took other steps to assure Snowden, then still an anonymous source, that she understood how to communicate securely. 'I felt pretty intrigued pretty quickly,' she says. 'At that point my thought was either it's legit or it's entrapment. There were two sides of my brain. One was holy shit, it feels kind of legit.'

Poitras wrote: 'I don't know if you are legit, crazy or trying to entrap me.'

Snowden replied: 'I'm not going to ask you anything. I'm just going to tell you things.'

Poitras asked if Snowden had seen her file, detailing her detentions entering the US. He said he hadn't. But he did explain that he had 'selected' her because of the harassment she had experienced. The security agencies had the capacity to track and monitor 'anyone', not just Poitras – across borders, city or streets, he said. 'I bet you don't like this system. Only you can tell this story.'

If anything, Poitras was even more paranoid than Snowden during this early period. She remained suspicious of an opaque government plot against her. Meanwhile, in Hawaii, Snowden was taking extreme precautions. He never made contact from home or office. 'He made it clear it was hard for him to communicate. He was going to another location to do so. He wasn't doing it from his regular networks. He created some kind of a cover,' Poitras says.

The emails continued to flow. There was one a week. They usually arrived at weekends, when Snowden was able to slip off. The tone was serious, though there were moments of humour. At one point Snowden advised

Poitras to put her mobile in the freezer. 'He's an amazing writer. His emails were good. Everything I got read like a thriller,' she recalls. Snowden was keen to keep up a regular correspondence but clearly found it difficult to find a secure spot to type. He gave little away. There were no personal details.

Then Snowden delivered a bombshell. He said he had got hold of Presidential Policy Directive 20, a top-secret 18-page document issued in October 2012. It said that Obama had secretly ordered his senior national security and intelligence officials to draw up a list of potential overseas targets for US cyber-attacks. Not defence, but attacks. The agency was tapping fibre-optic cables, intercepting telephony landing points and bugging on a global scale, he said. He could prove all of it. 'I almost fainted,' Poitras says.

At this point the film-maker sought out trusted contacts who might help her authenticate these claims. In New York she consulted the American Civil Liberties Union, the ACLU. Over dinner in the West Village she talked with the *Washington Post*'s Barton Gellman. Gellman, a national security expert, thought the source sounded real. But he was a tad noncommittal. Meanwhile, the source made it clear he wanted Greenwald on board.

Back in Germany, Poitras moved ultra-cautiously. It was a fair assumption that the US embassy in Berlin had her under some form of surveillance. In connection with her latest documentary, Poitras had been in touch with Julian Assange, Washington's *bête noire*, who since the summer of 2012 had been holed up in London's

Ecuadorean embassy. Given the company she'd been keeping and the many other reasons she was a person of interest to US security forces, she could be sure that any conventional means of communication would be monitored. Phones were no good; email was insecure. How could she contact her friend Greenwald about her mysterious correspondent?

It would have to be a personal meeting. In late March she returned to the States. From here she sent Greenwald a message, suggesting that they meet face to face, without any electronics.

Greenwald was already due to fly to New York to give a talk to the Council on American Islamic Relations (CAIR), the Muslim civil rights organisation. The pair met in the lobby of Greenwald's hotel, the Marriott in Yonkers – an unlikely, 'horrible' venue for what was to be the first step of the most significant leak in US intelligence history.

Poitras showed Greenwald two emails. She didn't know the unknown source had already tried to reach Greenwald himself. Was he real? Or an imposter, trying to entrap her? Poitras was excited, nervous and seeking verification. 'There were no details in the emails. The source didn't identify himself. He didn't say where he worked,' Greenwald says.

Instead of facts, the emails offered up a radical personal manifesto – an intellectual blueprint for why Snowden was prepared to leak classified material, and what the life-changing consequences of this action would inevitably be. 'It was philosophically what he wanted to achieve and why he was willing to take these risks,' Greenwald says. The source seemed credible: 'Somehow Laura and I instinctively felt there was so much authentic passion about it. We both realised the emails were real. [The tone] was smart and sophisticated, not rambling or crazy.'

A picture was forming – of an intelligent, politically savvy, rational individual, of someone who had been working on a plan for some time. The source was unfolding it, stage by stage. The journalists had to wait for each new episode. 'He was talking as though he was taking a huge risk, about disclosures that were very serious,' Greenwald says. 'He didn't seem frivolous or delusional.'

Chatting to Poitras, Greenwald sketched out a way forward of his own. For the story to have impact, people needed to care, Greenwald argued. They would only care if the source could demonstrate convincing evidence of illegality – of wrong behaviour by the NSA, which went way beyond any democratic mandate. The best way of doing this would be to get hold of the national security documents: without them it would be difficult to rattle the doors on these issues.

The source behaved in an unexpected way. Poitras had assumed that he would seek to remain anonymous. After all, coming forward would bring the law down on his head. But Snowden told her: 'I'm not cleaning the metadata. I hope you will paint a target on my back and tell the world I did this on my own.'

In another email Snowden said that the 'hard part' of pulling the documents was over, but that a different dangerous phase was beginning. 'I could sense the stakes,' says Poitras. 'He was very worried about his friends and family being implicated. He didn't want to remain anonymous. He didn't want other people to take the fall.'

Snowden, it seemed, knew his actions were likely to end with him going to jail. He warned: 'You need to manage your expectations. At a certain point I'm not going to be reachable.'

Once a relationship of trust had been established, Poitras told the source she would like to interview him. She told Snowden he needed to articulate 'why' he was taking these risks. This was important.

It hadn't occurred to Snowden to give an interview. But the idea was a good one: his goal was to get the documents out to the world. He had had a view to leaking this material for four years, he said. At one stage he had considered giving the material to Assange. Eventually he rejected the idea. WikiLeaks' submission site was down and Assange was under surveillance, stuck in a foreign embassy. Even with Assange's security skills, Snowden realised it would be difficult to punch through to him.

By late spring 2013, the idea of a conclusive meeting was in the air.

'I need six to eight weeks to get ready to do this,' Snowden wrote.

What exactly the 'this' meant was still tantalisingly unclear. Poitras returned to Berlin. Greenwald returned to Rio. He got on with his life. The shadowy source was interesting. But – as is so often the case with journalistic leads – the 'this' could have been less alluring than it seemed; one of journalism's many false starts. 'I didn't sit around fantasising about it. He could be fake,' Greenwald says. As the weeks went by it seemed less rather than more likely that something would happen. 'I gave it almost no thought. I really wasn't focused on it at all.'

In mid-April, Greenwald received an email from Poitras. It told him to expect a FedEx delivery. Neither of the two parties had communicated much in the interim; Greenwald still hadn't got encryption. But the FedEx parcel signalled that things were moving and that, as Greenwald puts it, 'the eagle had landed'.

The package arrived; inside it were two thumb drives. Greenwald at first imagined that the USB sticks contained top-secret documents 'wrapped in layers of encryption and Linux programs'. In fact, they contained a security kit, allowing Greenwald to install a basic encrypted chat program.

Snowden contacted Poitras again: 'You should come. I will meet with you. But it's risky.'

It was the next stage of their plan. Snowden intended to leak one actual document. The file would reveal collaboration between the NSA and giant internet corporations under a secret program called PRISM. 'Heart attacks will be had over this,' Snowden claimed.

Snowden didn't want Poitras directly involved; instead he asked her to recommend other journalists who might publish it without attribution to him. He wanted to spread his net wider.

Poitras flew across to NYC again for what she imagined would be her meeting with a senior intelligence bureaucrat. She assumed this would naturally take place somewhere on the US east coast – probably in Baltimore, or a country house in Maryland. She asked for a minimum of half a day to film, and ideally a whole day. The source then sent her an encrypted file. In it was the PRISM PowerPoint. And a second document. It came as a total surprise: 'Your destination is Hong Kong.'

The next day a further message arrived for Poitras, in which the source for the first time gave his name: 'Edward Snowden'.

The name meant nothing; Poitras knew that if she searched Snowden's name on Google this would immediately alert the NSA. Attached was a map, a set of protocols for how they would meet, and a message: 'This is who I am. This is what they will say about me. This is the information I have.'

Snowden now contacted Greenwald himself, using his new encrypted channel. 'I have been working with a friend of yours … We need to talk, urgently.'

The whistleblower finally had something he had been craving for nearly six months – a direct, secure connection to the elusive writer. The source was evidently familiar with Greenwald's work. The two messaged. Snowden wrote: 'Can you come to Hong Kong?'

The demand struck Greenwald as bizarre and it left him 'really confused': what would someone who worked for a US security agency be doing in a former British colony, part of communist China and far away from Fort Meade? 'I didn't understand what Hong Kong had to do with this,' Greenwald says. His instinct was to do nothing. He was working on things that appeared important at the time; a book deadline loomed. 'I kind of stalled a little bit,' he says.

Snowden tried again via Poitras, urging her to get Greenwald to fly to Hong Kong 'right now'.

Sitting alone in his Chinese hotel room, expecting exposure at any moment, Snowden was growing frantic. His plan to escape with a cache of top-secret NSA and GCHQ material had worked thus far with remarkable ease. That was supposed to be the hard part. But the easy bit – passing the material to sympathetic journalists – was proving tricky.

Greenwald contacted Snowden via chat. 'I would like some more substantial idea why I'm going and why this is worthwhile for me?'

Over the next two hours Snowden explained to Greenwald how he could boot up the Tails system, one of the securest forms of communication, which uses the anonymising Tor network. Eventually the task was done.

Snowden then wrote, with what can only be called bathos: 'I'm going to send you a few documents.'

Snowden's welcome package was around 20 documents from the NSA's inner sanctuaries, most stamped 'top secret'. Among them were the PRISM slides. There were files that filled in the gaps on STELLAR WIND, the main case study of top-level impunity in Greenwald's latest book.

It was, quite simply, treasure – a rich trove of extraordinary data. At a glance it suggested the NSA had misled Congress about the nature of its domestic spying activities, and quite possibly lied to it. Greenwald: 'I always equate things with dog behaviour. Snowden was treating me like a dog and putting a biscuit in front of my nose. He was showing me top-secret programs from the NSA. It was unbelievable. There are no leaks from the NSA. It was enough to make me hyperventilate.'

Snowden was smart enough to indicate this was just the start – and that he was in possession of a very large number of secrets. Greenwald now comprehended. He picked up the phone to Janine Gibson, the *Guardian* US's editor in New York. He said it was urgent. When Greenwald began explaining about the NSA documents, Gibson shut him down and said: 'I don't think we should be discussing this on the telephone.' She suggested he come to New York.

Two days later, on Friday 31 May, Greenwald flew from Rio's Galeão international airport to JFK, going directly to *Guardian* US's SoHo HQ. He sat in Gibson's office. He said a trip onwards to Hong Kong would enable the *Guardian* to find out about the mysterious source.

The source could help interpret the leaked documents. Many of them were technical – referring to programs, interception techniques, methods, that practically nobody outside the NSA knew existed. Most were not written in human language but in a kind of weird lexicon under-standable only to the initiated. A few made no sense at all, as comprehensible as ancient Assyrian tablets.

'This was a very serious thing. And the most exciting thing it was possible to imagine,' Greenwald says. 'Snowden had picked documents that got me completely excited. They worked with everyone at the *Guardian*. Some were mind-blowing. What we had was the tiniest tip of the iceberg.'

Stuart Millar, the deputy editor of *Guardian* US, joined the discussion. Both executives felt that Snowden's manifesto came across as overwrought. In portentous terms, the source was talking about his personal philosophy, and the cataclysmic no-way-back journey he was taking. With hindsight, Snowden's tone was understandable: he was, after all, about to become the world's most wanted man.

But for the *Guardian*'s editorial staff there was a realisation that they could be in for a difficult ride – about to incur the wrath of the NSA, the FBI, the CIA, the White House, the State Department, and probably many other government departments so secret they didn't officially exist.

Gibson and Millar agreed that the only way to establish the source's credentials was to meet him in person. Greenwald would take the 16-hour flight to Hong Kong the next day. Independently, Poitras was coming along, too. But Gibson ordered a third member on to the team, the *Guardian*'s veteran Washington correspondent Ewen MacAskill. MacAskill, a 61-year-old Scot and political reporter, was experienced and professional. He was calm. He was unfailingly modest. Everybody liked him.

Except Poitras. She was exceedingly upset. As Poitras saw it, an extra person might freak out the source, who was already on edge. MacAskill's presence might alienate him and even blow up the entire operation. 'She was insistent that this would not happen,' Greenwald says. 'She completely flipped out.' Greenwald tried to mediate, without success. On the eve of the trip, Poitras and Greenwald rowed for the first time ever. Tensions were high. At this point Greenwald was thinking of MacAskill as the *Guardian*'s corporate representative – as the cautious, dull guy. Later he discovered the Scot was the most radical of the three, prepared to publish much that was in the public interest.

At JFK airport, the ill-matched trio boarded a Cathay Pacific flight. Poitras sat at the back of the plane. She was funding her own trip. Greenwald and MacAskill, their bills picked up by the *Guardian*, were further up in Premium Economy. 'I hate coach!' Greenwald says, pointing out that he had slept little since arriving from Brazil 48 hours earlier.

As flight CX831 gained speed down the runway and took off, there was a feeling of liberation. Up in the air there is no internet – or at least there was not in June 2013. It was a space that, at that date, even the omnipotent NSA didn't penetrate. Once the seatbelt signs were off, Poitras joined Greenwald in Premium Economy: there was room in front of his seat. She brought a present they were both eager to open: a USB stick. Snowden had securely delivered to her a second cache of secret NSA documents. This latest data-set was far bigger than the initial 'welcome pack'. It contained 3–4,000 items.

For the rest of the journey Greenwald read the latest cache. Sleep was impossible. He was mesmerised: 'I didn't take my eyes off the screen for a second. The adrenaline was so extreme.' From time to time, while the other passengers slumbered, Poitras would come up from her seat in the rear and grin at Greenwald. 'We would just cackle and giggle like we were schoolchildren. We were screaming, and hugging and dancing with each other up and down,' he says. 'I was encouraging her loudness.' Their celebrations woke some of their neighbours up; they didn't care.

It had started as a gamble. But now the material was becoming a scoop to end all scoops. What Snowden revealed was looking more and more like a curtain dramatically pulled away to reveal the true nature of things. As the plane came in to land, the crowded lights of Hong Kong twinkling below, there was for the first time a sense of certainty. Greenwald had no more doubts. Snowden was real. His information was real. Everything was real.

4

PUZZLE PALACE

National Security Agency,
Fort Meade, Maryland
2001–2010

'That capability at any time could be turned
around on the American people, and no American
would have any privacy left, such is the capability to
monitor everything: telephone conversations, telegrams,
it doesn't matter. There would be no place to hide.'

SENATOR FRANK CHURCH

The origins of the dragnet surveillance of the world's
internet users can be clearly pinpointed. It started on
9/11, the day of the terrorist atrocities that so frightened
and enraged the US. Over the ensuing decade, both in
America and Britain, there came a new political will-
ingness to invade individual privacy. At the same time,
mushrooming technical developments started to make
mass eavesdropping much more feasible.

The intricate web of the internet secretly became what
Julian Assange of WikiLeaks was to call, with only some
exaggeration, 'the greatest spying machine the world
has ever seen'. But before the appearance of Edward
Snowden, very little of the truth about that had reached
the surface.

The NSA – the biggest and most secretive of the US intelligence agencies – failed on 11 September 2001 to give advance warning of al-Qaida's surprise attack against the Twin Towers in New York. Michael Hayden, an obscure air force general, was running the agency at the time.

George Tenet, the CIA director and nominal head of all 16 intelligence agencies, therefore had a question for Hayden. It was really Vice President Dick Cheney's question, and Tenet was merely the messenger. The query was simple: could Hayden do more? Tenet and Cheney wondered if it was possible for the general to be more aggressive with the NSA's extraordinary powers to vacuum up vast amounts of electronic communications and telephone information, and turn them against the terrorists.

For five decades, since its founding in 1952, the NSA has accumulated almost mythical technical and mathematical expertise. So much so that in the 1970s, the reformist senator Frank Church had warned that the NSA had the power 'to make tyranny total in America'.

Its neighbours in Maryland include a number of secret or sensitive US military sites, such as Fort Detrick, the home of the US bioweapons programme, and Edgewood Arsenal, where the US developed chemical weapons. But the NSA was the most secret of the lot. Its budget and personnel are a state secret too.

The NSA's mission is to collect signals intelligence from around the globe. This means anything electronic: radio, microwave, satellite intercepts. And internet communications. This clandestine monitoring is done without the target finding out. The agency has intercept stations around the world – in US military bases, embassies and elsewhere.

Its capabilities are boosted by a unique intelligence-sharing arrangement dating back to just after the second world war, known as 'Five Eyes'. Under Five Eyes, the NSA shares its intelligence product with four other Anglophone nations: the UK, Canada, Australia and New Zealand. In theory, these allies don't spy on each other. In practice, they do.

Legally, the NSA cannot just do as it pleases. The fourth amendment to the US constitution prohibits unreasonable searches and seizures against American citizens. Searches, which include communications intercepts, are only legal against a specific suspect, backed by 'probable cause' and the issue of a judicial warrant.

These safeguards are not just irrelevant or antiquarian restrictions. In the 1970s, President Nixon demonstrated how such power could be abused, by ordering the NSA to tap the phones of several fellow Americans he didn't like, under the notorious MINARET program. The NSA's illegal domestic targets included some US senators themselves, plus the boxer Muhammad Ali, the writer Benjamin Spock, the actress Jane Fonda, the black activists Whitney Young and Martin Luther King, and other critics of the misbegotten Vietnam war.

The MINARET scandal brought about the Foreign Intelligence Surveillance Act (FISA), a seminal 1978 law. Under it, the NSA was supposed to steer clear of communications inside the US or involving Americans, unless it had a warrant.

Life was easier for the NSA's smaller UK partners at GCHQ, who faced no written constitution, and who could pressurise government ministers to give them what they wanted under a cosy British blanket of secrecy. Britain's RIPA (the 2000 Regulation of Investigatory Powers Act) was soon to be 'interpreted' to give GCHQ legal carte blanche to carry out mass surveillance on British soil, and pass on the results to the NSA – provided only that one end of a communications link was foreign.

As GCHQ boasted internally, in documents later to be revealed: 'We have a light oversight regime compared with the US.'

That was certainly true in 2001. Within 72 hours of the devastating 9/11 attacks, Hayden had already taken the agency to the outer limits of its existing legal authorities.

In the midst of the emergency, Hayden secretly allowed his agency to match known terrorist phone numbers with US communications involving international calls. 'Mission Creep' rapidly occurred; within two weeks, the NSA was also cleared to give the FBI any US telephone number that contacted any Afghan telephone number. An internal NSA history would later call this 'a more aggressive use' of Hayden's powers than his predecessors tolerated.

And so, under questioning from Cheney and Tenet in 2001, Hayden had to provide an answer that his bosses would find unsatisfying. What more can you do? Nothing. Nothing more can be done within the NSA's existing authorities.

Later, Tenet asked Hayden a follow-up question over the phone. What *could* you do if you had more authorities?

As it happened, the NSA could do a tremendous amount.

Prior to the 9/11 attacks, the NSA had already been working on one experiment, which it had had to abandon because of FISA legal constraints. The idea was to perform something called 'contact chaining' on the records of communications, or metadata, it received. Contact chaining is a process of establishing connections between senders and recipients and their contacts. Done rigorously, it establishes a map of connections between people that doesn't involve actually listening to their phone calls or reading the contents of their emails. Long before Facebook ever existed, the NSA was toying with what the social network would later unveil as a 'social graph'.

But there was a problem. The Justice Department's intelligence policy branch determined in 1999 that metadata was covered under FISA's definition of electronic surveillance. That meant that contact chaining was kosher for non-American communications, but if it ensnared Americans, the NSA would be breaking the law.

Adding complexity, the transmission of electronic communications even between foreigners overseas could transit through the US, since the data splits apart into digital 'packets' rather than travelling from point to point over a telephone line. FISA protects transits inside the US. Yet, increasingly, that was how global telecommunications occurred.

There was, however, one avenue open to Hayden, Tenet, Cheney and George W Bush in the days after 9/11. They could go to Congress, which was rabid for war, and ask for more power by amending FISA. Congress was feeling generous to executive authority while the Twin Towers and the Pentagon still smouldered. In early October, representatives overwhelmingly passed the Patriot Act, granting federal investigators more authority to conduct searches in terrorism cases. Surely they would also wave through an amendment to the FISA regulations?

But the Bush administration decided against openly asking for more power. Instead, the White House simply instructed Hayden to go ahead in secret with more surveillance. The NSA's official history hazards a guess why. 'Anecdotal evidence suggests that government officials feared the public debate surrounding any changes to FISA would compromise intelligence sources and methods.'

So Hayden's NSA began preparing a new program, one that would be kept in the strictest confidence while transgressing traditional NSA boundaries. It had four aspects: telephone communications, telephone metadata, internet communications like emails and web searches, and internet metadata. The NSA would collect as much of it as it could. Contact chaining from foreigners to Americans was back on, and the NSA could scoop up foreign communications even when they traversed the USA. The program received the elegant codename STELLAR WIND, although some of the NSA's technologists took to calling it the Big Ass Graph. On 4 October

2001, STELLAR WIND began – the official covername would follow on the 31st, Halloween – thanks to an authorisation signed by President Bush and an initial outlay of $25 million.

Not many people knew about STELLAR WIND. Hayden kept Bush's directive in a safe. The NSA's top lawyer knew – along with approximately 90 NSA staff who implemented the program – and blessed it as legal. But there was no initial court approval: it would not be until January 2002 that the chief of the secret FISA court even heard of the effort; his colleagues, except for one, would not know about it for another four years. Even the NSA's internal watchdog, the inspector general, would not learn about STELLAR WIND until August 2002, nearly a year into the program's existence.

Nor would most members of Congress. Initial knowledge was limited to the top Democrat and Republican on the Senate and House intelligence committees. By January, the NSA included Democrat Ken Inouye and Republican Ted Stevens, the leaders of the Senate appropriations committee, which presides over the purse for the Senate. It would take until January 2007 for 60 people on Capitol Hill to be cleared to know the details of STELLAR WIND, out of 535 US legislators.

But from the start, STELLAR WIND appears to have had the enthusiastic support of the major telephone companies and internet service providers. This would prove to be crucial. Unlike in the old Soviet Union or modern-day China, the US government does not own and operate the internet's fibre-optic cables and switches, even the parts that pass through and out of the US. For the NSA to have a hope of harvesting phone and email records, it needed the co-operation of those companies.

The NSA's internal history records that unnamed 'private-sector partners' began providing the agency with phone and internet content from overseas in October 2001, the first month of the program, and phone and internet metadata from inside the US the following month.

The volume of communications traffic the companies opened up to the NSA was tremendous. Infrastructure controlled by three 'corporate partners', as the NSA referred to them, represented an estimated 81 per cent of international calls transiting through the United States. Close and secret partnership with telecoms is nothing new for the NSA: in fact, it is the way the NSA has operated since its inception. Those long-standing relationships, along with the patriotic sentiment of a nation wounded after 9/11, provided for a receptive audience from the firms. Two of the three 'corporate partners', for instance, contacted the NSA even before STELLAR WIND officially began and asked, 'What can we do to help?'

The following two years saw at least three more telecommunications firms approached to provide support to STELLAR WIND – although strains were beginning to emerge. The demand for this additional data did not occur, thanks to a judge's order. It was a unilateral request from the NSA, with nothing more official than a notice from Attorney General John Ashcroft – who periodically renewed the program – to back it up, and Ashcroft was no judge. One of the three firms provided merely 'minimal' support to the agency. Two others were even more hesitant. One, which the NSA wanted to provide it with email content, bucked the agency due to 'corporate liability concerns', according to an internal NSA draft history. Another wanted to bring in outside lawyers to review the legality of its compliance. The NSA, deeming the risk of exposure too great, withdrew the request.

There was unease within the Justice Department too, about the program's legality. The deputy attorney general, James Comey, was reported to have refused to sign off renewals during his boss Ashcroft's illness. Not only Hayden, the head of the NSA, but also President Bush himself were personally involved in a 2004 attempt to pressurise the *New York Times* to suppress a leak about the program. 'The Bush administration actively misled us, claiming there was never a doubt that the wiretapping operations were legal,' says Eric Lichtblau, one of the authors, along with Risen, of the subsequent exposé of the scandal in the newspaper.

In December 2005, the NSA's worst fear eventually came true. 'BUSH LETS US SPY ON CALLERS WITHOUT COURTS' read the front-page headline in the *New York Times*. The story gave only a fraction of the picture. It focused on the warrantless NSA interception of Americans' international phone calls and email traffic, without disclosing the bulk collection of the metadata that essentially provided the agency with a social network of everyone inside the US and their ties abroad.

While denouncing the *Times*, Bush publicly launched a vigorous defence of the program as one of the biggest post-9/11 intelligence successes. Even shrewder, Bush confirmed only the parts of STELLAR WIND that the *Times* had reported, and gave them a new, politically powerful name that would put its critics on the defensive: the Terrorist Surveillance Program.

As with nearly every element of Bush's national security policies, the subsequent furore was largely partisan and predictable: Republicans fell over themselves to defend the warrantless surveillance as necessary to thwart terrorists; Democrats just as quickly denounced it as a constitutional atrocity.

In October 2001, Nancy Pelosi, the liberal Californian House minority leader and parliamentary tactician, had been the ranking Democrat on the House intelligence committee, and she attended Hayden's initial briefings. Bush administration officials and allies, smelling hypocrisy and opportunism, accused Pelosi of abandoning a program she had safeguarded in secret.

Pelosi fought back. She declassified a letter she wrote to Hayden days after STELLAR WIND became operational, which expressed uneasiness: 'Until I understand better the legal analysis regarding the sufficiency of the authority which underlies your decision on the appropriate way to proceed on this matter, I will continue to be concerned.'

Pelosi was not the only one personally affected by the revelations. Vito Potenza had a problem on his hands the moment the *Times* ran with the story. As the general counsel for the NSA, one of Potenza's responsibilities was interacting with the telecoms and internet service providers, to reassure them that their co-operation was legal. But that was an easier arrangement to maintain in secret. Now that the media had run with the story, the telecoms worried about both their bottom lines and their legal exposure. But they also didn't contemplate ending the arrangement with the NSA.

One of the service providers passed on a potential solution to Potenza. Don't ask us to provide telephone metadata. Make us do it. 'The provider preferred to be compelled to do so by a court order,' the NSA's internal history noted.

So during the early months of 2006, the Justice Department and NSA lawyers worked together to craft a secret legal authorisation for domestic telephone metadata collection that would withstand the scrutiny of the equally secret FISA court, now briefed on STELLAR WIND. The answer was the so-called 'business records provision' of the Patriot Act, its now-notorious section 215.

Under section 215, passed after 9/11 and already detested by civil libertarians, the government had the power to compel businesses to turn over items 'relevant' to an 'ongoing' terrorism investigation. Shoehorning bulk metadata collection into that statutory requirement was tricky. It was questionable whether all Americans' phone records posed any relevance to any actual ongoing investigation. The metadata was more like a body of information that occurred prior to an investigation, creating the conditions for divining investigative threads.

Yet the newly briefed FISA court proved to be receptive. 'There are reasonable grounds to believe that the tangible things sought are relevant to authorised threat investigations ... being conducted by the FBI,' wrote Judge Michael Howard of the FISA court on 24 May 2006, in a classified decision, granting the court orders the companies wanted.

Keith Alexander, the next director of the NSA, was to describe these relationships with telecoms and internet service providers during a contentious hearing of the House intelligence committee on 29 October 2013: 'We've asked industry's help. Asked? OK, more accurately, we have compelled industry to help us in this manner by court order.'

It would have been more accurate, perhaps, to say 'industry' compelled Alexander to compel industry by court order.

The administration then wrote itself more legal cover in the hotly contested FISA Amendments Act (FAA). The FAA legalised and blessed any communications interception between an American and a foreigner. The foreigner did not have to be a terrorist suspect: he merely had to be 'reasonably' suspected of having foreign intelligence value. Nor did he even have to be actually overseas: he merely had to be 'reasonably' suspected of being overseas during the time of interception. Approvals came from the FISA court in bulk, annually.

In one of the most important provisions of the bill, the FAA granted explicit legal immunity to any telecommunications firm that participated in the bulk surveillance. The immunity was both retroactive and prospective. Essentially, no private-sector partner of the NSA's would ever face criminal charges or financial damages.

The FAA was passed in mid-2008, the thick of presidential election season. It was a tremendous success for the NSA. What had begun as a lawless secret, controlled entirely by the executive branch, had now won the explicit approval of Congress, many of whose members little understood its significance. There was now a new term in the NSA lexicon: '702', a reference to the legal text of FISA that the FAA changed, which would now be a wellspring for much of the NSA's overseas and ostensibly terrorism-related collection.

Civil libertarians rued a fight they bitterly contested and had now lost. Bulk collection of communications on a massive scale would follow, warned the ACLU, and some of it would inevitably be American, all without individual suspicion or a way to adequately challenge its occurrence. It sounded like the General Warrants issued by the British colonial authorities – the very unreasonable searches and seizures that had provoked the American Revolution and the constitution itself.

In the House of Representatives, where the FAA was passed by a 293–129 margin in June, the overwhelming majority of dissenting votes were Democrats. But the Democrats on the intelligence committee tended to vote for it. Among them were committee veteran Jane Harman and her predecessor, now the House speaker, Nancy Pelosi. It seemed she had overcome her earlier reservations.

In the Senate, the bill passed by a comfortable 69–28 margin. All 29 dissenters were Democrats. But what was notable were Democrats aligning with the NSA. One was

Dianne Feinstein, who would become the intelligence committee chairwoman the following year. Another was Jay Rockefeller, who held the position at the time – and who had denounced the same surveillance activities when the *Times* exposed them.

A third was the liberal hope of the early 21st century, a first-term senator from Illinois and constitutional law professor. Barack Obama, in a 2007 stump speech for his nascent presidential campaign, had pledged, 'No more illegal wiretapping of American citizens. No more National Security Letters to spy on American citizens who are not suspected of a crime. No more tracking citizens who do no more than protest a misguided war. No more ignoring the law when it is inconvenient.'

Obama, the Democratic nomination in sight, and from there the presidency, voted for the FAA on 9 July 2008.

With the passage of the FAA, political controversy over warrantless surveillance became marginal, the preoccupation of those already invested in one outcome or another. Periodically throughout the Obama administration, surveillance votes would occur – as with the renewal of the Patriot Act and the FAA itself – but relatively few paid attention. Obama paid no political price for any of the bulk surveillance activities he presided over.

One reason for that was that the FAA vote largely returned the veil of secrecy to the NSA's bulk collection activities. While a few obsessives knew the name STELLAR WIND, there was no public proof that the NSA was secretly hoarding the phone metadata of every American. There was no public proof that the NSA had entered into sweeping arrangements with every significant internet service provider, under a program that was getting off the ground called PRISM.

There was, however, a warning. In 2011, in an interview with *WIRED* reporter Spencer Ackerman – who would soon become the *Guardian*'s national security editor – and in a floor speech shortly before a critical vote on the Patriot Act, Senator Ron Wyden, an Oregon Democrat who sat on the intelligence committee, obliquely said that the government had a secret interpretation of the Patriot Act that was so different from what the text of the law said that it amounted to a new law – one that Congress had not voted to approve.

'We're getting to a gap between what the public thinks the law says and what the American government secretly thinks the law says,' Wyden said. 'When you've got that kind of a gap, you're going to have a problem on your hands.' If the American people saw the discrepancy, he added, they would be astonished – and horrified. But Wyden, sworn to protect classified information, refused to say exactly what he meant.

Despite all the suspicions and the arcane controversies, the developing facts about the country's biggest and most intrusive domestic and international surveillance programs were thus kept from the American public in whose name they were being carried out. When Edward Snowden got on a plane for Hong Kong in 2013, the material he held on his laptops was highly explosive.

5

THE MAN IN THE ROOM

Mira Hotel, Nathan Road, Hong Kong
Tuesday 4 June 2013

MACASKILL: 'What do you think is going
to happen to you?'
SNOWDEN: 'Nothing good.'

Ewen MacAskill was no stranger to Hong Kong. But during his trips to the then British colony in the early 1980s, his name had been 'Yuan Mai'. This was the official Chinese byline he used while writing for the *China Daily*. Back then, the young MacAskill lived in Beijing. He was, in theory at least, a member of the Chinese communist party's propaganda unit. In reality, he was on secondment from the respected *Scotsman* newspaper in Edinburgh. He had spotted an advert there for an English-speaking journalist.

Working for the *China Daily* was less stressful than it might have appeared, since all mention of politics was taboo. MacAskill's role was to mentor Chinese journalists. The hope was they would produce a modern English-language newspaper. There were charming tales to be told along the way. As well as obligatory stories on grain production in Tibet, MacAskill interviewed the brother of China's last emperor, and the first climber to reach the summit of Mount Everest from the Chinese face. He wrote about a Chinese nuclear physicist who later in life – maybe as repentance – designed playground rides for kids.

'People were still wearing Mao suits and riding bikes,' MacAskill recalls. It was an exotic world for a young Scot who had grown up in a tenement block in chilly Glasgow.

MacAskill had become one of the *Guardian*'s most respected journalists. Britain's Fleet Street trade may have been notorious for phone hacking, blagging, subterfuge and other acts of petty treachery, but MacAskill was one of the straight guys. In a highly regarded career he had never done anything devious. He was one of few to whom Humbert Wolfe's epigram didn't apply:

> One cannot hope to bribe or twist
> Thank God! the British journalist.
> But, seeing what the man will do
> Unbribed, there's no occasion to.

MacAskill's integrity perhaps owed something to his Scots parents, who belonged to the Free Presbyterian Church. The small sectarian group took an uncompromising view on sin. Family summers in the Hebridean island of Harris, a diehard Calvinist refuge, reinforced the evangelical creed. A working-class boy in the late 1950s, MacAskill learned that Sundays were for church. Dancing, music and fornication were forbidden. Lying was, of course, wrong.

Aged 15, MacAskill discovered books. He became an atheist. He stopped going to church. (The breach came one Sunday when the minister devoted an entire sermon to the evils of long hair; MacAskill was the only hirsute teenager in the congregation. The Beatles were increasingly hairy; beards were flourishing.) He won a place at Glasgow University to study history. 'It transformed my life,' he says. There, he realised the students who had been privately educated were no brighter than he was; that Britain's intractable postwar social divisions were more porous than he had thought.

After university, MacAskill joined the *Glasgow Herald*. He was a trainee. It was the 1970s. The period was one of old-school journalism, when the *Herald*'s reporters were kings, rather than its columnists, the stars of today's popular media, and there was a culture of Big Drinking. Reporters not working on stories would go to Ross's, a nearby bar down a dark, cobbled lane. If a story broke and you needed a reporter you went to the bar.

MacAskill thrived at the *Herald* but also had what the Germans call *Fernweh*, a longing to be far away. In 1978–9 he spent two years training journalists in remote Papua New Guinea. After China, he moved to the *Scotsman*, and then to London as the *Scotsman*'s political correspondent. In 1996 he applied for the same role at the *Guardian*. Ahead of his interview with Rusbridger, MacAskill was nervous; afterwards the editor told him: 'That's the worst interview I've heard in my life.'

Nevertheless he got it. MacAskill reported on Tony Blair's 1997 UK election landslide victory and in 2000 became diplomatic editor, covering Iraq and the Israel–Palestine intifada. In 2007 he moved to Washington.

At first his view of Obama was positive, 'a pretty good president'. Latterly, the administration's heavy-handed pursuit of journalists and their confidential sources disillusioned him. The relationship between the executive and the Fourth Estate was getting darker and more nasty, its battleground the control of digital information.

So Janine Gibson, the *Guardian*'s US editor, could certainly rely on MacAskill for imperturbable and honest advice. He now had a challenging assignment: to verify whether Greenwald's mysterious 'NSA whistleblower' was the real deal. On Monday 3 June, he stayed ensconced in the W Hotel in Kowloon while his pair of freelance companions went off to find their alleged intelligence source for the first time.

MacAskill whiled away the day taking the subway to Hong Kong Island, revisiting old haunts. It was hot and humid. Later that evening, Greenwald returned with his news – Snowden was plausible, if ridiculously young. He had agreed to meet MacAskill. They took a cab back to the Mira Hotel the next morning. Past its onyx entrance, they found Poitras in the lobby. She took them up to room 1014.

Inside 1014, MacAskill saw someone sitting on the bed. The young man was casually dressed in a white T-shirt, jeans and trainers. They shook hands, MacAskill saying: 'Ewen MacAskill from the *Guardian*. Pleased to meet you.' This was Snowden. His living conditions were cramped. There was a bed, and a bathroom; a small black suitcase lay on the floor. A large TV was on with the sound turned down. Through Snowden's window you could see Kowloon Park; mums and dads were strolling with their kids across a flash of green; it was drizzling, the sky dull and overcast.

The remains of lunch were on the table. When he left Hawaii Snowden clearly hadn't taken much with him. There were four laptops, with a hard case for the biggest of them. The previous day Poitras had given Snowden a book, *Angler: The Shadow Presidency of Dick Cheney*, by the *Washington Post*'s Barton Gellman. It told the story of how Vice President Cheney secretly brought in 'special programs' in the wake of 9/11; the STELLAR WIND affair, part-exposed by the *New York Times*.

Chapter six, well-thumbed by Snowden, read: 'The US government was sweeping in emails, faxes and telephone calls, made by its own citizens, in their own country ... Transactional data, such as telephone logs and email headers, were collected by the billions ... Analysts seldom found information even remotely pertinent to a terrorist threat.'

The encounter with MacAskill went smoothly until he produced his iPhone. He asked Snowden if he minded if he taped their interview, and perhaps took some photos? Snowden flung up his arms in alarm, as if prodded by an electric stick. 'I might as well have invited the NSA into his bedroom,' MacAskill says. The young technician explained that the spy agency was capable of turning a mobile phone into a microphone and tracking device; bringing it into the room was an elementary mistake in operational security, or op-sec. MacAskill exited, and dumped the phone outside.

Snowden's own precautions were remarkable. He piled pillows up against the door to stop anyone from eavesdropping from outside in the corridor; the pillows were stacked up in half-columns either side, and across the bottom. When putting passwords into computers, he placed a big red hood over his head and laptop – a sort of giant snood – so the passwords couldn't be picked up by hidden cameras. He was extremely reluctant to be parted from his laptops.

On the three occasions he left his room, Snowden employed a classic spy trick, updated for his Asian surroundings. He put a glass of water behind the door next to a piece of a tissue paper. The paper had a soy sauce mark with a distinctive pattern. If water fell on the paper it would change the pattern.

Snowden wasn't suffering from paranoia. He knew what he was up against. During his stay in Kowloon he had been half-expecting a knock on the door at any moment – a raid in which he would be dragged away. He explained: 'I could be rendered by the CIA. I could have people come after me – or any of their third-party partners. They work closely with a number of nations. Or they could pay off the triads, or any of their agents or assets. We've got a CIA station just down the road in the [US] consulate in Hong Kong. I'm sure they are going to be very busy for the next week. That's a fear I will live under for the rest of my life, however long that happens to be.'

He confided to MacAskill that one of his friends had taken part in a CIA rendition operation in Italy. This was almost certainly the 2003 snatch of Muslim cleric Abu

Omar, who was taken in broad daylight in Milan, flown from a local US airbase, and subsequently tortured. In 2009 an Italian judge convicted the CIA's Milan station chief, Robert Seldon Lady, and 22 other Americans, most CIA operatives, of kidnapping. Lady later admitted: 'Of course it was an illegal operation. But that's our job. We're at war against terrorism.'

Snowden felt extremely vulnerable right up until the first story on the bulk collection of US metadata from the phone company Verizon was published. (Once articles based on his NSA revelations appeared, the search for him heated up, but he felt the publicity would also offer him a measure of protection.) Before publication, there were risks for the journalists too, obviously. What would happen to them if they were caught with secret material?

With Poitras filming, and Snowden sitting on the bed, MacAskill began a formal interview. He had asked for one-and-a-half to two hours. Greenwald's questions the previous day had been those of a seasoned litigator verbally slapping and bombarding a doubtful witness; the breakthrough moment came when Snowden talked about comics and gaming.

MacAskill, by contrast, was methodical and reporterly, his journalistic style complementing Greenwald's. He asked Snowden for the basics. Could he produce his passport, social security number, driver's licence? What was his last address? What was his salary?

Snowden explained that his pay and housing allowance in Hawaii before he joined Booz Allen Hamilton as an infrastructure analyst came to $200,000. (He took a pay cut to join Booz. MacAskill conflated his former and current salary, leading some to wrongly accuse Snowden of exaggerating his income.)

Snowden anticipated he would encounter scepticism. He had brought with him from Kunia a heap of documents. 'He had a ridiculous amount of identification,' Greenwald says.

MacAskill asked a series of follow-ups. How had he got involved in intelligence work? What year had he joined the CIA? He told MacAskill of his foreign postings in Switzerland and Japan, and of his most recent assignment in Hawaii. What was his CIA ID? Snowden revealed that too. Most bafflingly, why was he in Hong Kong? Snowden said it had 'a reputation for freedom in spite of the People's Republic of China' and a tradition of free speech. It was 'really tragic' that as an American he'd been forced to end up there, he said.

And when did he make the fateful decision to become a whistleblower?

'You see things that may be disturbing. When you see everything, you realise that some of these things are abusive. The awareness of wrongdoing builds up. There was not one morning when I woke up [and decided this is it]. It was a natural process.'

Snowden said he hadn't voted for Obama in 2008 but had 'believed' in his promises. (He voted for a 'third party', instead, he said, a reference to the libertarian Ron Paul.) He had intended to 'disclose' what he had found out, but decided to wait and see following Obama's election. What did happen, he said, was profoundly disillusioning: 'He continued with the policies of his predecessor.'

All of this made sense. But some of Snowden's CV was a little odd. Snowden said that he hadn't been to university, and had instead attended a Maryland community college. This set off alarm bells for MacAskill – how could someone as smart as Snowden achieve such a high-profile job so quickly without a degree? In his career as a spy Snowden appeared to have worked for practically everybody in a remarkably short period of time: the NSA, CIA and the DIA, the Defense Intelligence Agency, either on contract or as a direct hire.

Snowden then mentioned that he had undergone basic training to join the US special forces, only to abandon the plan when he broke his legs. 'I thought, Christ, this sounds a bit like a fantasist,' MacAskill admits. 'The story was [like a] *Boy's Own* adventure.'

Yet gradually, MacAskill did become convinced that Snowden's account of his life was true, despite its unlikely and even picaresque moments. He moved on to a core issue: 'What you are doing is a crime. You are probably going to jail for the rest of your life. Why are you doing it? Is it really worth it?'

Snowden's answer was convincing to his questioner: 'We have seen enough criminality on the part of government. It is hypocritical to make this allegation against me. They have narrowed the public sphere of influence.' He acknowledged that 'nothing good' was likely to happen to him. But said he didn't regret his decision, or want to live in a world 'where everything I do and say is recorded'. As he explained: 'The NSA has built an infrastructure that allows it to intercept almost anything. With this capability, the vast majority of human communications are automatically ingested.' Federal agencies had hijacked the internet, he said. They had turned it into a machine for spying on whole populations.

MacAskill had met leakers before from his time as a correspondent in Britain's House of Commons. For the most part these were politicians. Some spilled information for reasons of ambition; others out of vengeance; many had a gripe, felt slighted, or had missed out on promotion. The reason was usually a pretty base one. But Snowden was different. 'He had a sense of idealism. It was a patriotic act,' MacAskill says.

Snowden stressed his overriding belief that the internet should be free. On one of his black laptops was an indicator to his stance: a sticker from the Electronic Freedom Forum, a US group that campaigns for internet transparency. It read: 'I support online rights.' Another sticker was for the anonymous router Tor, which is used to disguise the origin of internet messages.

As a Washington correspondent, MacAskill understood some of Snowden's fervour. The Scot had covered Obama's 2008 election campaign. He recognised that for Snowden and other Americans, the US constitution is special: it enshrines basic freedoms. Snowden believed that the US government's stealth attack on it was the equivalent of an attack that occupies land – a terrible and illegitimate invasion. He viewed his own deeds in explicitly patriotic terms. He saw his leak not as an act of betrayal but as a necessary corrective to a spy system that had grown dysfunctional.

'America is a fundamentally good country,' he maintained. 'We have good people with good values. But the structures of power that exist are working to their own ends, to extend their capability at the expense of the freedom of all publics.'

Critics would subsequently accuse Snowden of narcissism, claiming it was a desire for attention that had made him spill the NSA's beans. MacAskill formed another impression, of a diffident individual far more at home in front of his laptop than in the limelight. 'He was personable and courteous. His instinct is to be friendly. He is really shy,' he says. 'A lot of people are suggesting he was after celebrity status. He isn't.' When MacAskill took a few snaps of Snowden he was visibly uncomfortable. Snowden was in fact happiest when talking about the technical details of surveillance. 'He has got a real nerdy side to him. He's comfortable with computers. That's his world.'

Greenwald and MacAskill were internet bumpkins who knew little about how the web actually worked (although Poitras's technical skills were formidable). The two men struggled to make sense of many of the PRISM slides. Snowden talked them through the complex diagrams. He explained acronyms, pathways, interception techniques. He wasn't patronising but patient and articulate, MacAskill says, in his element among double-barrelled NSA program codenames. To outsiders they were gobbledygook, an impenetrable alphabet spaghetti.

Because he was British, MacAskill asked, almost as an afterthought, whether there was a UK role in this mass data collection. It didn't seem likely to him. Most Britons' benign mental image of GCHQ was of boffins in tweed jackets, puffing on pipes, cracking wartime Nazi codes and playing chess.

MacAskill knew that GCHQ had a long-standing intelligence-sharing relationship with the US, but he was taken aback by Snowden's vehement response. Snowden said: 'GCHQ is worse than the NSA. It's even more intrusive.'

It was another piece of sensational information.

Each time MacAskill and Greenwald went to visit Snowden they expected him to have gone, to have been arrested, press-ganged and taken to a dark modern gulag.

The following day, Wednesday 5 June, Snowden was still in place at the Mira Hotel. That was the good news. No one had grabbed him. The bad news was that the NSA and the police had been to see his girlfriend back at their home in Hawaii. Snowden's absence from work had been noted, an automatic procedure when NSA staff do not turn up. Snowden was calm, as usual, but outraged at the treatment of Lindsay Mills. He thought the police were badgering and intimidating her.

He had so far said little about his personal life; his focus was the story and what it said about the US surveillance state. His mother, Wendy, worked as a clerk at the district court back in Baltimore. Since he had vanished on 20 May, she had been trying to contact him. She realised something had gone wrong.

Now he agonised: 'My family does not know what is happening. My primary fear is that they will come after my family, my friends, my partner. Anyone I have a relationship with.' He admitted: 'That keeps me up at night.'

The NSA's unwelcome house call was hardly surprising. And as he was now on their radar, the chances of Snowden's Hong Kong hideout soon being busted seemed much higher. He had, after all, exfiltrated many thousands of the agency's most secret documents. MacAskill felt sympathy towards Snowden. Here was a young man in trouble. His future seemed bleak. Snowden was almost the same age as MacAskill's children. 'I would not like one of my kids to be in that predicament,' he says.

But the CIA hadn't found him yet. This was one of the more baffling aspects of the Snowden affair: why did the US authorities not close in on him earlier? Once they had spotted his absence, they might have pulled flight records showing he had fled to Hong Kong. There he was comparatively easy to trace. Snowden had checked into the £200-a-night Mira Hotel under his own name. He was even paying the bill with his personal credit card, now practically maxed out, and another source of worry for him: Snowden feared his pursuers might block it.

One explanation is that the US was reluctant to act in communist China. Another is that the US authorities were less omnipotent than they appeared. This view – bureaucratic ineptness rather than a Sino–US impasse – seems the more likely explanation in the light of the

White House's subsequent bungled attempts to extradite Snowden from Hong Kong.

The experience of flying half way across the world, meeting Snowden, and then working on a set of extraordinary stories created a close bond between three journalists who were quite ill-assorted: a disputatious gay American, an intense Oscar-nominated film-maker and a Brit professional reporter and mountaineer who said 'Aye' rather than 'Yes', just like Scottie from *Star Trek*. It was a camaraderie born out of something thrilling and uncertain. All three felt they were involved in a joint endeavour of high public importance, with a large degree of risk. MacAskill had climbed the Matterhorn, Mont Blanc and the Jungfrau. His calmness now stood him in good stead.

Poitras's earlier antipathy to MacAskill vanished. She grew fond of him. 'Ewen meshed into the team so seamlessly and perfectly and instantly,' Greenwald says. Rusbridger dubbed the triple working partnership 'a lovefest'.

That evening, Greenwald rapidly drafted a story about Verizon. Snowden's classified documents showed that the NSA was secretly collecting all the records from this major US telecoms company. The trio intended this story to be only the first in a series of seismic disclosures. But they feared that time was not on their side. Mac-Askill and Greenwald discussed the text until late. They sat in Greenwald's room in the W Hotel, overlooking the harbour and the hills of the Chinese mainland. The view took in skyscrapers on Hong Kong Island and the bridge towards the airport – a crowded, twinkling cityscape.

Greenwald would work on his laptop, then pass it to MacAskill. MacAskill would type on his computer and hand Greenwald his articles on a memory stick; the sticks flowed back and forth. Nothing went on email. The journalists lost track of the hours. MacAskill went to bed for a while. When he got up, Greenwald was still working. Snowden told the *New York Times*'s Peter Maass, 'I was particularly impressed by Glenn's ability to operate without sleep for days at a time.' (In fact, Greenwald would crash out in the afternoons.)

They sent their final version of the story over to Janine Gibson in New York. Its appearance would certainly start an unprecedented and unpredictable uproar.

But the question now was whether the *Guardian* was actually prepared to publish it.

6

SCOOP!

Guardian US office, SoHo, New York
June 2013

HIGGINS: 'You can walk, but will they publish?'
TURNER: 'They'll publish.'
Three Days of the Condor, 1975

For over a decade, 33-year-old Spencer Ackerman had been covering the US national security beat. He had been building contacts, schmoozing senators and tracking the post 9/11 policies of the Bush and Obama administrations. This could be frustrating. True, in 2005 the *New York Times* had revealed the existence of an aspect of President Bush's warrantless surveillance program, codenamed STELLAR WIND. But this leak was highly unusual, a ray of light chinking out from an otherwise impenetrable secret world. (The *Times* had sat on the story for a year. It had eventually published, but only after its hand was forced when *Times* reporter James Risen planned to write about it in a book.)

A rambunctious character, prone to performing push-ups during moments of high stress, Ackerman came from New York. He was nearby in New Jersey at college – aged 21 – when the planes crashed into the Twin Towers. 'It was the big story,' he says, explaining his interest in national security. Working first for *The New Republic*, and then for *WIRED* magazine, and its national security blog 'Danger Room', he had devoted much of his energies to probing the NSA's surveillance programs. There were clues. But few facts. And the NSA was silent about its work, as remote as an order of mute Carthusian monks.

In 2011, Ackerman got a call from the office of Ron Wyden, the Oregon Democrat and a leading critic of government surveillance. Speaking obliquely during an interview in the senator's office – he couldn't disclose classified information, after all – Wyden said he was deeply concerned about the Patriot Act, which Congress was about to reauthorise. More specifically, the senator said the executive branch had come up with a legal inter-pretation drastically at odds with what the act actually *said*. Conveniently, the government had classified its own interpretation. So nobody could challenge it. But, Wyden hinted, the White House was using casuistic means to conceal the scale of its data-gathering programs.

What was going on? In a post for *WIRED*, Ackerman speculated that the government was hoovering up massive amounts of information on private citizens. But the NSA flatly rejected suggestions it spied on Americans. In 2012, General Alexander made an unlikely appearance at a Las Vegas hacker convention. It was the first time the US's top spy boss had visited the DefCon event. Swap-ping his crisply ironed general's uniform for a crumpled T-shirt and down-with-the-kidz jeans, Alexander took incongruously to the stage. He assured his audience that the agency 'absolutely' didn't keep 'files' or 'dossiers' on 'millions or hundreds of millions' of Americans.

Was this a barefaced lie? Or a semantic evasion in which 'files' meant something different from, say, bulk collection of telephone records? For Ackerman, and other national security journalists, these were tantalising pieces of a large puzzle. The post-9/11 Patriot Act gave the edges. But the overall design remained unclear. Officials might well be using a mixture of secret courts, obfuscation and classification to fend off legitimate requests for information. But there was no proof. And since hardly anyone ever leaked from the NSA, there seemed little prospect the true extent of government surveillance would be revealed any time soon.

In late May, Ackerman, a prolific tweeter, quit his job at *WIRED*. An opportunity came up with a new operation, to become US national security editor at the *Guardian*. The job would be based at the paper's DC office in Farragut Square, a mere three blocks away from the White House. US editor Janine Gibson asked Ackerman to come first to New York. She told him she would like him to spend a week undergoing 'orientation'. It wasn't entirely clear what 'orientation' meant. Nonetheless, keen to impress and brimming with ideas, Ackerman travelled to NYC to report for duty.

His start date, Monday 3 June 2013, turned out to be exceptionally fortuitous.

Ackerman reported to the sixth floor at 536 Broadway. Compared to, say, the *New York Times*, the *Guardian* US's SoHo office is small and low-key – an open-plan room shaped like an inverted L; with some computers, meeting areas and a kitchen containing PG Tips tea, biscuits and a coffee machine. On the wall are black and white portraits by the world-famous *Observer* photographer, Jane Bown. A picture of a young Rupert Murdoch also once hung in the editor's office; the ironic Rupe was later to disappear to make way for framed *Guardian* front pages of its NSA scoops.

Below is the hubbub of Broadway: boutiques, cafes, tourists. Five minutes' walk away down Spring Street is Mother's Ruin, a favoured bar, with a stuccoed cream-coloured ceiling.

Guardian US is, perhaps, a vision of how media might look once print newspapers have gone the way of the dinosaurs. It is an exclusively digital operation, run with 31 editorial staff and a shoestring $5 million budget. (The *NYT*, by contrast, has 1,150 news-department employees.) About half of its journalists are Americans, mostly young and digitally native. Many have half-sleeve tattoos, one bold soul the full arm. The mission, as Gibson puts it, is to be an entirely US version of the London *Guardian*, offering a dissenting voice about the world.

Since its July 2011 start-up, the US audience had grown. Even so, the Brit interlopers seemed way too low down the Washington food chain to compete with news giants like the *NYT*, the *Post* or the *Wall Street Journal*. (The in-house joke was that at the annual 2012 White House press dinner, *Guardian* US had been allocated just two tickets, next to the toilets and the dumb waiter.)

As the week's events would dramatically illustrate, not being part of the Washington club had its advantages. Gibson put it frankly: 'Nobody takes our calls anyway. So we have literally nothing to lose in terms of access.'

The *Guardian* was the third-largest newspaper website in the world, well before Edward Snowden came along. But seemingly the White House had little idea what the title was – a newspaper, a free sheet, a blog? – or about the nature of its innovative British editor, Janine Gibson.

Ackerman never got the 'orientation' Gibson promised him. He watched for several hours as Gibson and her Scottish deputy Stuart Millar sat closeted inside her office. The door remained firmly closed. Occasionally she would emerge, heading briskly across the newsroom, before vanishing again behind frosted glass. As Millar, a 41-year-old who moved from London to NYC in 2011, put it: 'Every time we came out to go to the bathroom or get a glass of water it was like meerkats popping up at desks, nodding to each other and sending out alarm signals.' Clearly a big story was in the offing.

At lunch, Gibson finally asked Ackerman to join her and Millar: the three walked round the corner to Ed's Lobster Bar in Lafayette Street. The restaurant was full; the three jammed up against other diners and ordered lobster rolls. Ackerman launched into chit-chat, only for the two Brits to cut him off. The editor then dropped her bombshell. She told him: 'There is no orientation. We've got a good story that we need you to be involved in.' Gibson laid out what was really going on – a whistleblower, in an unidentified third country. The whistleblower was working with Greenwald and Mac-Askill. They were preparing stories on … NSA surveillance. Holy shit!

Ackerman was stunned. 'I went silent for a little while,' he says. He adds: 'I had been reporting on this stuff, on warrantless surveillance programs, for seven years. I got so deep into the weeds on this.'

Gibson briefed him on the PRISM slides, and the secret court order compelling Verizon to hand over the phone records of all of its US customers. Ackerman grasped his head in his hands and began rocking up and down, muttering, 'Oh fuck! Oh fuck!' before recovering his composure.

He was excited that his long-held suspicions were correct: the Obama administration was secretly continuing and even expanding Bush-era surveillance practices. Ackerman asked Gibson if the words STELLAR WIND meant anything to her. It did. 'Birds sang. Butterflies fluttered,' he recalls dreamily. 'It was everything I had been trying to find for seven years.' He went on: 'I thought this white whale was coming to the tip of my harpoon. It turned out there was a pod of stories.'

The implications were massive. The Verizon secret court order was dated 25 April 2013. It forced one of the US's largest telecoms providers to hand over to the NSA the telephone records of millions of its US customers. Verizon was passing on private details on an 'ongoing, daily basis'. It was giving the NSA information on all calls in its systems, both inside the US and between the US and other countries. It was sensational apparent proof that the NSA was a dragnet collecting the records of millions of US citizens, regardless of whether they had committed any crime or been involved in terrorism.

The document was from the Foreign Intelligence Surveillance Act [FISA] court. Signed by Judge Roger Vinson, it gave the US administration unlimited authority to suck up telephone metadata for a 90-day period. The period ended on 19 July. 'It was the most exciting thing I have ever seen. No one who is not authorised has seen a FISA court order,' Ackerman says. 'In my most fevered and conspiratorial imaginings I didn't think they [the government] would be doing something like this.' Was the three-month request a one-off? Were there other similar orders? There was no answer to that. Snowden had provided one recent document. But the suspicion was that the NSA compelled other major mobile phone networks to share their data in the same way.

At the New York office, Gibson drew up a careful plan. It had three basic components: seek legal advice; work out a strategy for approaching the White House; get draft copy from the reporters in Hong Kong. The NSA seemed so far unaware of the tsunami about to engulf it. Ironically, the *Guardian* was itself beginning to operate like a classic intelligence agency – working in secrecy, with compartmentalised cells and furtive encrypted communications. Email and conversations on open lines were out. Gibson wrote a tentative schedule on a whiteboard. (It was later titled 'The Legend of the Phoenix', in foot-tapping homage to the summer's hit by the French electro duo Daft Punk.)

Those with knowledge of the Snowden project were a tiny group, burrowing into the heart of US secrecy. Newspaper people are, by their natures, incorrigible gossips. On this occasion all information was as tightly controlled as in a Leninist cell. Most staff were quite unaware their colleagues were strapping into a journal-istic roller-coaster.

The paper intended to publish the Verizon story first. Of all the thousands of documents, these were the most comprehensible. 'It was unequivocal, crystal-clear,' Millar says. Next would come a story about the internet project codenamed PRISM. Then the revelation that the US was actively engaged in cyber-warfare. Last, if the paper made it that far, the truth behind a covername, BOUNDLESS INFORMANT.

The task was made fraught by the fact that the journal-ists working on the scoop were strung across the world – in Hong Kong, in the US, in Britain. Ackerman was sent back to Washington DC. He was told to get ready to contact Verizon. And, when the moment came, to liaise with the White House. In London, Alan Rusbridger, the *Guardian*'s editor-in-chief, headed for the airport with diplomatic editor Julian Borger, for the next available New York flight.

For Janine Gibson, formerly the online editor of guardian.co.uk, the paper's website, this would certainly be a white-knuckle ride. Could a mistake blow every-thing? There were multiple problems. 'Nobody had ever seen these documents before. The FISA court documents were so secret there was nothing to compare them with,' she says. She was wondering uneasily whether the text of the court order was too good to be true – a possible hoax.

One of the biggest problems was the US Espionage Act. The US regulatory regime was looser than its British counterpart. Back at the *Guardian*'s UK base, the British government could simply go for a court injunction – a gag order to stop publication. But even in the US, home of the first amendment, the potential ramifications of publishing super-sensitive classified NSA material were grave. This was the biggest intelligence leak ever.

It seemed highly possible that the US government might seek a subpoena. And assemble a grand jury. The aim would be to force the *Guardian* to disclose the identity of its source. Millar and Gibson met with two leading media lawyers – initially David Korzenick and later David Schulz. The pair helped sketch a way forward.

The Espionage Act was a curious piece of legislation written during the first world war. It made it a crime to 'furnish, transmit or communicate' US intelligence material to a foreign government. The statute was rather vague. It was unclear, for example, whether the law did or didn't apply to journalists who might publish national security items. Case law wasn't much help, either: there were very few precedents for a prosecution of this kind.

There were some grounds for optimism. First, during its 96 years, the Espionage Act had never been used against a news organisation. It seemed unlikely this administration would want to be the first. Second, the political context was propitious. The White House had found itself at the centre of a firestorm over what critics said was its repeated persecution of investigative journalists. The Justice Department had obtained telephone records from reporters working for the Associated Press, who had written about a failed al-Qaida plot – an astonishing intrusion into a news-gathering operation. In another leaked inquiry it had targeted a reporter from Fox News. Following an outcry, attorney general Eric Holder told Congress his department would not prosecute journalists for engaging in journalism.

Nonetheless, it was important for the *Guardian* to demonstrate that it was behaving responsibly. The paper had to show it was taking every reasonable step to avoid hurting US national security. And that it published only material which revealed the broad outlines of the government's surveillance policies, rather than damaging operational details. The test was: does the public have a genuine right to know under the first amendment? The paper's sole aim was to enable the debate that Snowden and persistent critics in the Senate such as Wyden, and his Senate intelligence committee colleague Mark Udall, had long wanted.

Events were moving at speed. The *Guardian*'s MacAskill had tapped out a four-word text from Hong Kong. It said: 'The Guinness is good.' This code phrase meant that he was now convinced Snowden was genuine. Gibson decided to give the NSA a four-hour window to comment, so the agency had an opportunity to disavow it. By British standards the deadline was fair – long enough to make a few calls, agree a line. But viewed from Washington, where journalist–administration relations were cosy and sometimes resembled a country club, this was nothing short of outrageous, even considering briefing spokesmen on complicated material.

In DC on Wednesday, Ackerman's official first day began in the Washington office. He said hello to his new colleague Dan Roberts, the *Guardian*'s Washington bureau chief, but could disclose nothing of his surreal mission. At around 1pm he put a call in to Verizon. He then rang the White House's Caitlin Hayden. Hayden was chief spokesperson for the National Security Council (NSC), the powerful body in charge of co-ordinating US national security and foreign policy strategy, chaired by the president. Hayden didn't pick up.

Ackerman sent an urgent email. It had the subject: 'need to talk ASAP':

> 'Hi Caitlin,
> Just left you a voicemail – on what I *hope* was your voicemail extension. I'm now with the *Guardian*, and I need to speak with you urgently concerning a story about US surveillance activities. I think it's best we speak by phone … Please do call as soon as you can.'

Hayden was busy. It was, coincidentally, the day the White House announced Ambassador Susan Rice would become Obama's national security adviser, director of the National Security Council. Hayden emailed to say she would come back to him in an hour. Mid-afternoon, she did call. Ackerman told her what the *Guardian* had – a secret FISA court document – and what it intended to do – publish it, the same day, at 4.30pm. 'Caitlin was extremely upset,' Ackerman says.

After her initial shock, Hayden professionally noted down the details. She promised to 'take this to her people'. Those people's mood must have been one of confusion – what precisely was the *Guardian* and where the hell had these pesky Brits got the leak from?

At 4pm, Hayden emailed and said the White House would like him to speak 'as soon as possible' to the relevant agencies, the Department of Justice and the NSA. Ackerman called the DoJ and spoke to NSA press officer Judy Emmel. Emmel betrayed no reaction. 'My heart was racing,' Ackerman says.

At Gibson's instruction, Ackerman now emailed Hayden to say his editor had authorised him to push the deadline back 'until 5.15pm'.

Hayden then called Gibson herself, direct from the White House. She had a proposal – a 5.15pm conference call. The White House was sending in its top guns. The team included FBI deputy director Sean M Joyce, a Boston native with an action-man resumé – investigator against Columbian narcotics, counter-terrorism officer, legal attaché in Prague. Joyce was responsible for the FBI's 75 overseas and domestic missions fighting crime and threats to national security. He was now the FBI's lead on intelligence.

Also patched in was Chris Inglis, the NSA's deputy director. Inglis was a man who interacted with journalists so rarely he was considered by many to be a mythical entity, like the unicorn. Inglis's career was illustrious. He had degrees in mechanical engineering and computer science, and had climbed rapidly through the NSA. Before becoming General Alexander's civilian number two, he was posted between 2003 and 2006 to London as senior US liaison officer (SUSLO), the US's top-ranking intelligence official liaising with GCHQ and British intelligence. Presumably during his London stint he would have seen the *Guardian*.

Then there was Robert S Litt – known as Bob – the general counsel to the Office of the Director of National Intelligence. A Harvard and Yale graduate, Litt knew how the FISA court worked from his six years in the mid and late 1990s at the Department of Justice. Litt was clever, likeable, voluble, dramatic, lawyerly and prone to rhetorical flourishes. 'He knows what he's doing. Smart. The smartest of the bunch,' in Ackerman's judgement.

On the *Guardian* side were Gibson and Millar, two British journalists, sitting in Gibson's small office, with its cheap sofa and unimpressive view of Broadway. Ackerman was routed in as well from DC. But it seemed poor odds – a couple of out-of-towners ranged against a Washington behemoth.

By fielding heavyweights, the White House had perhaps reckoned it could flatter – and if necessary bully – the *Guardian* into delaying publication of the Verizon story, certainly for a few days, and possibly forever. The strategy was a rational one. But it made a few presumptions. It assumed the White House was in control of the situation. And it perhaps underestimated Gibson. 'It's in these moments you see what your editors are made of,' Ackerman observes.

The general theme of the official representations – all 'on background', of course – was that their Verizon story was far from impartial. It was misleading and inaccurate. But the administration high-ups were willing to sit down and explain the bigger picture. The offer, in essence, was that Gibson would be invited for a chat in the White House.

This sort of gambit had worked with US publications in the past, most notably with the *New York Times* back in 2004 when the paper first discovered President Bush's warrantless surveillance programs. After 'the chat', it was made clear the *Guardian* might feel less enthusiastic about publishing. The subtext was: you don't really understand how things work around here. 'I think they thought they could flannel through me,' Gibson says.

Her agenda was different. As she saw it, this encounter was a reasonable opportunity for government to raise 'specific' national security concerns. She told Bob and co she believed there was an overwhelming public interest in revealing the secret court order. The order, she said, was very general, with no operational detail, facts or findings. It was hard to see a prima facie case where it might cause damage. But she was open to listening to their concerns.

The men were used to getting their own way and seemed nonplussed by Gibson's manner. Even in moments of high stress such as this, the editor's tone was convivial and breezy – a disarming mix. In her previous incarnation as the *Guardian*'s media editor, Gibson had dealt with many other people who tried to throw their weight about. They included the noisy CNN anchor Piers Morgan and the UK Prime Minister David Cameron – back then a mere public relations man for Carlton, a none-too-distinguished TV channel.

As the pressure was piled on, Gibson felt her accent growing more and more starchily British. 'I began to sound like Mary Poppins,' she jokes. Millar, meanwhile, Googled 'DNI', 'Bob Litt', 'Chris Inglis', 'Sean Joyce'. What exactly were their backgrounds? Sitting over in DC, Ackerman was impressed by Gibson's performance; he sent words of cheery encouragement by G-chat.

After 20 minutes the White House was frustrated. The conversation was going in circles. Litt and Inglis refused to raise any specific concerns on the grounds that even 'discussing' the secret Verizon document on the telephone amounted to a felony. Finally one of the team could take no more. Losing his temper, and growling in a thick accent, as if the star of a cop show, he shouted: 'You don't need to publish this! No serious news organisation would publish this!'

Gibson stiffened; the earlier grace and lightness of touch disappeared. She replied icily: 'With the greatest respect, we will take the decisions about what we publish.'

'It was: "How dare you talk to us like this?"' Millar says. He adds: 'It was clear that the administration wasn't going to offer anything of substance. We were going to publish. It was game on.'

The White House team indicated they might escalate the issue. Gibson replied that the editor-in-chief – half way across the Atlantic – was unavailable. She said: 'I'm the final decision maker.' A deflated group wrapped up the conference call: 'We seem to have reached an impasse we can't get past.'

Gibson had resisted the administration's attempts to cajole her, keeping her cool while sticking to the legal playbook. Ackerman says: 'She didn't budge. She was ramrod.' He adds: 'It took the Obama administration a long time to acclimate to the fact that they were not the ones in control, that she was ... How often do they interact with people who are not part of their club?'

The encounter demonstrated the difference between newspaper cultures on either side of the pond. In the US, three big newspapers enjoy a virtual monopoly. With little competition, they are free to pursue leads at a leisurely, even gentlemanly, pace. The political culture is different too, with the press generally deferential towards the president. If anyone asked Obama a tough or embarrassing question, this was itself news.

In what used to be Fleet Street, by contrast, the media landscape was very different. In London, there were 12 UK national titles locked in a permanent, exhausting battle for survival, a Darwinian struggle to the death. The rivalry had grown more intense as print newspaper circulations declined. If you had a scoop, you published. If you didn't, someone else would. It was dog-eat-dog, then grind up its bones.

The US authorities now tried to exert pressure in the UK. The British security service MI5 called Nick Hopkins, the paper's security editor at the *Guardian*'s London headquarters; the FBI's people similarly called the paper's no. 2, the deputy editor Paul Johnson.

(Deputy director Joyce began: 'Hello Paul, are you having a good day? We've been talking to Ms Gibson. We don't feel we've been making progress … ') Attempts to reach Rusbridger personally were unsuccessful. The editor-in-chief was still on a plane. He had made it clear this was Gibson's call.

The federal officials now acted sad rather than angry. But in DC, Ackerman was getting nervous. He was wondering whether guys with guns and wraparound shades might be standing outside his apartment in Dupont Circle, ready to whisk him away and interrogate him in a dark cell. He reasoned: 'We had got off the phone with three extremely powerful and extremely displeased men, one of whom was the deputy head of the FBI.'

Over in Hong Kong, Snowden and Greenwald were restless; they were sceptical that the *Guardian* would have the sheer finger-in-your-eye chutzpah to publish. Greenwald signalled that he was ready and willing to self-publish or take the scoop elsewhere if the *Guardian* hesitated. Time was running out. And Snowden could be uncovered at any minute.

Just after 7pm, *Guardian* US went ahead and ran the story. It was, by any standards, an extraordinary scoop, but it was to be just the first one of many.

The article, with Greenwald's byline on it, began: 'The National Security Agency is currently collecting the telephone records of millions of US customers of Verizon, one of America's largest telecoms providers, under a top-secret court order issued in April.'

Despite the failure of their conference call, the White House must never have really believed that the *Guardian* would have the audacity to publish the secret order. A few minutes after the story went live, Hayden sent a note to Ackerman, asking: 'Are you guys going ahead?'

Being behind the curve in this way was to characterise the White House's interactions in the days ahead. Senior officials were incredulous at the breakneck speed of publication. The NSA must have been chasing down the leak but was unaware the *Guardian* didn't just have one top-secret document, but thousands. Gibson says: 'We were absolutely moving at speed. We knew we had a really limited window to get stories out before it became a manhunt.'

Snowden had maintained the Verizon revelations would set off a public storm. Gibson and Millar were less persuaded; it was a good story, for sure, but how big would it go? The day's tasks finished, Ackerman met his wife Mandy for dinner, sat down in a Korean restaurant, and ordered a large, calming beer. He pulled up the newly published Verizon piece on his iPhone. He showed Mandy. 'Holy shit,' she exclaimed. Ackerman looked at Twitter: the *Guardian* revelation was suddenly everywhere. 'It was rapidly becoming a thunderclap,' he says. He looked around. Could the two men sitting at the next table be FBI?

The paranoia was understandable. From now on the *Guardian* found itself the target of intense NSA scrutiny. Suddenly the world felt different. Jitteriness set in. It was unclear on what legal basis the NSA was spying on journalists going about their job and protected by the first amendment. But it was evident that whatever electronic privacy they had once enjoyed had now vanished. At 7.50pm Millar ran out of the office, got on the subway and returned to his home in Brooklyn; his twins were celebrating their fifth birthday, and he wanted to see them before they went to bed. (Millar told his daughter: 'I didn't want to miss you on your birthday, darling.' She replied: 'You've already missed my birthday, Daddy.')

Millar headed off back to work a mere 20 minutes later, to discover that diggers had mysteriously arrived at 536 Broadway. They were tearing up the pavement immediately in front of the *Guardian*'s office, a strange activity for a Wednesday evening. With smooth efficiency, they replaced it. More diggers arrived outside Gibson's home in Brooklyn. Construction crews also began very loud work outside the *Guardian*'s Washington bureau. Soon, every member of the Snowden team was able to recount similar unusual moments – 'taxi drivers' who didn't know the way and forgot to ask for money, 'window cleaners' who lingered and re-lingered next to the editor's office.

In the coming days the *Guardian*'s laptops repeatedly stopped working. Gibson was especially unlucky. Her mere presence had a disastrous effect on technology. Often her encrypted chats with Greenwald and others would collapse, raising fears of possible hacking. She stuck a Post-it note on one compromised machine. It read: 'Middlemanned! Do not use.' Having glimpsed Snowden's documents, it was clear the NSA could 'middleman' practically anything, in other words insert itself in the middle of a conversation between two parties and siphon off private data. All the players involved in the Snowden story went from being encryption novices to encryption mavens. 'Very quickly, we had to get better at spycraft,' Gibson says.

That evening, the bleary-eyed journalists began pulling into shape the next exclusive on PRISM. At midnight Rusbridger and Borger walked in; on the plane over, Rusbridger had been mugging up on US law and the Espionage Act. The following morning on the subway to Spring Street station, the nearest to the New York office, the pair had overshot their stop. They ran up the stairs, and dived into a train heading in the opposite direction. 'That will shake them off,' Rusbridger joked. The mood was jubilant as Rusbridger read through the draft of the next story, about PRISM.

That story, too, was remarkable. The NSA was claiming it had secret direct access to the systems of Google, Facebook, Apple and other US internet giants. Under the program, previously undisclosed, analysts were able to collect email content, search histories, live chats and file transfers. The *Guardian* had a 41-slide PowerPoint presentation, classified as top secret and not to be shown to foreign allies. It was apparently used to train analysts. The document claimed 'collection directly from the servers' of major US service providers. Silicon Valley would vehemently deny this.

As the team reassembled the next morning there were still difficult editorial decisions to make. How many of the slides, if any, should the *Guardian* publish? Several gave details of previously undisclosed intelligence operations abroad. There was no public interest in betraying them. It was also important – legally, and in the interests of fairness – to approach the US tech companies for reaction. Dominic Rushe, the *Guardian*'s US business reporter, was assigned the task. And then there was the White House. PRISM was an even bigger secret than Verizon. How much warning should the White House get ahead of publication?

Gibson picked up the phone for another difficult conversation. On the other end of the line was Bob Litt and the director of national intelligence's press spokesman Shawn Turner; other security agencies were patched in. Gibson explained this was another opportunity for the White House to raise specific national security concerns. She was asked, in tones of friendly banter: 'Could you send us a copy of your story and we'll take a look at it for you?' It was maybe worth a shot. Gibson replied: 'We're not going to do that.'

There were issues with many of the slides. The problem was that the White House's and the *Guardian*'s slide-decks didn't quite match up; the colours were different. At one point Gibson said: 'I'm really sorry. It's just inherently comedic when you say the words purple box.' From the *Guardian* side laughter, from the White House bemusement. It was another moment of cross-cultural confusion.

The NSA, not surprisingly, was against publication of any of the slides; the agency's bad week was morphing into full-blown disaster. Gibson, however, was insistent the *Guardian* should disclose the dates when Microsoft, Yahoo and other tech giants had apparently signed up to the aggressive PRISM program; it was a key slide. 'We need to publish this. That's my bottom line,' she said, stressing: 'We've taken out anything operational.'

The Obama team had apparently still not entirely grasped that they had lost control irrevocably of a large cache of top-secret NSA material. As Gibson put it, reflecting on the non-existent leverage available to the US authorities: 'I could not understand what the "or else" in this was.' The *Guardian* decided it would publish only three out of the 41 slides, a conservative approach. The White House had been told the story would go live at 6pm. A few minutes earlier, the *Washington Post*, which had been sitting on some similar material, published its own version of the PRISM story. The immediate suspicion was that someone inside the administration had tipped off the *Post*. The *Post* article, however, lacked one crucial element: howling denials from Facebook and others that they were complicit in NSA surveillance.

In mid-afternoon, Gibson, Rusbridger and the others gathered in the large meeting room at the end of the office. The area had been jokingly dubbed the 'Cronut'. The reference was to GCHQ's doughnut-shaped head-quarters in England, and to the latest SoHo craze for 'cronuts', a cross between a croissant and a doughnut. Several young interns had been liquidising cronuts at a nearby desk; they were writing a feature. Cronut was, perhaps, not the funniest pun in the world. But in these febrile times it stuck.

The mood was lightening – two massive stories, Snowden still in play, an engagement process of sorts with the White House. After a succession of long days merging into muggy nights, the working environment resembled an unkempt student dormitory. Cardboard rectangles of grubby pizza boxes littered the tables; there were take-away cups and other detritus. Someone knocked over a cappuccino. This was Rusbridger's cue. He reached down for the nearest newspaper, began theatrically mopping up the coffee, and declared: 'We are literally wiping the floor with the *New York Times*.'

The Snowden revelations were becoming a deluge. On Friday morning the *Guardian* published an 18-page presidential policy directive, dated October 2012 – the document Snowden had revealed to Poitras. It showed that Obama had ordered officials to draw up a list of potential overseas targets for offensive US cyber-attacks. Like other top-secret programs, the policy had its own acronym – OCEO – or Offensive Cyber Effects Operations. The directive promised 'unique and uncon-ventional capabilities to advance US national objectives around the world with little or no warning to the adver-sary or target.' The potential effects, it boasted, ranged 'from subtle to severely damaging'.

The story was a double embarrassment for the White House. First, the US had complained persistently about invasive and damaging cyber-attacks from Beijing, directed against American military infrastructure, the Pentagon and other targets. These complaints now looked distinctly hypocritical; the US was doing exactly the same. Second, and more piquantly, Obama was due later that day to meet his Chinese counterpart Xi Jinping at a summit in California. Beijing had already hit back at US criticism. Senior officials claimed to have 'mountains' of evidence of US cyber-attacks, every bit as serious as the ones allegedly carried out by rampant Chinese hackers.

As the day unfolded it became clear that the leaks had got the president's attention. The NSA programs helped defend America against terrorist attacks, Obama said. He added that it was impossible to have 100 per cent security and 100 per cent privacy: 'We have struck the right balance.'

Rusbridger and Gibson watched Obama on the TV monitor: the immensity of what the *Guardian* had initiated was sinking in. Gibson says: 'Suddenly he was talking about us. We felt: "Oh shit. There's no going back."'

Gibson called Hayden again to warn her that another story was coming down the runway, this time on BOUNDLESS INFORMANT. The top-secret program allows the NSA to map country by country the voluminous amount of information it collects from computer and telephone networks. Using the NSA's own metadata, the tool gives a portrait of where the agency's ubiquitous spying activities are concentrated – chiefly, Iran, Pakistan and Jordan. This came from a 'global heat map' slide leaked by Snowden. It revealed that in March 2013 the agency collected a staggering 97 billion intelligence data points from computer networks worldwide.

Gibson launched into her legalistic script, inviting the White House to air its latest concerns. 'I'm just going to say my thing,' she told Hayden brightly. Hayden replied: 'Please don't.' From the NSC, there was, perhaps, a grudging acceptance that the *Guardian* had behaved responsibly. The tone was cordial. That evening, Inglis himself rang. The subject was BOUNDLESS INFORMANT. The NSA deputy chief's response to Gibson was a half-hour lecture on how the internet worked – a patronising tutorial. Still, Gibson notes: 'They had moved into a place where they were trying to engage with us.'

Like most of the Snowden files, the BOUNDLESS INFORMANT documents were highly specialised, and not easy to parse. The plan had been to publish later on Friday. With journalists gathered round, Rusbridger read the draft story out aloud, line by line.

He stopped several times. 'I don't quite get that,' Millar said.

Very quickly it emerged that more work was needed. In Hong Kong, Greenwald went off to search for more documents that might help. He found several, and the story was then re-written and posted the following morning. Gibson told her non-Snowden staff that they were free to take the weekend off. But practically all journalists came in. They wanted to witness the extraordinary denouement to an extraordinary week.

For Snowden himself now declared his intention to go public. He proposed, he said, to reveal his own identity to the world.

7

THE PLANET'S
MOST WANTED MAN

Mira Hotel, Nathan Road, Hong Kong
Wednesday 5 June 2013

'If I were a Chinese spy, why wouldn't I have flown
directly into Beijing? I could be living in a palace,
petting a phoenix, by now.'

EDWARD SNOWDEN

It had been around 3am local time when the *Guardian*
broke the first of Snowden's NSA stories. Returning to
his Hong Kong hotel room early the next morning, the
three reporters found the whistleblower ecstatic.

His revelation was there, running on CNN at the top
of the news. Snowden turned the sound up on his hotel
TV. Wolf Blitzer, CNN's anchor, was sitting with a panel
of three pundits: they were discussing the possible identity of the *Guardian*'s mysterious source. Who was the
leaker? Someone in the White House, perhaps? A disaffected general? A KGB super-mole? It was a moment of
some irony. 'It was funny watching them speculate who
might have leaked it when you are sitting beside that
person,' MacAskill said.

The public response surprised even Snowden. Posts
on the internet were massively supportive; already a

grassroots movement, Restore the Fourth Amendment, was springing up. The rapid publication was good for his relations with the *Guardian*: it demonstrated to Snowden that the paper was acting in good faith. All along his goal had been to spark a debate; he felt that the Verizon story was achieving that, making a big splash.

MacAskill wondered if the leaker was going to be smug, thrilled or proprietary to find himself at the centre of world events. Remarkably, he was totally impassive; he listened to CNN intently. He seemed to understand the enormity of what had happened. From this moment there was no way back. If he flew home to Hawaii now, arrest and incarceration would follow. Snowden's life was never going to be the same again.

So what next specifically? The most likely scenario for him, as Snowden sketched it, was that the Chinese police would arrest him in Hong Kong. There would be a legal tussle. Possibly for a few months. Maybe even a year. At the end of this he would be sent back to the US. And then … well, decades and decades in jail.

Snowden had turned over an enormous quantity of material on portable drives. This included not only the NSA's internal files, but also British material emanating from GCHQ and apparently trustingly handed over by the Brits to their US colleagues.

'How many British documents are on these?' Mac-Askill asked.

Snowden said, 'About 50,000 to 60,000.'

He had given months of thought to his planned dealings with the media. He was fastidious. He wanted a series of strict conditions for handling secret material. He was insistent that NSA/GCHQ documents disclosing spying should go to the respective subjects of surveillance. He felt Hong Kong media should have information relating to spying on Hong Kong, the Brazilian material to Brazilian media and so on. He was categorical on this point. If, on the other hand, the material fell into the hands of third-party adversaries such as the Russians or the Chinese, this would lay him open to the damaging charge that he was little more than a defector or foreign agent – which he wasn't.

Snowden was alert to the possibility that foreign intelligence services would seek his files, and was determined to prevent this. As a spy, one of his jobs had been to defend American secrets from Chinese attack. He knew the capabilities of America's foes. Snowden made clear repeatedly that he didn't want to damage US intelligence operations abroad.

'I had access to full rosters of anybody working at the NSA. The entire intelligence community and undercover assets around the world. The locations of every station we have, all of their missions … If I just wanted to damage the US I could have shut down the surveillance system in an afternoon. That was never my intention,' he said.

He put it in even more vivid terms, when subsequently accused of 'treachery': 'Ask yourself: if I were a Chinese spy, why wouldn't I have flown directly into Beijing? I could be living in a palace, petting a phoenix, by now.'

During the days of debriefing in Hong Kong, Snowden said citizens in countries that recognised whistleblowing and public-interest reporting had a right to know what was going on. He wanted the *Guardian* and other media partners to filter out anything that was operational and might damage legitimate intelligence activities. These were his conditions. All agreed.

Technical precautions were taken. The files were on memory cards. They were strongly encrypted with multiple passwords. No one person knew all the passwords to access a file.

The US freelance journalists approached by Snowden now had in their possession a large treasure trove of classified material. The WikiLeaks disclosures, published by the *Guardian* in London in 2010, were of US diplomatic cables and war-logs from Afghanistan and Iraq leaked by the US private Chelsea Manning. A few – just 6 per cent – were classified at the relatively modest level of 'secret'. The Snowden files were in a different league. They were 'top secret' and above. There had once been a melodramatic defection of Cambridge-educated spies to Soviet Moscow – Burgess, Maclean and Philby. But there had never been a mass documentary leak at this vertiginous altitude before.

Snowden generally wore just a casual T-shirt in his room, but on Thursday 6 June, Greenwald organised a switch. Snowden put on a grey, ironed shirt. He moved from his regular perch on the hotel bed to a chair: behind him a mirror was positioned. It made the room seem less tiny and cramped.

Snowden was about to record his first public interview. It would be the moment when he would introduce himself to the world and would confess – or, rather, proudly own up – to being the source behind the NSA leaks. He told Greenwald: 'I have no intention of hiding who I am, because I know I have done nothing wrong.'

It was a bold and counterintuitive move, and one that Snowden had contemplated for a long time. His reasons impressed his journalist partners as sound. First, he told MacAskill, he had seen close up the disastrous impact on colleagues of leak inquiries pursuing anonymous sources. He had witnessed the 'terrible consequences for people under suspicion'. He said he didn't want to put his colleagues through such an ordeal.

Second, he was aware of the NSA's ferocious technical capacities; it was only a matter of time before they tracked him down. His plan all along had been that after the first few stories, he would make himself known. This didn't mean, however, that Snowden wished to emulate Chelsea Manning, whose arrest in 2010 and harsh jail treatment he had followed closely. Snowden said: 'Manning was a classic whistleblower. He was inspired by the public good.' As a result, Manning was due to face a court martial in Fort Meade, next door to the NSA's headquarters – one that was shortly to sentence the young soldier to 35 years in prison.

Snowden intimated that Manning had proved the point that it was impossible for a whistleblower to get a fair trial in the US. A long spell in jail would also stymie the public debate Snowden wanted.

Poitras had been filming Snowden from the first encounter; her camera had had a freezing effect on their early interactions, but now Snowden agreed to talk directly into her lens. He was, as he put it, a 'virgin source'. Snowden had previously shunned all contact with reporters and the media. He had even avoided showing his face in his girlfriend's blog. But he was also acutely aware of how much was at stake. What was ultimately important, Snowden accepted, was the public's verdict. In this context, an interview would help shape perceptions.

Greenwald sat opposite Snowden. He asked the questions. As a lawyer and experienced broadcaster, Greenwald was comfortable with televised interviews. But Snowden's own on-screen manner would be an unknown quantity.

Snowden, however, gave a remarkable performance for a media newbie, with fluent answers and a cogent account of what had motivated him to take such a radical step. Most importantly, he appeared eminently sane.

Asked why he had decided to become a whistleblower, Snowden said he had struggled inside the system, before finally concluding he had no alternative but to go outside it: 'When you're in positions of privileged access like a systems administrator for these sort of intelligence community agencies, you're exposed to a lot more information on a broader scale than the average employee.'

What he saw had 'disturbed' him deeply. 'Even if you're not doing anything wrong you're being watched and recorded,' he told the *Guardian*. 'The storage capability of these systems increases every year consistently by orders of magnitude to where it's getting to the point … you don't have to have done anything wrong. You simply have to eventually fall under suspicion from somebody, even by a wrong call. And then they can use this system to go back in time and scrutinise every decision you've ever made, every friend you've ever discussed something with. And attack you on that basis to sort of derive suspicion from an innocent life and paint anyone in the context of a wrongdoer.'

He added, by way of explaining his own decision to blow the whistle, with all the foreseeable consequences for the rest of his life: 'You realise that that's the world you helped create and it's gonna get worse with the next generation and the next generation who extend the capabilities of this sort of architecture of oppression.'

MacAskill, who watched, gripped, as Poitras filmed, felt Snowden came across even better on camera than in person.

For the three journalists, those Hong Kong nights and days blurred into one another: a succession of gruelling work periods, fuelled by excitement, adrenaline and paranoia.

At the Mira, Poitras was soon able to show her video edit to the other two. She had turned Snowden's interview into a 17-minute film, beautifully framed and with a set-up shot at the beginning showing Hong Kong harbour and a velvety sky. Its title said simply: 'PRISM Whistleblower'. They discussed possible cuts, with Poitras eventually crunching the interview down to 12-and-a-half minutes, and releasing a second interview later.

'I felt as if he had been thrust into the middle of a spy movie,' MacAskill says. How on earth were they safely to ship the key material over to New York and London?

Talking to the *Guardian*'s editor via encrypted chat, MacAskill said the group needed technical help. David Blishen, the *Guardian*'s systems editor, was a man who had skills that few working journalists possessed. He also understood how the editorial process functioned. During the WikiLeaks investigation, Blishen helped co-ordinate the redaction of names of sources who had talked to US diplomats and might be at risk if exposed in countries such as Afghanistan, Iraq or Belarus. (This was an important but ultimately futile exercise; in the summer of 2011, six months after the first stories appeared based on US diplomatic cables, Julian Assange released the entire un-redacted cache of documents.)

Blishen was summoned, headed for the airport, and arrived in Hong Kong the next day. For him, too, the trip was nostalgic. He was born in the then colony in 1972; his father, a British official, had been stationed there. When MacAskill joined him the two talked about Scottish newspapers where they had both worked. 'I was none the wiser why I was really there,' Blishen says. 'Ewen gave nothing away.' Afterwards, MacAskill told Blishen to leave his mobile at the hotel reception, and proposed a walk. Once they were outside, MacAskill gave him a memory card; a small, flat, square chip. The SD card didn't look much. Though it was pretty large – 32 gigabytes.

Blishen needed to transmit Snowden's video back to *Guardian* US in New York. Blishen watched the video first, and he was impressed: 'He [Snowden] is articulate. He seemed principled. With Assange and Manning, people can question if they are rational. Ed seemed completely normal and plausible.' Taking the edited version, he anxiously jumped into a taxi to get back to his own hotel in Central.

The cabbie asked Blishen in sing-song English: 'Do you want to go and see girls? They cheap. Very pretty. Do you like Asian girls?'

Blishen needed to get to his room fast. He made clear his lack of interest. The cabbie thought for a moment. His face brightened: 'Oh, you like boys! Boys! Like me?' Blishen replied wearily: 'I'm very boring. I just want to go to my hotel.' The cabbie persisted: 'What do you want to do at your hotel?' Even though it was only 7.30pm, Blishen told the driver he wanted to sleep. 'I was his worst, dullest passenger ever.'

Back at the Lan Kwai Fong Hotel, Blishen crypto-messaged the *Guardian*'s James Ball, in New York. He uploaded the video file via a secure connection in an encrypted folder. He sent over the password separately. Disaster ensued. The *Guardian* US team proved unable to open the file. Time was running out. In the end, the video file had to go again unencrypted, and potentially hackable by the NSA, though still via secure connection. To everyone's relief, it arrived unmolested.

All along, Snowden had made clear that he planned to reveal himself. In New York, the record of Snowden actually speaking was nevertheless cathartic. And reassuring. 'We were completely blown away. We thought he was cool and plausible. Everything about him seemed credible,' Millar says. When the moment arrived, with the video ready to go live, the atmosphere in the news-room was deeply emotional. 'It was a terrifying moment,' Gibson adds. The editorial question remained: was this the right thing to do? Once again Snowden was making his own strategic choices – playing his increasingly limited hand of cards his own way.

Five people, including Rusbridger, were in the office. The video went up around 3pm local time. 'It was like a bomb going off,' says Rusbridger. 'There are a silent few seconds after a bomb explodes when nothing happens.' The TV monitors were set to different channels; for almost an hour they carried pre-recorded Sunday news. Then at 4pm, the top of the hour, the story erupted. Each network carried Snowden's image. CNN aired the entire 12-minute video.

It was 3am in Hong Kong when the video was posted online. Twitter instantly exploded. It was to become the most viewed story in the *Guardian*'s history.

'It's a rare thing for a source to come out in public like that. So we knew this video was going to be big,' MacAskill recalls. 'The choreography of several huge stories followed by the video was terrific.'

One moment, Snowden was known only to his friends and family, and a few colleagues. Then suddenly he became a global phenomenon, no longer just an indi-vidual but a lightning rod for all sorts of conflicting views about the state, the boundaries of privacy and security, and even the entire modern condition.

Snowden took all of this with sangfroid and humour. Sitting in room 1014 he chatted online with Greenwald and MacAskill, and joked wryly about his appearance, and the online comments it provoked. It was the first time he had seen the video. (Poitras had sent it to him before but he had had problems with his internet connection and couldn't access it.) There was one inescapable corollary: now Snowden's identity was out, he had just become the most hunted man on the planet.

The chase was already on. Greenwald, in one of his many TV interviews, had been captioned by CNN as 'Glenn Greenwald, Hong Kong' – a pretty big clue to everyone watching as to the location of the *Guardian*'s source. The local Chinese media and international journalists now studied every frame of the video for clues. They were initially thrown off by Poitras's opening shot, filmed from the W Hotel. They assumed Snowden was there too. But one enterprising hack then used Twitter to identify the Mira from its lamps.

By Monday 10 June, Snowden was packing his belongings to leave the hotel, as Poitras filmed him for the last time. She felt protective towards him. She had known him the longest, and had believed in him from the beginning. She gave him a hug. 'I don't know what he planned for that moment. I had no idea what his next move was,' she says.

Snowden vanished.

At the W Hotel, MacAskill popped out to get a cup of coffee, and to buy himself a suit and a shirt. He had brought enough clothes for a two-day assignment. A crew from CNN doorstepped him. When he returned from Marks and Spencer he found a scene of chaos. TV crews and reporters had staked out the lobby. Not only that but the management said the hotel was now 'full' and asked them to leave. They slipped out via a service lift to a waiting taxi and moved into the Sheraton. By the evening, the hacks had found them again. Before going to sleep, MacAskill piled chairs in front of his door. This might give him some warning if someone came for him, he reasoned.

Two days passed. Greenwald, MacAskill and Poitras marked the end of their trip with wine and cheese in Poitras's room, overlooking the harbour. MacAskill crashed out, exhausted. In the early hours, Poitras rang with alarming news. Snowden had sent a message saying he was in danger. He hinted that he was about to be arrested, and signed off ominously. MacAskill phoned Snowden's Hong Kong lawyers, who were now dealing with his case. No response. He called the police station. Recorded message. Two hours later one of the lawyers phoned back to say Snowden was OK. The details were hazy but it appeared Snowden had survived a close call.

How much longer could he hold out until the US grabbed him?

8

ALL OF THE SIGNALS
ALL OF THE TIME

Bude, North Cornwall
2007 onwards

'We have the brains: they have the money.
It's a collaboration that's worked very well.'
SIR DAVID OMAND, FORMER GCHQ DIRECTOR

It is visible from miles around on its cliff-top. Standing spectacularly exposed on Cornwall's geographical 'foot', which protrudes far into the Atlantic, the eavesdropping station is impossible to hide. Some of the otherworldly array of gigantic satellite dishes are 30 metres across. The dishes are set around a white golf ball-shaped radome: votive objects laid before a faceless god. A high-security fence encircles the complex. Every few metres are CCTV cameras. A sign at the entrance reads: 'GCHQ Bude'. There are guards. Visitors are unwelcome.

Near the front gate is Cleave Crescent, a miserable-looking hamlet of terraced houses. Around is a wooded valley, with ash trees, gorse and brambles. From the coast path there are stunning views: scudding waves, a steel-grey sea, and the jagged rock strata at Lower Sharpnose Point. There are gulls and sometimes a sparrowhawk, hovering against a wind-bashed headland.

One of the more charming files scraped by Snowden from the GCHQ intranet repository is a write-up of a trip to Bude by a group of spying trainees. They got the tour. They were allowed to peek inside the radome, climb up one of the larger satellite dishes, nicknamed Ocean Breeze, and peer at the antennae. On the way home they stopped off for an ice cream and dipped their toes in the Atlantic. The travel blog makes reference to Bude's original role – contributing 'Comsat to the SIGINT machine'. In other words, feeding intercepted satellite communications back to British and American intelligence.

This dramatic look-out on the UK coast has long been used for surveillance. Eighteenth-century customs officers kept watch for smugglers. The Victorian vicar Robert Stephen Hawker built himself a wooden hut to spot shipwrecks. He and his parishioners would fetch the bodies of drowned sailors up the sheer cliffs. During the second world war a military base was constructed, called Cleave Camp: there is a ghostly pillbox where gunners looked out for Nazi invaders.

GCHQ put a station here on government property in the late 1960s, in order to eavesdrop on commercial satellite links from Goonhilly Downs on the Lizard peninsula, 60 miles down the road. Goonhilly carried much of the world's international telephone traffic, but became obsolete and closed in 2008.

However, Bude is now at the heart of a new and most ambitious secret project, developed by the UK. Its fruits are handed over to London's US paymasters. The program is so sensitive that exposures of it by Edward

Snowden drive British officials into fits of anxiety and rage. Those officials' dream is to 'master the internet'. This phrase of theirs was what Snowden meant when he told the startled journalists in Hong Kong that Britain's GCHQ was worse and more intrusive even than the NSA.

Bude itself is a small seaside resort, popular with surfers and swimmers. It has a golf course, a high street with shops selling fresh crabs, an open-air swimming pool and a Sainsbury's store. But its most important role is invisible. Just down the road is Widemouth Bay. Few of the holidaymakers who splash in its bracing waters know of the beach's significance. But major undersea telecommunications cables from the US's eastern seaboard emerge here. They are called Apollo North, TAT-8, TAT-14 and Yellow/Atlantic Crossing-2, also known as AC-2. Other transatlantic cables come ashore at nearby Land's End. Thousands of miles long, the fibre-optic cables are operated by big private telecoms firms, often in consortia.

The landing points of these submarine cables are so important that the American Department of Homeland Security lists them as critical American national infrastructure (according to leaked US diplomatic messages). In this new world of internet-driven communications, Britain's position on the eastern edge of the Atlantic makes it a hub. As much as 25 per cent of the world's current internet traffic crosses British territory via the cables, en route between the US, Europe, Africa and all points east. Much of the remaining traffic has landing or departure points in the US. So between them Britain and the US play host to most of the planet's burgeoning data flows.

Unsurprisingly, given their history, both countries' spy agencies wanted to exploit their good luck and tap into all these submarine cables in order to eavesdrop. As technology changed, the two organisations had successively intercepted radio traffic, then microwave beams and ultimately satellite links. It was logical to seek now to break into the floods of internet and phone data which were travelling by the latest fibre-optic systems.

Postwar Britain originally won its place in the so-called 'Five Eyes' electronic spying team, along with Australia, Canada and New Zealand, by handing over access to a network of listening stations across the globe in Cyprus, Ceylon, Hong Kong, South Africa, Diego Garcia, Ascension Island and such Middle East client states as Oman. But with the loss of empire, some of that advantage evaporated.

Britain also gave the US two satellite stations of its own on British soil – Menwith Hill (known as 'MHS'), on the southern edge of the Yorkshire Dales, and Croughton, which handles CIA communications. But the Brits constantly had their hands held out for cash. As one GCHQ chief, Sir David Omand, was heard to say optimistically: 'We have the brains: they have the money.'

Thanks to Snowden we know to what extent, at least partially. In the period 2009 to 2012 the US government paid GCHQ at least £100m. In 2009 the NSA gave GCHQ £22.9m. The following year the NSA's payments rose to £39.9m. This included £4m to support GCHQ's work for NATO forces in Afghanistan, and £17.2m for 'mastering the internet'. The NSA paid a further £15.5m towards redevelopments at GCHQ Bude. The gesture 'protected (GCHQ's core) budget', at a time of austerity by David Cameron's coalition. In 2011/2012 the NSA gave another £34.7m to GCHQ.

British officials sniff that the sums are tiny. 'In a 60-year alliance it is entirely unsurprising that there are joint projects in which resources and expertise are pooled,' a Cabinet Office spokesman says. But the cash gives the NSA further leverage. In one 2010 document, GCHQ acknowledges that Fort Meade had 'raised a number of issues with regards to meeting NSA's minimum expectations'. It said GCHQ 'still remains short of the full NSA ask'.

Lurking always is the spectre of US displeasure. One internal paper warns: 'The NSA ask is not static and retaining "equability" will remain a challenge in the near future.' The UK's biggest fear, says another, is that 'US perceptions of the ... partnership diminish, leading to loss of access and/or reduction in investment ... to the UK.'

In other words, the British needed to keep up and demonstrate their worth. They were only a tenth of the size of their US partners. If they fell behind technically, the mighty NSA might cease intelligence-sharing, and Britain's ability to punch above its weight in the world could end ignominiously.

It was against this background that the GCHQ director in charge of 'mastering the internet' wrote a pitch for a new British project on 19 May 2009. He asserted that the agency had been struggling with changes in technology: 'It's becoming increasingly difficult for GCHQ to acquire the rich source of traffic needed to enable our support to partners within HMG [Her Majesty's government], the armed forces and overseas.'

But a breakthrough was in sight, he said. Experiments had been taking place for two years at Bude, and had been crowned with success.

The problem was not so much to tap into the internet pipes – both the US and the UK could do that. It was to find a method of reading and analysing the torrents of data within the tapped cables, as they rushed past at speeds of at least 10 gigabytes per second.

GCHQ's achievement was to be able to build a gigantic computerised internet buffer. The buffer could store traffic. Analysts and data miners would then be able retrospectively to sort through this vast pool of digital material. Full content, such as email messages, could be kept available for three days, and the less bulky metadata, such as email contacts and subject lines, for as much as 30 days. Uninteresting material such as peer-to-peer downloads of movies would be filtered out.

From the residue the spy agencies would, with luck, glean usable intelligence about targets of interest. The system was analogous to a gargantuan catch-up TV service where you could go back and watch any broadcast you'd previously missed.

At Bude, several key transatlantic fibre-optic cables made landfall close by. They could therefore be tapped into relatively cheaply and the data diverted the short distance to RPC-1 – a new 'Regional Processing Centre' secretly constructed on-site by a consortium of private firms, led by Lockheed Martin with BAE Systems' subsidiary Detica and software company Logica. The process of furtive extraction had its own acronym: SSE, for special source exploitation.

By March 2010, analysts from the NSA had been allowed some preliminary access to the Bude project, initially codenamed TINT, then christened TEMPORA. It was described as a 'joint GCHQ/NSA research initiative'. It uniquely 'allows retrospective analysis' of internet traffic.

Soon GCHQ was boasting of major achievements. 'We are starting to "master the internet". And our current capability is quite impressive.' One document spoke of 2 billion users of the internet worldwide, with over 400 million regular users of Facebook, and a 600 per cent increase in mobile phone traffic from the year before. The agency believed it was on top of these developments. The report claimed the UK now had the 'biggest internet access in Five Eyes'.

Not everything was perfect. The memo noted that American service providers were moving to Malaysia and India, with the NSA 'buying up real estate in these places' in a scramble to keep up. 'We won't see this traffic crossing the UK. Oh dear,' the author said, suggesting Britain should follow suit and 'buy facilities overseas'.

But the general tone of GCHQ's 2010–2011 mid-year review was cheery. It stated that in one 24-hour period the agency had been able to process and store 'more than 39 billion events', 'increasing our capability to produce unique intelligence from our targets' use of the internet'. Apparently this meant GCHQ had managed to collect 39 billion pieces of information in a single day.

The NSA was impressed with British efforts. In a 2011 'Joint Collaboration Activity' report it said that the UK now 'produced larger amounts of metadata than the NSA'. By May 2012 it was reported that a second internet buffering centre had been constructed at Cheltenham, within the vast circular state-of-the-art headquarters complex its 6,000 staff generally referred to as 'the doughnut'. A third overseas processing centre was also successfully organised and built at a location in the Middle East. The whole program was capable of collecting 'a lot of data!' Using TEMPORA, more than '300 GCHQ and 250 NSA analysts' now had access to 'huge amounts of data to support the target discovery mission'.

Snowden's files show just how closely British and US intelligence personnel work alongside each other. While working for the CIA in Geneva, Snowden himself visited Croughton, the CIA communications base 30 miles north of Oxford in rustic Northamptonshire. Writing as TheTrueHOOHA, Snowden said he was struck by the large number of sheep grazing nearby in green fields – a classic English scene.

The NSA has had its own operations branch at GCHQ Cheltenham since the 1950s, as well as in London; GCHQ staff work at MHS. With some advance warning other GCHQ employees from Cheltenham can visit the heavily protected US outpost.

The NSA has a senior US liaison officer attached to the UK intelligence community known as SUSLO; his British counterpart operating in Washington under diplomatic cover is called SUKLO. Lesser GCHQ employees are assigned to practically all NSA facilities; they are called 'integrees'. There is even a GCHQ staffer at the NSA's tropical base in Hawaii, where Snowden worked.

Typically GCHQ employees do at least one stint at an NSA facility. The agency provides a helpful glossary for the Brits on American life; it gives tips on car hire and points out that in the US a boot is a 'trunk'. There are joint meetings, training courses, exchange visits, cryptological workshops and celebratory dinners. And, one suspects – though Snowden's documents don't tell us this – the odd inter-agency romance.

This intelligence-swapping arrangement dating back to 1947 has been a success story. One document speaks of 'another fine example of NSA and GCHQ working well together'. The Anglo-American SIGINT partnership is often warm on a personal level, beneficial to both parties and historically enduring. You might call it a marriage.

The files, meanwhile, offer a rare insight into the cloistered world of British spying. Salaries of GCHQ staff may be low but the organisation offers its linguists and mathematicians lots of leisure activities: pub quiz nights, cake sales, trips to Disneyland Paris and an internal puzzle letter called *Kryptos*. It even has its own social networking site, SpySpace. The main drawback to a GCHQ career is the agency's provincial location. 'Be prepared to describe where Gloucestershire is,' a GCHQ recruitment guide says.

*

One particularly sensitive aspect of TEMPORA is the secret role played by telecoms companies which own or manage the fibre-optic cables. GCHQ calls them 'intercept partners', liaison with whom is handled by 'sensitive relationship teams'. They include some of the world's leading firms. BT, the main intercept partner, is code-named 'REMEDY', Verizon Business 'DACRON', and Vodafone Cable 'GERONTIC'. Four smaller providers also have codenames. In 2009, Global Crossing was 'PINNAGE', Level 3 'LITTLE', Viatel 'VITREOUS' and Interoute 'STREETCAR'.

Between them these companies help intercept most of the cable links touching the UK. They have British landing points at Lowestoft, Pevensey Bay, Holyhead (linking the UK to the Republic of Ireland), Whitesands Bay, Goonhilly and other seaside towns.

The company names are classified even higher than top secret, as 'Strap 2 ECI' – 'exceptionally controlled information'. Exposure might presumably lead to customer unhappiness. One leaked document warns of potential 'high-level political fallout' if the firms' identities become public. Intelligence sources stress that the companies have no choice. As in the US, they can use the excuse that they are compelled by law.

Thanks to this corporate co-operation, for which the telecoms companies are paid substantially by the British taxpayer, GCHQ was handling 600 million 'telephone events' a day by 2012. It had tapped more than 200 fibre-optic cables which touched the UK. It was able to process data from at least 46 of them at a time. This is indeed a lot of data – more than 21 petabytes a day – and the equivalent of sending all the information in the British Library 192 times every 24 hours.

Yet inside GCHQ there is still anxiety that the organisation will fall behind. One of the team responsible for managing TEMPORA sets out how the agency's 'mission role' grew. New techniques had given GCHQ access to huge amounts of new data or 'light' – emails, phone calls and Skype conversations. 'Over the last five years, GCHQ's access to "light" [has] increased by 7,000 per cent.' The amount of material being analysed and processed had increased by 3,000 per cent, he said – an astonishing figure. The agency was 'breaking new ground' but also struggling to keep up. 'The complexity of our mission has evolved to the point where existing management capability is no longer fit for purpose.'

An internal review for 2011/2012 also warns: 'The two major technology risks that GCHQ has to face next year are the spread of ubiquitous encryption on the internet and the explosion in the use of smartphones as mobile internet devices. Over time, both of these technologies could have significant effect on our current tradecraft.'

The agency predicts that by 2015, 90 per cent of all internet traffic will come from mobile phones. There were already 100 million smartphones around the world in 2012. The mobile was the 'most prolific customer product ever invented'. GCHQ was launching a new project to 'exploit mobile devices', the document said. It meant 'getting intelligence from all the extra functionality that iPhones and BlackBerrys offer'. GCHQ's end goal was: 'to exploit any phone, anywhere, anytime'.

TEMPORA and allied projects may be impressive. But in inventing them, the western espionage agencies seemed oblivious to the larger picture: that the state was now indiscriminately collecting the communications of millions of people, without their knowledge or consent.

In the past, British spooks attached crocodile clips on copper wires to eavesdrop on the phone calls of thieves and villains or Irish Republican terrorists. These were individual targets approved on individual ministerial warrants: the identifiable bad guys. Now, though, the NSA and GCHQ were hoovering up data from everyone on a Brobdingnagian scale. This included data from a majority of people who were entirely innocent.

Officials insist they don't have the analysts to sift through all this private correspondence. One told the *Guardian*: 'The vast majority of the data is discarded without being looked at ... we simply don't have the resources.' He said: 'If you had the impression we are reading millions of emails, we are not. There is no intention in this whole program to use it for looking at UK domestic traffic – British people talking to each other.' The head of GCHQ, Sir Iain Lobban, publicly repeats the spies' favourite analogy of a 'vast haystack of data', containing needles.

The haystack does, of course, consist of the communications of both Britons and foreigners. GCHQ's mass sweepings included among other things the contents of cables linking the international data centres belonging to Google and Yahoo, where they passed across British territory.

The British spies quote obscure UK legislation dating from 2000, which permits unrestrained foreign intelligence-gathering. They say this Regulation of Investigatory Powers Act (RIPA) allows them to bulk-collect all 'external' internet communications. 'We turn somersaults to obey its spirit and letter,' one said. The word 'external' is interpreted – some would say twisted – to mean anything tapped from a cable that has at least one foreign end. Because of the way internet links work, this means that anyone in Britain who sends an email is often also talking to GCHQ. Not something the ordinary paying customer who signs up to BT and Google can find on their contract, even in the very smallest print.

Both the British and the Americans can make secret searches inside this 'haystack' of mass data for patterns of behaviour, for contact chaining of groups of friends and for target individuals. Secret letters signed by British foreign secretaries – the first was Labour's David Miliband in 2009, the next the Conservatives' William Hague – apparently authorise queries made with a view to investigating foreign political intentions, nuclear proliferation, terrorism, serious financial crime and the UK's 'economic wellbeing'. How is this policed? Government lawyers have since demonstrated in British cases that the word 'terrorism' is capable of being interpreted very widely.

When GCHQ staff succeed in supplying their US partner with valuable intelligence, they brag about it. This happened, they say, on at least two recent occasions: the first involved underwear bomber Umar Farouk

Abdulmutallab, who in 2009 tried to blow up an airliner bound for Detroit. The second took place five months later when Faizal Shahzad, a 30-year-old US citizen who was born in Pakistan, attempted a car bombing in New York's Times Square.

The NSA was 'delighted' with GCHQ's 'unique contributions' against the US bombers. There is no clue as to what these exact contributions were. For its part, the NSA helped GCHQ with the investigation following the devastating 7/7 atrocities in London in 2005. It was the worst attack in London since the second world war. Four suicide bombers blew up three Tube trains and a bus, killing 52 people.

GCHQ denies routinely circumventing the Five Eyes' own self-denying rules and carrying out spying on US citizens on the NSA's behalf. And the NSA denies providing the same 'revolving door' service when it comes to collecting intelligence on UK nationals.

Unfortunately, Snowden's documents appear to give the lie to such claims. He unearthed NSA memos from 2005 and 2007 implying that sometimes the two agencies do target each other's citizens. The NSA is allowed to include Britons in its mass surveillance databases, 'when it is in the best interest of both nations'. Furthermore, a procedure is detailed under which the NSA will even spy on UK citizens behind the backs of the British. 'Under certain circumstances it may be advisable and allowable to target second-party persons and second-party communications systems unilaterally, when it is in the best interests of the US, and necessary for US national security.'

So the Five Eyes' claim that the gentlemanly western partners do not spy on each other seems simply false. All these dismaying disclosures and the subsequent international uproar meant that – as the leakers and journalists involved were soon to discover – their boldness was making the secret spymasters on both sides of the Atlantic very angry indeed. Snowden himself, Glenn Greenwald and the British reporters back in London at the *Guardian* were all shortly to feel the effects of that rage.

9

YOU'VE HAD YOUR FUN

The *Guardian* offices, Kings Place, London
June 2013

'Give me the liberty to know, to utter,
and to argue freely according to
conscience, above all liberties.'

JOHN MILTON,
Areopagitica

Up on the otherwise silent third floor of Kings Place, a late-night cleaner steered his Hoover around the group clustered at a computer. He was busy chatting in Spanish on his mobile as he passed, and did not seem to register their unease at the sight of him.

Under the eye of deputy editor Paul Johnson, a painfully slow assembly and formatting process was taking place through the night, not to the normal online *Guardian* network, but on to a big orange LaCie external hard drive – one of the few unused items on the premises capable of holding scores of gigabytes. The stuff was Snowden's – thousands of highly classified leaked documents in a heavily encrypted form.

It included more than 50,000 files belonging to British intelligence. GCHQ had apparently exported them over to the US, and allowed them to fall into the hands of this junior US private contractor. But one of the reasons for Johnson's nervousness was that possession of these documents back in Britain presented special – and scary – legal problems.

The *Guardian*'s current sleek glass-walled London offices give little hint of the paper's nonconformist Manchester origins back in 1821. But the lobby does have a bust of a formidable bearded figure; this is CP Scott, legendary editor for 57 and a half years. His famous dictum 'comment is free, but facts are sacred' is still the *Guardian*'s animating principle.

Inspired by CP Scott's tough-mindedness, editor-in-chief Alan Rusbridger had handled some big leaks in the past, of which WikiLeaks had been the most recent and famous. But this one was without precedent.

British journalists do not enjoy the constitutional free speech protection of their US counterparts. There is also a strong cultural understanding in the US that journalism has a key function in society. Although this can lead to establishment-minded behaviour sometimes, it has also made possible a tradition of investigative reporting in the spirit of Watergate, when two young *Washington Post* journalists brought down President Nixon in the 1970s.

Britain, by contrast, has a repressive culture of state secrecy. At the very moment Woodward and Bernstein were being fêted in Washington for their Watergate disclosures, some young journalists in Britain wrote an article called 'The Eavesdroppers'. It revealed for the first time the mere existence of GCHQ as a British radio spying agency. They were promptly had up and convicted at the Old Bailey under the Official Secrets Act. One, a US citizen named Mark Hosenball, was deported without a right to trial as a purported 'threat to British national security'.

Against this history, the challenge of publishing top-secret GCHQ documents in a British paper was a sizeable one.

The Official Secrets Act, passed amid fears of German espionage in 1911 and updated in 1989, makes it a crime for British officials to leak intelligence information. But it also has clauses that potentially criminalise journalists. While there is no specific public interest defence so the *Guardian*'s editor could be caught by provisions that make it an offence to publish intelligence information, such a disclosure has to be deemed damaging. The only arguable defence would be that the published article was not in fact damaging or, at any rate, not intentionally so. Police moves could therefore be just round the corner.

Mere possession of the Snowden files in London could also lead to a civil gag order, if the British government got to hear about their presence. The files were undoubtedly highly confidential and, while unlikely to identify James Bond-style undercover secret agents, they were certainly the property of the government. National security was at stake.

Under the UK's law of confidence, a judge could quite possibly be persuaded to grant a government request for an immediate injunction banning all publication of such material, and demanding the files' return. The paper could challenge this through the courts, by arguing there was a public interest in what it was disclosing. But at best, the case could embroil Rusbridger in a lengthy, uncertain and costly legal battle. In the meantime the paper would be unable to report on any of the documents' contents. An injunction would therefore be a journalistic disaster.

Hunkered down the next day with prominent media QC Gavin Millar, Rusbridger considered his legal options. The 100 per cent safe course was to destroy all the UK files at once. Another safe alternative was to hand the files to a security-cleared politician and call for an inquiry into their contents – the obvious recipient was former Conservative foreign secretary Malcolm Rifkind. He now chaired the notoriously weak parliamentary intelligence and security committee which was supposed to oversee bodies such as GCHQ. Rifkind would probably hand the files straight back to the spies themselves, unread.

Millar's advice was one thing. But Rusbridger also had to take into consideration his obligations towards Snowden. Snowden 'had risked his life to get hold of this stuff', the editor felt. Furthermore, Snowden had given the material to the *Guardian* because he believed Congress couldn't be trusted. The special US courts that dealt with intelligence matters met in secret. Only a newspaper could begin the debate he wanted. And it couldn't take place if the public remained clueless as to the extent of the state's suspicion-less surveillance.

'Of all the journalist ethical dilemmas you have to face in life, it was a fairly big one,' Rusbridger says.

He decided to ask some trusted staff to make a detailed study of the files. The data-set was unwieldy. A few documents were obviously sensitive. But the majority were confusing and corporate: PowerPoints, training slides, management reports, diagrams of data-mining programs. Much was unclear, although it was evident that GCHQ's technical capacities and sheer ambition were very great. And that GCHQ's 'special relationship' with its sister organisation the NSA went surprisingly deep.

The *Guardian* team set up a small 'war room' and were tough about security. A guard was posted 24 hours a day on the corridor to check IDs against a highly limited list. All phones were banned: a row of BlackBerrys and smartphones sat on a table outside with their owners' names on yellow Post-it notes. The windows of the bunker were papered over. All the computers were new. None had ever been connected to the internet or any other network – a precaution against hacking or phishing attacks. They were to remain 'air-gapped' throughout.

Multiple passwords were needed to log in; no staff member knew more than one password. Work was written and saved on USB sticks; nothing went on the network. In the corner an air-conditioning unit gave off a low hum. There was also a shredder.

Without natural light and strictly off-limits to cleaners, the bunker soon became frowsty. 'It smells like a teenage boy's bedroom in here,' said one visitor.

Posted onto a whiteboard was a memo from Rusbridger: 'Edward Snowden approached the *Guardian* because he says people have no idea of the extent of what he regards as the surveillance state. He argues that technology has run ahead of the law or the ability of anyone – citizens, courts, press or Congress – to have meaningful oversight of what is happening. This is why we have the documents.'

The memo added: 'We should search for material relevant to these concerns which are of high public importance. We are not engaged in a general fishing expedition.'

The team interrogating Snowden's material was made up of trusted senior journalists. It included Nick Hopkins, the *Guardian*'s defence and security editor, data editor James Ball, veteran Nick Davies and Julian Borger, who shuttled between London and New York. Greenwald in Brazil was lead reporter. MacAskill operated out of the US.

Having the material was one thing, making sense of it another. At first the reporters had no idea what 'strap one' and 'strap two' meant. It was only later they realised these were classifications beyond top secret. Snowden had given MacAskill one helpful clue – look for a program called TEMPORA. On day one the team stayed until midnight, returning the next day at 8am. The process became easier when TEMPORA led them to GCHQ's internal 'Wiki', which Snowden had uploaded. Mostly, it was written in plain English.

Soon the board was covered in the codenames of NSA/GCHQ programs – SAMUEL PEPYS, BIG PIGGY, BAD WOLF. The early stages of document analysis were heavy-going. 'The documents were seriously technical, fantastically dull and utterly brilliant,' Hopkins says. Hopkins would shout: 'What does QFD mean?'

Someone would answer: 'Query-focused database.' And what's a '10gps Bearer'? Or MUTANT BROTH? MUSCULAR? EGOTISTICAL GIRAFFE? And so on.

One of the first shocks revealed was that GCHQ had bugged foreign leaders at two G20 summit meetings hosted in London in 2009. Labour premier Gordon Brown and foreign secretary David Miliband apparently authorised this spying.

The agency had set up fake local internet cafes equipped with key-logging software. This allowed GCHQ to hack delegates' passwords, which could be exploited later. GCHQ also penetrated their BlackBerrys to monitor email messages and phone calls. A team of 45 analysts kept a real-time log of who phoned whom during the summit. Turkey's finance minister and 15 other members of his delegation were among the targets. This had, of course, nothing whatever to do with terrorism.

The timing of the *Guardian*'s discovery was piquant. David Cameron was about to host another international summit for G8 countries on the picturesque banks of Lough Erne in Northern Ireland. Presidents Obama and Putin would be dropping in, and other heads of state. Would GCHQ bug them too?

Fearing an injunction any moment, Paul Johnson decided to rush a print edition on to the British streets. On Sunday 16 June, he rolled 200 special copies off the press in the early evening. Another 30,000 copies were printed at 9.15pm. This made it harder for any late-night judge to order 'Stop the presses!' and prevent distribution. They would be too late.

That evening Rusbridger's phone rang. Retired Air Vice-Marshal Andrew Vallance was on the line. Vallance ran the uniquely British 'D-Notice' system, under which the government discreetly discourages the media from publishing stories said to endanger national security.

In 1993, as part of a tentative move towards glasnost, they were rebranded Defence Advisory (DA) notices. This change was meant to reflect the fact that it was voluntary whether or not to seek government advice.

Whether 'voluntary' or not, DA notices could be generally relied on to dampen media coverage. Vallance had already issued a 'private and confidential' notice not only to the *Guardian* itself but to the BBC, Sky and other UK broadcasters and newspapers. On behalf of GCHQ it discouraged them from following up *Guardian* US's original PRISM scoops. British media largely complied and barely covered the story. Now, he made clear his concern that the *Guardian* had failed to consult him in advance before telling the world of the G20 snooping.

This was the beginning of a struggle between the British government and the *Guardian*. Since David Cameron became Conservative prime minister in 2010, Rusbridger had barely spent half an hour with him. 'It wasn't a warm or constructive relationship,' he says. But the following day, while Cameron was hosting the G8 leaders at Lough Erne, his press officer Craig Oliver slipped out and called Rusbridger. With Oliver, a former BBC editor, was Sir Kim Darroch, a senior diplomat and the government's national security adviser.

Sniffing – he was suffering from hay fever – Oliver said the *Guardian*'s G20 story risked 'inadvertent damage' to national security. He said officials were unhappy with the G20 revelations, and some of them wanted to chuck Rusbridger in jail. 'But we are not going to do that.'

Rusbridger said that the *Guardian* was handling Snowden's leaked material in a responsible manner. Its focus wasn't operations or names, but the boundaries between security and privacy. The paper was willing to engage with Downing Street on future stories, he added, and to listen to any specific security concerns.

Coming down the pipeline was the TEMPORA article, about Britain's feats of 'Global Telecoms Exploitation'. This, as Rusbridger knew, might provoke even more trouble from Britain's spymasters.

He offered Oliver a conference call in which the *Guardian* would lay out key details of the TEMPORA story in advance. The aim was to avoid genuine national security damage – and an injunction. Gibson had used the same approach in the US in her dealings with the White House, and Rusbridger had a similar dialogue with the US State Department in 2010, in advance of publishing some of its WikiLeaks cables. Oliver agreed the government wanted a 'sensible conversation'. But, asked about possible injunctions, he refused to give any assurances, saying vaguely: 'Well, if the story is mega … '

The *Guardian* went ahead and told Sir Kim Darroch, the national security adviser, about TEMPORA. Two days later, the government came up with a formal response. Oliver said, apologetically: 'Things move at a very slow pace.' He said the prime minister had only recently been briefed on Snowden after Putin and the other guests had gone. And he was 'concerned'. Oliver added: 'We are working on the assumption you have got rather a lot of stuff.'

The upshot was a personal visit from Cameron's most lofty emissary, the cabinet secretary Sir Jeremy Heywood. This top official had advised three prime ministers and three chancellors. Assured, urbane and intelligent, Oxford- and Harvard-educated Heywood was used to having his own way.

In a 2012 profile, the *Mirror* had dubbed Heywood 'the most powerful unelected figure in Britain ... and you will never have heard of him.' Heywood lived in some style in Clapham, south London, it reported (he was building a wine cellar and a gym). Nick Pearce, the former head of Downing Street's policy unit, told the *Mirror* jokingly: 'If we had a written constitution in this country, it would have to say something like, "Not withstanding the fact that Jeremy Heywood will always be at the centre of power, we are free and equal citizens."'

There was an unhappy precedent for using cabinet secretaries on these sorts of missions. In 1986, the then prime minister Margaret Thatcher dispatched Sir Robert Armstrong all the way to Australia, in a vain legal attempt to quell intelligence agency leaks. MI5 were seeking to halt the publication of *Spycatcher*, a memoir by disgruntled former MI5 officer Peter Wright. In it, Wright alleged that MI5's former director general Sir Roger Hollis had been a Soviet spy, and that MI5 had 'bugged and burgled' its way across London, and eavesdropped on Commonwealth conferences. There were echoes here of GCHQ's bugging of the G20.

Thatcher's move was a debacle. Armstrong was ridiculed in the witness box, not least for his smug phrase that civil servants were sometimes 'economical with the truth'. Wright's memoir sold hundreds of thousands of copies worldwide on the back of the publicity.

At 8.30am on Friday 21 June, Heywood arrived at the *Guardian*'s Kings Place office. 'He was clearly quite irritated,' Johnson says. The prime minister, the deputy PM Nick Clegg, the foreign secretary William Hague, the attorney general and 'others in government' were all 'deeply concerned', said Sir Jeremy. (The reference to attorney general Dominic Grieve was deliberate; it was he who would decide any Official Secrets Act prosecution.)

Heywood wanted reassurances that locations of troops in Afghanistan wouldn't be revealed, or 'our agents undercover'. 'Absolutely,' Rusbridger agreed. The government was 'grateful' to the *Guardian* for the reasonable way it had behaved so far, Heywood conceded. But further publication could help paedophiles and endanger MI5 agents.

The editor said the *Guardian*'s surveillance revelations were dominating the news agenda in the US and had sparked a huge debate. Everyone was concerned, from Al Gore to Glenn Beck; from Mitt Romney to the American Civil Liberties Union. Tim Berners-Lee, the founder of the internet, and Jim Sensenbrenner, the congressman who drew up the Patriot Act, were also supportive. Even President Obama had said he welcomed the debate.

'We are hoping you will take the same view as Obama. It's a good debate,' said Rusbridger.

Heywood responded: 'You have had your debate. Debate is raging. You don't need to publish any more articles. We can't have a drip drip drip of this material into the public domain.'

He left the threat of legal action against the *Guardian* open. He said it was now up to the attorney general and the police to decide whether to take things 'further'. 'You are in possession of stolen property,' he emphasised.

Rusbridger explained that British action would be futile. Snowden's material now existed in several non-British jurisdictions. Had he heard of Glenn Greenwald? Greenwald lived in Brazil. If the *Guardian* were restrained, Greenwald would certainly resign and carry on publishing. Heywood: 'The PM worries a lot more about the *Guardian* than an American blogger. You should be flattered the PM thinks you are important.'

The *Guardian* was now a target for foreign powers, he went on. It might be penetrated by Chinese agents. Or Russians. 'Do you know how many Chinese agents are on your staff?' He gestured at the modern flats visible from the window across muggy Regent's Canal. The *Guardian* sits at a busy crossroads: in one direction King's Cross and St Pancras stations, between them an old goods yard, soon to be Google's new European HQ. On the canal are barges, coots and moorhens. Heywood pointed at the flats opposite and remarked, 'I wonder where our guys are?' It was impossible to tell if he was joking.

Behind the scenes, a lot of people were apparently furious with the *Guardian*. And willing to take extreme steps. 'What do you know about Snowden anyway? A lot of people in government believe you should be closed down, and that the Chinese are behind this.'

Rusbridger responded that this top-secret GCHQ material was already shared with … well, thousands of Americans. It wasn't, after all, the *Guardian* that had sprung a leak but GCHQ's transatlantic partners. Heywood rolled his eyes, signalling 'Tell me about it.' But he insisted that the UK's own vetting procedures were rigorous. 'It isn't in the public interest to be writing about this. All this stuff is scrutinised by parliament. We are asking you to curb your enthusiasms.'

Rusbridger reminded Sir Jeremy politely of the basic principles of press freedom. He pointed out that 40 years earlier similar arguments had raged over the *New York Times* and the Pentagon Papers. US officials asserted it was the job of Congress to debate the conduct of the Vietnam war, not the Fourth Estate. The *Times* had published anyway. 'Do you think now it was wrong to publish?' Rusbridger asked the mandarin.

The encounter was inconclusive. For the government, it proved that the *Guardian* was obdurate. For the *Guardian*, it showed that the government was willing to bully behind the scenes, to try and shut down debate. Heywood's charges – you are helping paedophiles and so on – were by their nature unprovable. And as was later to become plain, the British government was not in fact at all keen to use its draconian legal powers. The reason, presumably, was simple: they feared Snowden and Greenwald had some kind of nuclear insurance policy. If HMG called in the police, maybe every single sensitive document would be spilled out online, WikiLeaks-style.

Oliver Robbins later hinted at the government's thinking in a witness statement, saying 'so long as the newspaper showed cooperation, engagement was the best strategy.' In return for the *Guardian* having a dialogue about a forthcoming story, the two men offered a high-level briefing. After that briefing, the *Guardian* published the TEMPORA story with a few modifications.

It went live on the *Guardian*'s website at 5.28pm. The reaction was instant. There was a rolling wave of public indignation. One comment read: 'Who gave them [GCHQ] permission to spy on us and hand our private information to a foreign power without our consent?'

Nick Hopkins, the *Guardian*'s defence and security editor, had liaison with the intelligence agencies as one of his regular tasks. After the TEMPORA disclosures, Hopkins suggested a peace meeting with a GCHQ official to clear the air. He replied: 'I would rather gouge my eyes out than be seen with you.' Hopkins responded: 'If you do that you won't be able to read our next scoop.' Another GCHQ staffer suggested – with tongue in cheek – that he should consider emigration to Australia.

The journalists feared that their paper's continued reporting might come under some serious legal strain. 'I thought at some point this story is going to get impossible for us,' Rusbridger says. Some footwork was required.

In 2010 the *Guardian* had successfully partnered with the *New York Times*, and other international titles including Germany's *Der Spiegel*, to report on the

WikiLeaks leak of classified US diplomatic cables and war-logs.

There were similar advantages to collaboration now, particularly with US partners. The *Guardian* could take advantage of first-amendment protection. And, if necessary, offshore its entire reporting operation to New York where most stories were already being written under Gibson's deft stewardship.

Rusbridger got in touch with Paul Steiger, founder of the independent news website ProPublica. It was a good fit. The non-profit ProPublica had a reputation for rigour; its newsroom had won two Pulitzers. A small selection of edited documents was sent off to him, heavily encrypted, via FedEx. This simple low-tech method proved inconspicuous, and perfectly safe. ProPublica's technology reporter Jeff Larson joined the bunker in London. A computer science graduate, Larson knew his stuff. Using diagrams, he could explain the NSA's complex data-mining programs – no mean feat.

Rusbridger had been in dialogue with Jill Abramson, the executive editor of the *New York Times*. Rusbriger had known her predecessor Bill Keller, and was on friendly terms with Abramson. The conversation was a strange one. In theory the *Times* and the *Guardian* were rivals. The *Guardian* had, in effect, just carried out a major US land-grab, raiding deep into traditional *Times* territory by publishing a series of high-profile national security scoops. To its credit, the *Times* had followed up the NSA story and produced some notable work of its own.

Would the *Times* be prepared to partner with the *Guardian* on the Snowden files? Rusbridger told Abramson bluntly that this was extremely hot material. There were no guarantees the *Times* would ever be able to look at it. There would be strict conditions around their use. 'The temperature [here in the UK] is rising,' he said. As with the collaboration over Wikileaks, both sides could benefit from the deal: the *Times* got the thumb drive; the *Guardian* got the first amendment. Abramson agreed.

What would Snowden make of this arrangement? It was unlikely he would be pleased. Snowden had repeatedly inveighed against the *New York Times*. The paper, he felt, was perfidious, too close to US power.

The alternative, however, was worse. The *Guardian* was in a tight spot; at any moment police could charge up the stairs and seize Snowden's material. Inevitably, experts would then carry out detailed forensic tests on the hard drive. The result could conceivably strengthen the ongoing US criminal investigation against Snowden, their source.

Two weeks passed, with the *Guardian* continuing to publish. For those in the bunker it was a demanding and stressful period. They couldn't talk to friends or colleagues, only to those in the circle of trust. Then on Friday 12 July, Heywood reappeared, accompanied by Craig Oliver, who was wearing a pink striped shirt. Their message was that the *Guardian* must hand the GCHQ files back; the mood in government seemed to be hardening, although scarcely more well-informed. 'We are pretty aware of what you have got,' said Sir Jeremy. 'We believe you have about 30 to 40 documents. We are worried about their security.'

Rusbridger said: 'You do realise there is a copy [of the documents] in America?' Heywood: 'We can do this nicely or we can go to law.' Then Rusbridger suggested an apparent compromise: that GCHQ could send technical experts to the *Guardian* to advise staff how the material could be handled securely. And possibly, in due course, destroyed. He made it clear that the *Guardian* didn't intend to hand the files over. 'We are still working on them,' he said. Heywood and Oliver said they would think about this over the weekend, but they wanted Rusbridger to reconsider his refusal to hand the stuff back.

Three evenings later, Rusbridger was having a quiet beer in the Crown, a Victorian pub in nearby Islington. A text arrived from Oliver, the premier's press secretary. Had the editor set up a meeting with Oliver Robbins, Cameron's deputy national security adviser?

'JH [Heywood] is concerned you have not agreed the meeting he suggested.'

Rusbridger was nonplussed. He texted back: 'About security measures?'

Oliver: 'About handing the material back.'

Rusbridger: 'I thought he suggested meeting about security measures?'

Oliver: 'No. He is very clear. The meeting is about getting the material back.'

It appeared that over the weekend something had

changed. Rusbridger told the press secretary there hadn't been a deal to return the Snowden files.

Oliver was blunt: 'You've had your fun. Now it's time to hand the files back.'

Rusbridger replied: 'We are obviously talking about different meetings. That's not what we agreed. If you've changed your mind that's fine.'

Oliver then went for the big stick: 'If you won't return it we will have to talk to "other people" this evening … '

The conversation left Rusbridger amazed. Since the first Snowden story six weeks earlier Downing Street had treated the leak non-urgently – often taking days to respond. It was bureaucratic delay verging on sloth. Now it wanted a resolution within hours. 'We just sat up and thought "Oh my God",' one insider said. It was possible the security services had detected an imminent threat from an enemy power. Or the securocrats had grown exasperated. Or Cameron had given a languid order to deal with it.

The next morning, Robbins called. Aged 38, Robbins had enjoyed a sharp vertical rise – Oxford, the Treasury, principal private secretary to Tony Blair, director of intelligence in the Cabinet Office. Robbins announced it 'was all over'. Ministers needed urgent assurances Snowden's files had been 'destroyed'. He said GCHQ technicians also wanted to inspect the files to ascertain their 'journey': to see if a third party had intercepted them.

Rusbridger repeated: 'This doesn't make sense. It's in US hands. We will go on reporting from the US. You are going to lose any sense of control over the conditions. You're not going to have this chat with US news organisations.'

Rusbridger then asked, 'Are you saying explicitly, if we don't do this you will close us down?'

'I'm saying this,' Robbins agreed.

That afternoon, Jill Abramson of the *New York Times* and her managing editor, Dean Baquet, slipped into the *Guardian*'s London office.

The *Guardian* had 14 conditions, set out on a sheet of A4, for the collaboration.

They stipulated that both papers would work together on the material. Rusbridger knew the *Times* newsroom included reporters with deep expert knowledge of national security matters. 'This guy is our source. I think you should treat him as your source,' Rusbridger said. He added that neither Snowden nor Greenwald were exactly fans of the *Times*. British journalists would move in and work alongside their *Times* colleagues.

Abramson gave him a wry smile. She agreed to the conditions.

Later Abramson and Baquet arrived at Heathrow airport to fly home. Security officers pulled them to one side. Was this a random stop? Or were they looking for the GCHQ files? They didn't find them. The documents had already been spirited across the Atlantic.

Rusbridger himself was due to go off to his regular summer 'piano camp' in the Lot Valley in central France.

He had recently published a book entitled *Play it Again*, an account of how he had combined demanding editing duties and the WikiLeaks story with learning Chopin's most exacting work, 'Ballade No. 1'. After consulting with Johnson, Rusbridger decided he might as well still go, despite all the dramas. He boarded the Eurostar train bound for Bordeaux. At first it was hard to concentrate on music. Soon, however, he immersed himself completely in Debussy.

As he worked on his piano technique, events in London now moved towards what Rusbridger would later describe as one of the strangest episodes in the *Guardian*'s long history. Robbins reappeared. 'He was punctiliously polite, very well-mannered. There was no obvious aggression,' Johnson says. But the official said the government wanted to seize the *Guardian*'s computers and subject them to forensic analysis. Johnson refused. He cited a duty to Snowden and to *Guardian* journalists. The deputy editor offered another way forward: to avoid being closed down, the *Guardian* would bash up its own 'war room' computers under GCHQ's tutelage. Robbins agreed.

It was a parody of Luddism: men were sent in to smash the machines.

On Friday 19 July two men from GCHQ paid a visit to the *Guardian*. Their names were 'Ian' and 'Chris'. They met with *Guardian* executive Sheila Fitzsimons. The Kremlin was apparently capable of techniques straight from the pages of James Bond, Ian told her: 'You have got plastic cups on your table. Plastic cups can be turned into microphones. The Russians can send a laser beam through your window and turn them into a listening device.' The *Guardian* nicknamed the pair the hobbits.

Two days later the hobbits came back, this time with Robbins and a formidable civil servant called Kata. Ian, the senior of the two, was short, bubbly and dressed in shirt and chinos. His accent hinted at Yorkshire. Chris was taller and more taciturn. They carried a large and mysterious rucksack. Neither had previously spent any time with journalists; this was a new experience for them. In normal circumstances fraternising with the media was forbidden.

Ian explained how he would have broken into the *Guardian*'s secret war room: 'I would have given the guard £5k and got him to install a dummy keyboard. Black ops would have got it back. We would have seen everything you did.' (The plan made several wildly optimistic assumptions.) At this Kata shook her head: apparently Ian's *Boy's Own* contribution was unwelcome.

Ian then asked: 'Can we have a look at the documents?' Johnson said he couldn't.

Next, the GCHQ team opened up their rucksack. Inside was what looked like a large microwave oven. This strange object was a degausser. Its purpose is to destroy magnetic fields, thereby erasing hard drives and data. The electronics company Thales made it. (Degaussers were named after Carl Friedrich Gauss, who gave his name to the Gauss unit of magnetism.)

The pair were not so much good cop/bad cop – more bad cop/silent cop.

Ian: 'You'll need one of these.'

Johnson: 'We'll buy our own degausser, thanks.'

Ian: 'No you won't. It costs £30,000.'

Johnson: 'OK, we probably won't then.'

The *Guardian* did agree to purchase everything else the government spy agency recommended: angle-grinders, Dremels – a drill with a revolving bit, masks. 'There will be a lot of smoke and fire,' Ian warned, adding, with grim relish: 'We can call off the black helicopters now … '

At midday the next day, Saturday 20 July, the hobbits came back again. They joined Johnson, Blishen and Fitz-simons in a windowless concrete basement three floors down. The room was unoccupied, but crowded with relics from a bygone newspaper age: linotype machines used for setting pages in the 1970s, and giant letters spelling 'The Guardian' which had once adorned the paper's old office in the Farringdon Road.

Dressed in jeans and T-shirts and directed by Ian, the three *Guardian* staff took it in turns to smash up bits of computer: black squares, circuit boards, chips. It was sweaty work. Soon there were sparks and flames. And a lot of dust.

Ian lamented that because of the GCHQ revelations he would no longer be able to tell his favourite joke. Ian used to go to graduate recruitment fairs looking to attract bright candidates to a career in government spying. He wrapped up his speech by saying: 'If you want to take it further, telephone your mum and tell her. We will do the rest!' Now, he complained, the spy agency's press office had forbidden the gag.

As the bashing and deconstruction continued, Ian revealed he was a mathematician – and a pretty exceptional one. He said that 700 people had applied the year he joined GCHQ, 100 had been interviewed, and just three hired. 'You must be quite clever,' Fitzsimons observed. 'Some people say so,' Ian answered. Chris rolled his eyes. The two GCHQ men took photos with their iPhones. When the smashing was finally completed, the journalists fed the pieces into the degausser, like small children posting shapes into a box. Everyone stood back. Ian bent forward and watched. Nothing happened. And still nothing. Then finally a loud pop.

It had taken three hours. The data was destroyed, beyond the reach of Russian spies with trigonometric lasers. The hobbits were pleased. Blishen felt wistful. 'There was this thing we had been protecting. It had been completely trashed,' he says. The spooks and the *Guardian* team shook hands; Ian dashed off. (He said he was in a bit of a rush, because he had a wedding the next day.) The hobbits obviously didn't come down to London often. They left carrying bags of shopping: presents for their families.

'It was an extremely bizarre situation,' Johnson says. The British government had compelled a major newspaper to smash up its own computers. This extraordinary moment was half pantomime, half-Stasi. But it was not yet the high tide of British official heavy-handedness. That was still to come.

10

DON'T BE EVIL

Silicon Valley, California
Summer 2013

'Until they become conscious, they will never rebel.'
GEORGE ORWELL,
1984

It was an iconic commercial. To accompany the launch of the Macintosh in 1984, Steve Jobs created an advert that would captivate the world. It would take the theme of George Orwell's celebrated dystopian novel and recast it – with Apple as Winston Smith. His plucky company would fight the tyranny of Big Brother.

As Walter Isaacson recounts in his biography of Jobs, the Apple founder was a child of the counterculture. He practised Zen Buddhism, smoked pot, walked around barefoot and pursued faddish vegetarian diets. He embodied the 'fusion of flower power and processor power'. Even as Apple grew into a multi-billion dollar corporation, Jobs continued to identify with computing's early subversives and long-haired pioneers – the hackers, pirates, geeks and freaks that made the future possible.

Ridley Scott of *Blade Runner* fame directed the commercial. It shows Big Brother projected on a screen, addressing lines of workers. These skinhead drones wear identical uniforms. Into the grey nightmare bursts an attractive young woman. She wears orange shorts and a white tank top. She is carrying a hammer! Police in riot gear run after her. As Big Brother announces 'We shall prevail', the heroine hurls the hammer at him. The screen explodes in a blaze of light; the workers are open-mouthed. A voice announces smoothly: 'On January 24th, Apple Computer will introduce Macintosh. And you'll see why 1984 won't be like *1984*.'

The 60-second advert was screened to nearly 100 million Americans during the Super Bowl, and was subsequently hailed as one of the best ever. Isaacson writes: 'Initially the technologists and hippies didn't interface well. Many in the counterculture saw computers as ominous and Orwellian, the province of the Pentagon and the power culture.'

The commercial asserted the opposite – that computers were cool, revolutionary and empowering, instruments of self-expression. The Macintosh was a way of asserting freedom against an all-seeing state.

Almost 30 years later, following Jobs's death in 2011, an NSA analyst came up with a smirking rejoinder. He prepared a top-secret presentation and, to illustrate the opening slide, he pulled up a couple of stills from Jobs's commercial – one of Big Brother, the other of the blonde heroine with the hammer and the orange shorts.

Under the heading 'iPhone Location Services' he typed: 'Who knew in 1984 … '

The next slide showed the late Jobs, holding up an iPhone.

'... that this would be Big Brother ...'

A third slide showed crowds of whooping customers celebrating after buying the iPhone 4; one fan had inked the name on his cheek. The analyst's pay-off line read:

'... and the zombies would be paying customers.'

The zombies were the public, unaware that the iPhone offered the spy agency new snooping capabilities beyond the imagination of the original Big Brother. The 'paying customers' had become Orwell's mindless drones.

For anyone who thought the digital age was about creative expression and flower power, the presentation was a shocker, and an insult to Steve Jobs's vision. It threw dirt on the hippy kaftan and trampled on the tambourine. The identity of the NSA's analyst is unknown. But the view appeared to reflect the thinking of an agency that in the aftermath of 9/11 grew arrogant and unaccountable. Snowden called the NSA 'self-certifying'. In the debate over who ruled the internet, the NSA provided a dismaying answer: 'We do.'

The slides, given to Poitras and published by *Der Spiegel* magazine, show that the NSA had developed techniques to hack into iPhones. The agency assigned specialised teams to work on other smartphones too, such as Android. It targeted BlackBerry, previously regarded as the impregnable device of choice for White House aides. The NSA can hoover up photos and voicemail. It can hack Facebook, Google Earth and Yahoo Messenger. Particularly useful is geo-data, which locates where a target has been and when. The agency collects billions of records a day showing the location of mobile phone users across the world. It sifts them – using powerful analytics – to discover 'co-travellers'. These are previously unknown associates of a target.

Another secret program had a logo that owed a debt to the classic 1970s Pink Floyd album *Dark Side of the Moon*. It showed a white triangle splitting light into a colourful spectrum. The program's name was PRISM. Snowden leaked a 41-slide PowerPoint presentation explaining PRISM's function.

One slide emphasised the dates when Silicon Valley's technology companies apparently signed up and become corporate partners of the spy agency. The first to provide PRISM material was Microsoft. The date was 11 September 2007. This was six years after 9/11. Next came Yahoo (March 2008) and Google (January 2009). Then Facebook (June 2009), PalTalk (December 2009), YouTube (September 2010), Skype (February 2011) and AOL (March 2011). For reasons unknown, Apple held out for five years. It was the last major tech company to sign up. It joined in October 2012 – exactly a year after Jobs's death.

The top-secret PRISM program allows the US intelligence community to gain access to a large amount of digital information – emails, Facebook posts and instant messages. The rationale is that PRISM is needed to track foreign terrorists living outside the US. The data-collection program does not apparently require individual warrants. Rather, federal judges give their broad approval to PRISM under the FISA. By the time Snowden revealed PRISM, at least nine technology companies were on board. (The slides show Dropbox was slated to join; Twitter was missing.)

The most bitter and contentious question is how the NSA accesses this personal data. The key slide claims the data is collected 'directly from the servers' of the nine 'US service providers', Google, Yahoo and the rest.

Speaking in Hong Kong, Snowden was adamant this 'direct access' was indeed how PRISM worked. He told Greenwald: 'The US government co-opts US corporate power to its own ends. Companies such as Google, Facebook, Apple and Microsoft all get together with the NSA. [They] provide the NSA direct access to the back-ends of all of the systems you use to communicate, to store data, to put things in the cloud, and even just to send birthday wishes and keep a record of your life. They give [the] NSA direct access, so that they don't need to oversee, so they can't be held liable for it.'

The leaked PRISM documents come from a training manual for NSA staff. It sets out several steps. First, a complex 'tasking' process. Analysts use or 'task' PRISM to find a new surveillance target. Next, a supervisor reviews the analyst's search terms, known as selectors. After that the supervisor then has to agree with the analyst's 'reasonable belief' the target lives outside the US. (This bar is pretty low, and defined as '51 per cent confidence'.)

Once the target has been agreed, PRISM gets to work. Sophisticated FBI equipment at the tech companies extracts matching information. The FBI has its own database to weed out – or 'research and validate', as the slide puts it – US persons whose data may have been sucked up by mistake. (This system, however, isn't foolproof.) The FBI then gives this data to the NSA. An array of NSA analytical tools processes it. These include MARINA, which sifts and stores internet records, MAINWAY for call records, PINWALE which does video, and NUCLEON, voice.

Another slide says that the NSA has 'real-time reporting capability'. In other words, the agency is notified each time a target sends an email, writes a text, begins a chat, or even fires up their computer.

Snowden's slide gives some sense of just how important PRISM has become to US intelligence efforts. As of 5 April 2013, the US had 117,675 active surveillance targets in its PRISM database. According to the *Washington Post*, much PRISM-derived intelligence ends up on President Obama's desk; it accounts for one in seven intelligence reports. British spies get to read it too.

The training manual gives the impression that Silicon Valley is actively collaborating with the NSA, albeit with varying degrees of enthusiasm. The corporate logos of all nine tech companies appear on the top of each PRISM slide. Jobs's Apple is among them. The logos look like shiny, colourful butterflies.

Snowden says it was his concerns over PRISM that pushed him towards whistleblowing. It was one of the first documents he leaked to Greenwald and Poitras. But PRISM was only one important element in a troubling picture. Over the last decade the US had been secretly working to gather practically all communications entering and leaving the US.

The NSA's original mission was to collect foreign intelligence. But it appears to have drifted away from its original goal, like a vast supertanker floating away from its anchor. It is now sucking in a lot of domestic communications. In this new era of Big Data, the agency moved from the specific to the general; from foreign targeting to what Snowden called 'omniscient, automatic, mass surveillance'.

The agency's other big operation, its highly sensitive cable-tapping program, ran parallel to GCHQ'S British TEMPORA project and was codenamed UPSTREAM. It gives the NSA direct access to the fibre-optic cables carrying internet and telephone data into, out of and around the US.

UPSTREAM is explained in one slide 'as the collection of communications on fibre cables and infrastructure as data flows past'. The slide shows a map of the US with brown cables extending in both directions across the Pacific and Atlantic oceans. The diagram looks like the thick tentacles of an enormous sea creature. Seemingly, the US has international cable taps in South America, East Africa and the Indian Ocean. There are green loops around the cables. They link to a box marked UPSTREAM. Below is a second box labelled PRISM. Linking both boxes is an instruction to the agency's data collectors: 'You should use both.'

According to author James Bamford, citing earlier NSA whistleblower William Binney, UPSTREAM captures 80 per cent of communications. PRISM scoops up anything that UPSTREAM may have missed.

Snowden referred to UPSTREAM when he told Greenwald: 'The NSA doesn't limit itself to foreign intelligence. It collects all communications that transit the US. There are literally no ingress or egress points anywhere in the continental US where communications can enter or exit without being monitored and collected and analysed.'

Since a large amount of the world's internet traffic travels through the US and 25 per cent of it also crosses Britain, the two spy agencies between them have the ability to hack most of the globe's key communications. A 2009 report by the NSA's inspector general, leaked by Snowden, acknowledges this. It says: 'The United States carries out foreign intelligence activities through a variety of means. One of the most effective means is to partner with commercial entities to obtain access to information that otherwise would not be available.'

The report refers to 'America's homefield advantage as the primary hub for worldwide telecommunications'. It says that the NSA currently has relationships with over '100 US companies'. This private sector/spy agency collaboration stretches 'as far back as World War Two'.

Thanks to ties to two unnamed companies in particular, the NSA is able to eavesdrop on the world, or as the inspector general puts it, access 'large volumes of foreign-to-foreign communications transiting the United States through fibre-optic cables, gateway switches and data networks'.

The US has the same 'advantage' when it comes to international telephone calls. Most international calls are routed through a small number of switches or 'choke-points' in the international telephone system, en route to their final destination. Many are in the US. The country is a 'major crossroads for international switched telephone traffic', the report says. It gives striking figures: of the 180 billion minutes of telephone communications in 2003, 20 per cent came from or terminated in the US, and 13 per cent transited the US. The internet numbers are bigger. In 2002 only a small fraction of international internet traffic went via non-US routes.

The NSA–telecoms partnership was highly lucrative. In return for access to 81 per cent of international telephone calls, Washington pays the private telecom giants many hundred millions of dollars a year. It is not known how much the British government pays its own domestic 'intercept partners', particularly the formerly state-owned BT, and Vodafone. But the sums will be similar and substantial.

By the end of the last decade, the NSA's capabilities were astonishing. The agency, backed by Britain and its other Five Eyes allies, had access to fibre-optic cables, telephone metadata and the servers of Google and Hotmail. The NSA's analysts were the most powerful spies in human history. Snowden maintains they were able to target practically anybody, at any time, including the president.

'The NSA and the intelligence community in general is focused on getting intelligence everywhere and by any means possible,' he says. 'Originally we saw this focus very narrowly targeted on foreign intelligence. Now we see it's happening domestically. To do that the NSA specifically targets the communications of everyone. It ingests them by default. It collects them in its systems. It filters them and it analyses them and it measures them and it *stores* them for periods of time simply because that's the easiest and most efficient and most valuable way to achieve these ends.'

Looked at as a whole, the files lend weight to Snowden's assertion that as an NSA analyst he had super-powers.

'While they may be intending to target someone associated with a foreign government or someone they suspect of terrorism, they are collecting your communications to do so. Any analyst at any time can target anyone. Any selector, anywhere. Whether these communications may be picked up depends on the range of the sensor networks and the authorities an analyst is empowered with. Not all analysts have the ability to target everybody. But I, sitting at my desk, certainly had the authority to wiretap anyone, from you, to your accountant, to a federal judge, and even the president, if I had a personal email [address].'

The PRISM revelations provoked a howling response from the hi-tech denizens of San Francisco's Bay Area. First there was bafflement, then denial, followed by anger. The Santa Clara valley, where most of the big tech firms are situated, likes to see itself as anti-government. The philosophical currents that waft through Cupertino and

Palo Alto are libertarian and anti-establishment, a legacy of Silicon Valley's roots in the hacker community. At the same time, these firms vie for government contracts, hire ex-Washington staff for the inside track and spend millions lobbying for legislation in their favour.

Clearly, the allegation that they were co-operating with America's most powerful spy agency was a corporate disaster, as well as being an affront to the Valley's self-image, and to the view of the tech industry as innovative and iconoclastic. Google prided itself on its mission statement 'Don't be evil'; Apple used the Jobsian imperative 'Think Different'; Microsoft had the motto 'Your privacy is our priority'. These corporate slogans now seemed to rebound upon their originators with mocking laughter.

Before the *Guardian* published the PRISM story the paper's US business reporter, Dominic Rushe, went through his contacts book. He called Sarah Steinberg, a former Obama administration official, and now Facebook's PR, as well as Steve Dowling, the head of PR at Apple. He rang Microsoft, PalTalk and the others. All denied any voluntary collaboration with the NSA.

'There was total panic. They said they had never heard of it [PRISM],' Rushe recalls. 'They said they hadn't given direct access to anybody. I was totally bombarded with telephone calls from increasingly senior tech executives who had more questions than answers.'

The tech companies said that they only released information to the NSA in response to a specific court order. There were no blanket policies, they said. Facebook revealed that in the last six months of 2012 it gave the personal data of between 18,000 and 19,000 users to various US law-enforcement bodies, not just to the NSA but also to the FBI, federal agencies and local police.

Several of the companies stressed they had mounted legal challenges in the FISA courts to try and say more about secret government requests for information. Google insisted: 'We do not provide any government, including the US government, with access to our systems.' Google's chief architect Yonatan Zunger remarked: 'We didn't fight the cold war just so we could rebuild the Stasi ourselves.' Yahoo said it had fought a two-year battle for greater disclosure, and had challenged amendments to the 2008 Foreign Intelligence Surveillance Act. Its efforts were thus far unsuccessful.

The NSA documents, though, look explicit. They say 'direct access'.

Asked how he might explain the discrepancy, one Google executive called it a 'conundrum'. He dismissed the PRISM slides as a piece of flimsy 'internal marketing'. He added: 'There is no back-door way of giving data to the NSA. It's all through the front door. They send us court orders. We are obliged by law to follow them.'

But in October 2013 it emerged there was indeed a back door – just one that the companies involved knew nothing about. The *Washington Post* revealed that the NSA was secretly tapping data from Yahoo and Google. The method was ingenious: 'on British territory', the agency had hacked into the private fibre-optic links that inter-connect Yahoo and Google's own data centres around the world.

The NSA codename for this tapping operation is MUSCULAR. It appears to be the British who are doing the actual hacking on the US's behalf. (One MUSCULAR slide says 'Operational July 2009', and adds: 'Large international access located in the United Kingdom.')

The firms go to great lengths to keep their customers' data safe. However, they transfer their information between data centres situated in Europe and America, along leased private internet cables protected by company-specific protocols. It was these cables that the NSA had managed to hack, as they transit the UK. Curiosity focused on Level 3, reported to have been hired as a cable operator by Yahoo and Google: Level 3 is named in the top-secret British documents as an 'intercept partner' with the codename LITTLE. The Colorado-based corporation's response is to say it complies with legal requests in the countries where it operates.

An NSA analyst drew a child-like sketch explaining how the program works; it shows two regions marked 'Public Internet' and 'Google Cloud'. There is a smiley face at the interface where the NSA hacks data. The sketch provoked a thousand Twitter parodies. 'With so many of these slides you get the feeling people inside the NSA are bragging about their programs,' ProPublica's Jeff Larson says. 'They are saying: 'We can break encryption! We can grab protocols!''

A document from the NSA's acquisitions directorate reports that thanks to its back-door access the agency can break into hundreds of millions of user accounts. The data is sent back to the NSA's Fort Meade headquarters and stored. The volumes are remarkable. In a 30-day period in late 2012, 181,280,466 new records were funnelled back to the Puzzle Palace, including metadata.

Google and Yahoo reacted with apoplexy to the tapping disclosures. Google's chief legal officer David Drummond said he was outraged at the lengths to which the US government had gone to 'intercept data from our private fibre networks'. Yahoo repeated that it had no knowledge of the NSA's back-door cyber-theft.

By the autumn of 2013 all the tech companies said they were scrambling to defend their systems from this kind of NSA snooping. They stood some chance of success. For the NSA's power to suck up the world's communications is not quite as awesome as Snowden has made it seem. Tapping into global flows of data is one thing: being able actually to read them is quite another. Particularly if they start to be encrypted.

On 23 October 1642, two armies clashed in the English fields north of Oxford. One belonged to King Charles, the other to Parliament. The battle of Edge Hill was the first in the bloody English civil war. The fight was messy. Parliament forces fired their cannons; the royalists led a cavalry charge; inexperienced soldiers on both sides ran away. Some were keener on looting than defeating the enemy. Neither side really won. The war dragged on for another four years.

Two centuries later, on 21 July 1861, another skirmish took place. This time the Union Army was fighting the Confederates, in the first major land encounter of the

American civil war. The location was Bull Run, a tributary of the Potomac in Virginia. The Northern forces expected a quick victory. Instead, the Confederate army launched a ferocious counter-attack. Brigadier General Irvin McDowell and his Union soldiers fled in the direction of Washington DC. The battle revealed there would be no easy knockout.

Many years later, American and British spies were mulling over names for two top-secret programs. Their new battles were electronic rather than territorial. It was the growing practice of encryption that was their enemy. The names they chose for their new battles were BULLRUN and EDGEHILL. Did the emphasis on civil wars have a special significance? Certainly, the spies were now about to declare war on their own domestic corporations.

Cryptography was first used in ancient Egypt and Mesopotamia. The aim, then as now, was to protect secrets. During the first and second world wars, military cryptography and cryptanalysis – the ability to decrypt coded information on enemy movements – played a key role. But it was largely the preserve of embattled nation states. Typically, those interested in codes were the British mathematicians working in secret to defeat the Nazis at wartime Bletchley Park, and the Soviets subsequently.

By the 1970s, however, encryption software such as Pretty Good Privacy (or PGP) was available to private individuals, as well as commercial organisations. Encryption thus posed an obvious challenge to western intelligence agencies, anxious to continue reading their adversaries' messages. The Clinton administration responded by trying to insert a back door into commercial encryption systems. This would let the NSA in. The attempt met with political defeat. A bipartisan group of senators and tech executives argued this would be bad for the Valley. Plus it would violate the fourth amendment.

By 2000, as encryption was increasingly employed by service providers and individuals in everyday online communications, the NSA was spending billions of dollars finding ways to get round it. Its encrypted targets included web searches, internet chats, emails, personal data, phone calls, even banking and medical records. The challenge was to convert 'ciphertext' – what encrypted data looks like in its raw form: that is, mathematical nonsense – into 'cleartext'.

In 2010 a British GCHQ document warned that over time the allies' capacities could degrade as 'information flows change' and 'widespread encryption becomes more commonplace'.

At first, the eavesdroppers seemed to face defeat, or at least stalemate. One of the leaked documents from 2006 shows that, at that date, the agency had only broken the encryption of one foreign state's nuclear ministry, a single travel reservation system, and three foreign airlines.

It was not until 2010 that the NSA made dramatic progress, thanks to BULLRUN and EDGEHILL. It used super-computers to crack algorithms, encryption's basic building blocks. (Algorithms generate the key which can encrypt and decrypt messages. The longer the key, the better the encryption.)

But most importantly, the Snowden files show that the NSA cheated. Despite the political defeat on back doors, the agency simply went ahead and secretly introduced 'trapdoors' into commercial encryption software used by millions of people. It collaborated with developers and technology companies to insert deliberate, exploitable flaws into both hardware and software. Sometimes this co-operation was voluntary; sometimes bullying legal orders enforced it. The NSA, if necessary, would steal encryption keys, almost certainly by hacking into servers where the keys were kept.

Unsurprisingly, the NSA and GCHQ were keen to keep details of these most shadowy of programs under wraps. A 2010 document from Snowden shows just how restricted knowledge was of BULLRUN – and how effective it was. The PowerPoint was used to brief British staff in Cheltenham on the NSA's recent breakthroughs, as a result of which decrypted internet traffic was suddenly streaming across the desks of analysts.

It says: 'For the past decade the NSA has led an aggressive, multi-pronged effort to break widely used internet encryption technologies. Cryptanalytic capabilities are now coming online. Vast amounts of encrypted internet data which up to till now have been discarded are now exploitable.'

The slide says 'major new processing systems' must be put in place 'to capitalise on this opportunity'. GCHQ staff previously kept in the dark about BULLRUN were astonished by the NSA's formidable new capabilities. One internal British memo reports: 'Those not already briefed were gobsmacked.'

Snowden's first batch of published files did not disclose details of which companies work with the NSA on counter-encryption. Or which commercial products may have back doors. But the files do give some idea of BULLRUN's massive dimensions. A budget report for the entire US intelligence community says that 2013 funding for the program was $254.9m. (PRISM, by contrast, costs just $20m annually.) Since 2009, the agency has splashed more than $800m on 'SIGINT [signals intelligence] enabling'. The program 'actively engages US and foreign IT industries to covertly influence and/or overtly leverage their commercial products' designs', the report says.

The joy of the program, the NSA says, is that ordinary citizens have no idea that their everyday encrypted communications are now hackable. When the NSA inserts 'design changes' into commercial encryption systems, the 178-page report for the fiscal year notes, 'To the consumer and other adversaries ... the systems' security remains intact.'

James Clapper, the director of national intelligence, stresses the importance of crypto. 'We are investing in groundbreaking cryptanalytic capabilities to defeat adversarial cryptography and exploit internet traffic,' he writes.

The agency is not lacking in ambition. The files show the NSA is breaking the encryption systems of 4G phones. It targets online protocols used in secure banking and business transactions, such as HTTPS and Secure Sockets Layer (SSL). It wants to 'shape' the worldwide encryption marketplace. Soon it expects to get access to 'data flowing through a hub for a major communications provider' and to a 'major internet peer-to-peer voice and text communications system'. That sounds like Skype.

Meanwhile, the British were pressing on with their own parallel EDGEHILL project. One file shows that the British spies have succeeded in breaking into three internet providers and 30 types of Virtual Private Networks (VPN) used by businesses to access their systems remotely. By 2015 it hoped to have penetrated 15 internet companies and 300 VPNs.

The spy agencies insist that their ability to defeat encryption is essential to their mission, and that without it they would be unable to track terrorists or gather valuable foreign intelligence. The problem, as the *New York Times* points out, is that the NSA's anti-encryption stealth campaign may have disastrous unwanted consequences.

By inserting deliberate weaknesses into encryption systems, the agency has made those systems exploitable. Not just by government agencies, who may be acting with good intentions, but by anybody who can get hold of encryption keys – such as hackers or hostile intelligence agencies. Paradoxically, in its quest to make Americans more secure, the NSA has made American communications less secure; it has undermined the safety of the entire internet.

The main US agency for setting security norms in cyberspace is the National Institute of Standards and Technology (NIST). It appears the NSA has corrupted this, too. A Snowden document reveals that in 2006 the NSA put a back door into one of the institute's main encryption standards. (The standard generates random prime numbers used to encode text.) The agency then encouraged another international standards body – and the rest of the world – to adopt it, boasting: 'Eventually the NSA became the sole editor.'

Both US and UK agencies have also devoted considerable efforts to cracking Tor, the popular tool to protect online anonymity. Ironically, the US government is one of Tor's biggest backers. The State Department and the Department of Defense – which houses the NSA – provide around 60 per cent of its funding. The reason is simple: journalists, activists and campaigners in authoritarian countries such as Iran use Tor to protect themselves from political reprisals and online censorship.

Thus far, however, the NSA and GCHQ have been unable to de-anonymise most Tor traffic. Instead, the agencies have attacked web browsers such as Firefox, which allows them control over a target's end computer. They have also developed the ability to 'stain' some traffic as it bounces around the Tor system.

Despite their best endeavours, the truth appears to be that NSA and GCHQ have not yet won cryptography's new civil war. With the right training and some technical expertise, corporations and individuals (as well, no doubt, as terrorists and paedophiles) are still successfully using cryptography to protect their privacy.

In a Q&A with *Guardian* readers while in hiding in Hong Kong, Snowden himself said: 'Encryption works. Properly implemented strong crypto systems are one of the few things that you can rely on.'

And he should know.

11

FLIGHT

Terminal F, Sheremetyevo International Airport,
Moscow, Russian Federation
Sunday 23 June 2013

'We always imagine eternity as something beyond
our conception, something vast. But why must it be
vast? Instead of all that, what if it's one little room, like
a bath house in the country, black and grimy and
spiders in every corner, and that's all eternity is?'

FYODOR DOSTOYEVSKY,
Crime and Punishment

Ed Snowden went underground after hastily checking
out of the Mira Hotel in Hong Kong. His local legal
team, barrister Robert Tibbo and solicitor Jonathan Man, knew where he was. So did someone else.
Snowden had a mystery guardian angel – a well-con-
nected Hong Kong resident. The American's interest in
China was long-standing. The precise details are murky.
But it appears this benefactor invited Snowden to stay
with one of his friends. Another lawyer, Albert Ho, says
that Snowden shifted between several homes, staying in
at least one house in the New Territories area, close to
the border with mainland China. He was lost in a densely
packed metropolis of seven million people.

Tibbo, a human rights lawyer, was used to dealing with clients in bad situations. A Canadian by nationality, with a pleasant manner, a smart blazer and a receding hairline, Tibbo represented the vulnerable and the down-trodden – Sri Lankans facing deportation, Pakistanis wrongly denied asylum, abused refugees.

One of his cases dated back to the darkest chapter of the Tony Blair era. In 2004, the Libyan Islamist Sami al-Saadi arrived in Hong Kong with his wife and family. He thought he was travelling back to the UK, his old home. Instead, MI6, working closely with Muammar Gaddafi's intelligence services, bundled him on a plane back to Tripoli. There, Saadi was interrogated, tortured and imprisoned. Shortly afterwards, Blair, the then British prime minister, struck a deal with the Libyan dictator. MI6's discreditable role in the affair emerged after Gaddafi's 2011 fall.

Like Saadi, Snowden was another client whom, he feared, western intelligence services would render and then imprison in a dark, damp hole. Tibbo and Snowden first met after he slipped out of the Mira Hotel. The lawyer refuses to talk about the details, citing client confidentiality. But he evidently considered Snowden to be bright, a rational actor who was making his own conscience-driven choices. And a young man in a whole pile of trouble. Over the next two weeks Tibbo would juggle his regular case-load while working on Snowden's behalf, often through the night.

The lawyers were soon sucked into Snowden's cloak-and-dagger world. Albert Ho describes a rendezvous.

He got into a car one night at an agreed spot and found Snowden inside, wearing a hat and sunglasses. Snowden didn't speak, the lawyer told the *Washington Post*. When they arrived at the home where Snowden was staying he whispered that everyone had to hide their phones in the refrigerator. Over the next two hours the lawyers went through his options with him. Ho brought dinner: pizza, sausages and chicken wings, washed down with Pepsi. 'I don't think he ever had a well-thought-out plan. I really think he's a kid,' Ho said afterwards.

The lawyers' assessment was negative. It was possible that Snowden might eventually prevail in a battle against US extradition. But in the meantime the most likely option was that he would sit in jail while the Hong Kong courts considered his asylum claim. This legal tussle could drag on for years. Snowden was horrified to discover that behind bars he would have no access to a computer.

He didn't mind being confined in a small room. But the idea of being exiled from the internet was repugnant to him. 'He didn't go out, he spent all his time inside a tiny space, but he said it was OK because he had his computer,' Ho told the *New York Times*. 'If you were to deprive him of his computer, that would be totally intolerable.'

After the meeting, Ho was asked to take soundings from the Hong Kong government. Would Snowden get bail if arrested? Could he somehow flee the country? The whistleblower presented a dilemma for Hong Kong's administrators. The territory is part of China but governed under the 'one country, two systems' framework; it has notional autonomy but Beijing retains ultimate responsibility for foreign affairs.

On the one hand, China's spies would certainly be interested in keeping Snowden, if they could get access to his tens of thousands of highly sensitive NSA documents, revealing the ambit and protocols of American surveillance. On the other hand, if Hong Kong refused to repatriate him, this would place Sino–American relations under great strain. Already the US was piling on the pressure. A major international row would be an unwelcome distraction.

There were other factors, too. Snowden's case might raise uncomfortable questions at home for the Chinese authorities. Many Chinese citizens were unaware that their own security services also engaged in domestic spying, with phone hacking, email and postal interception rampant, not to mention censorship. Holding on to Snowden could set off an uncomfortable internal debate over matters currently under the table.

Hong Kong's chief executive Leung Chun-ying held numerous meetings with his top advisers, it was reported, struggling to decide what to do over a thorny US request for Snowden's detention.

Public opinion in Hong Kong was largely pro-Snowden, boosted by some carefully targeted disclosures. On 12 June Snowden gave an interview from hiding to the *South China Morning Post*. In it, he revealed that the US hacked millions of China's private text messages. 'The NSA does all kinds of things like hack Chinese mobile phone companies to steal all of your SMS data,' he told the paper. The agency had also, he alleged, attacked China's prestigious Tsinghua University, the hub of a major digital network from which the data on millions of Chinese citizens could be harvested.

For years, Washington had complained bitterly about Beijing's industrial-scale stealing and spying in cyber-space. In numerous documents GCHQ and NSA identify China and Russia as the two nations responsible for most cyber-espionage. Now it appeared the NSA did the same thing, only worse.

Snowden must have hoped that in the wake of his leaks the Hong Kong government would treat his case sympathetically. After Ho's approach to the authorities, an intermediary contacted Snowden. The intermediary delivered a message. The message was that Hong Kong's judiciary was independent. And, yes, it was possible he would spend time in jail. But – and this was the crucial bit – it also said the government would welcome his departure.

Ho sought further assurances. He told the *Guardian*'s Beijing correspondent Tania Branigan, who had flown to Hong Kong: 'I talked to government officials seeking verification of whether they really wanted him to go, and in case they really wanted him to go, whether he would be given safe passage.'

On Friday 21 June the US government formally indicted Snowden with espionage. It sent an urgent official extradition request. 'If Hong Kong doesn't act soon, it will complicate our bilateral relations and raise questions about Hong Kong's commitment to the rule of law,' a senior Obama administration official said.

With his legal options shrinking by the hour, Snowden made a fateful decision. He would leave.

Six thousand miles away, someone else in hiding had been taking a close interest in these developments. Julian Assange had been frantically trying to make contact with the fugitive NSA contractor. Assange is the self-styled editor-in-chief of WikiLeaks. He had been holed up in the tiny Ecuadorean embassy in London for over a year.

Assange had taken refuge inside the apartment building – Flat 3b, 3 Hans Crescent – after his own legal options ran out. In summer 2012, Britain's supreme court ruled that an extradition warrant served by authorities in Sweden was valid. Assange should be extradited to answer complaints from August 2010 that he sexually assaulted two Swedish women, the court said.

Assange promptly walked into the embassy and was granted political asylum by Ecuador's leftist government. The tactic seemed extravagant to some. During the cold war, Hungary's dissident Cardinal Mindszenty spent 15 years in the US embassy. But this was 2012, not 1956. There were few signs of state brutality amid the penthouses of London's Knightsbridge; instead of Soviet tanks there were Bentleys and Ferraris. Thanks to his going to ground in this way, WikiLeaks had released little of significance for some time. Assange, as the *New York Times*'s David Carr put it, 'looked like a forgotten man'.

Now, Assange barged his way into Snowden's drama. Much is mysterious. But it is known his approaches came via intermediaries and through his Hong Kong lawyers.

These pre-dated Snowden's video confession, and they grew more intense after it.

From Assange's perspective the approach was logical. Snowden was another anti-US whistleblower in trouble, apparently just like him. In 2010, Assange had leaked the thousands of classified documents obtained from the US private Chelsea Manning. Their publication, in collaboration with the *Guardian* and other newspapers, had caused a global furore. Manning was jailed and a grand jury reportedly investigated Assange over the leaks. Assange's woes with Swedish women were a separate matter, though the former hacker would frequently – and some would say cynically – confuse the two. But Assange did have some claim to specialised expertise in asylum issues. And the Snowden story also opened up a chance for him to step back into the limelight.

Ideologically, the two had much in common: a passionate commitment to the internet and transparency, a libertarian philosophy when it came to information, and strong digital defence skills. Snowden had at one point considered leaking his NSA files to Assange. He later reconsidered on the grounds of risk. Assange's confined situation at the embassy in London, right under the nose of the British authorities and their NSA allies, meant inevitably that he was bugged and constantly monitored.

In terms of temperament, Snowden was nothing like Assange. He was shy, allergic to cameras, and reluctant to become the focus of media attention. He never sought celebrity. The world of journalism was utterly alien to him. Assange was the polar opposite. He liked the public gaze. Charming, he was capable of deadpan humour and wit, but could also be waspish, flying into recrimination and anger. Assange's mercurial temperament spawned both groupies and ill-wishers: his supporters saw him as a radical paladin fighting state secrecy, his enemies as an insufferable narcissist.

Assange hatched a plan with two key elements. The first was to secure the same sort of asylum for Snowden as he had himself, from Ecuador's populist president Rafael Correa, one of a string of leftist Latin American leaders unfriendly to US power. The second was to help get Snowden physically from Hong Kong to Quito. This was no easy thing, given that the CIA and practically every other intelligence agency on the planet were on his trail.

Assange began personal discussions with his friend Fidel Narváez, Ecuador's London consul. The two had become close. The goal was to secure Snowden some kind of official paper – a temporary travel document, or better still a diplomatic passport, that would speed him to the cool and grey Andes. Eventually, Assange dispatched his sometime girlfriend Sarah Harrison to Hong Kong, carrying safe-conduct papers for Ecuador signed by Narváez. A 31-year-old would-be journalist and WikiLeaks activist, Harrison was thoroughly loyal.

Snowden's first choice for exile had always been Iceland. He believed the island had some of the most progressive media laws in the world. But reaching Reykjavik from Hong Kong would require passage through the US, or through European states which might arrest him on the US warrant. Ecuador, on the other hand, could safely be reached via Cuba and Venezuela, who were unlikely to obey US instructions.

Unfortunately, the trip also apparently required transit through Russia.

Whose idea was it for Snowden to go to Moscow? This is the million-rouble question. Tibbo, Snowden's lawyer, won't answer. He says merely that the situation was 'complicated'. Harrison says she and Snowden wanted to avoid flying over western Europe. Most connections also involved changing planes in the US, clearly not an option. Snowden's itinerary does, however, seem to bear the fingerprints of Julian Assange.

Assange was often quick to criticise the US and other western nations when they abused human rights. But he was reluctant to speak out against governments that supported his personal efforts to avoid extradition. This was especially true of Russia. US diplomatic cables released by WikiLeaks paint a dismal portrait of Russia under Vladimir Putin. They suggest that the Kremlin, its powerful spy agencies and organised crime have grown practically indistinguishable, with Russia in effect a 'virtual mafia state'.

And yet in 2011 Assange signed a lucrative TV deal with Russia Today (RT), Putin's English-language global propaganda channel. The channel's mission is to accuse the west of hypocrisy while staying mute about Russia's own failings. The fate of Russia's own whistleblowers was grimly evident. The list of Russian opposition journalists killed in murky circumstances is a long one. It includes the investigative journalist Anna Politkovskaya (shot dead in

2006) and the human rights activist Natalia Estemirova (abducted in Grozny in 2009 and murdered).

Assange's view of the world was essentially self-regarding and Manichaean, with countries divided up into those that supported him (Russia, Ecuador, Latin America generally) and those that didn't (the US, Sweden and the UK). As Jemima Khan, one of many demoralised former WikiLeaks supporters, put it: 'The problem with Camp Assange is that, in the words of George W Bush, it sees the world as being "with us or against us".'

On Sunday 23 June 2013, Snowden's lanky figure, wearing a grey shirt and carrying a backpack, arrived at Hong Kong's Chek Lap Kok airport. With him was the young WikiLeaks worker, Sarah Harrison. It was a hot and humid morning. The pair were nervous. They checked in at the Aeroflot counter for flight SU213 to Moscow, and made their way through normal departure channels. Snowden was holding the safe-conduct pass issued by Narvaez, Assange's friend, and couriered to him by Harrison. Several plain-clothes Chinese officials observed them closely. For any CIA officers watching, this departure must have been exasperating.

In theory, Snowden's audacious exit should have been impossible. The previous day US authorities had annulled Snowden's US passport. They had also faxed over extradition papers to the Hong Kong authorities, demanding his immediate arrest. But Hong Kong claimed that there were 'irregularities' in the American paperwork, and they were powerless to halt Snowden's departure until the errors were rectified.

Shortly afterwards, some 40,000 feet in the air, Snowden and his companion tucked into the first of their two airline hot meals. Aeroflot was working hard to overcome its past Soviet reputation for non-existent customer service. On the ground was a scene of international mayhem, as American officials discovered that Snowden had escaped the net and was en route to Moscow. The bastard had got away! For the world's greatest superpower, Hong Kong's not-very-plausible legalistic explanation was humiliating stuff. Not only had Snowden vamoosed, but he now appeared to be heading straight into the embrace of Washington's adversaries – Russia, Cuba, Venezuela!

Capitol Hill made little secret of its rage. 'Every one of those nations is hostile to the United States,' Mike Rogers, chair of the House intelligence committee, fumed. 'The US government must exhaust all legal options to get him back. When you think about what he says he wants and what his actions are, it defies logic.' Democrat senator Charles Schumer was equally scathing: 'Vladimir Putin always seems eager to stick a finger in the eye of the United States, whether it is Syria, Iran and now, of course, with Snowden.'

General Keith Alexander, the NSA's director and Snowden's former boss, was no happier: '[Snowden] is clearly an individual who's betrayed the trust and confidence we had in him. This is an individual who is not acting, in my opinion, with noble intent.'

The Chinese, however, were unapologetic. By way of reply the official Xinhua news agency lambasted the US for its 'hypocritical' spying: 'The United States, which has long been trying to play innocent as a victim of cyber-attacks, has turned out to be the biggest villain of our age.'

With Snowden safely on board the Airbus A330-300, Assange put out a statement. He claimed personal credit for the entire rescue operation. He said WikiLeaks had paid for Snowden's ticket. While in Hong Kong, the organisation had also given Snowden legal advice. Assange would subsequently liken his role, in an interview with the *South China Morning Post*, to that of a 'people smuggler'.

Proprietorially claiming Snowden as the latest star player for Team WikiLeaks, the statement said: 'Mr Edward Snowden, the American whistleblower who exposed evidence of a global surveillance regime conducted by US and UK intelligence agencies, has left Hong Kong legally. He is bound for a democratic nation via a safe route for the purposes of asylum, and is being escorted by diplomats and legal advisers from WikiLeaks.'

Moscow journalists dumped their Sunday leisure plans and scrambled to Terminal F of Sheremetyevo International Airport, where Snowden was due to transit. The airport was named after Russia's most celebrated aristocratic dynasty, the Sheremetevs. The Sheremetevs served numerous tsars, grew fabulously rich, and built two Moscow palaces, Ostankino and Kuskovo. Count Nikolai Sheremetev fell in love with and secretly married his former serf, Praskovya. The romance had spawned a thousand cultural histories.

A large scrum of Russian and international correspondents gathered in front of a small door. It was from here that arriving passengers would emerge; the cleverer reporters had brought pictures of Snowden to show his fellow travellers from Hong Kong.

Plain-clothes Russian agents also trawled the terminal, deflecting questions about which state agency they represented by pretending to be businessmen from Munich and journalists from state-run NTV. A Venezuelan contingent was also said to be there, fuelling speculation that Caracas could be Snowden's eventual destination. Ecuador's ambassador turned up, arriving at the airport in his 7-series BMW. He appeared lost as he wandered around the terminal, asking one group of journalists: 'Do you know where he is? Is he coming here?' A reporter replied: 'We thought you did.'

When the plane landed in Moscow at 5pm local time, Russian security vehicles were waiting. From Vietnam, Ecuador's foreign minister Ricardo Patino tweeted that Snowden had sought political asylum in his country. But where was he? The news agency Interfax announced that Snowden was booked on an Aeroflot flight to Cuba the following day. He appeared to be holed up in Moscow's transit zone. An Aeroflot source claimed – wrongly, it would turn out – he was staying in a small overnight hotel 'capsule' room in Terminal E.

What did the Kremlin know of Snowden's arrival? President Putin claimed that he was informed of Snowden's presence on a Moscow-bound flight just two hours before he landed. He observed that by cancelling his passport the Americans had made an elementary mistake in tradecraft, making his onward flight options impossible.

In characteristic fashion, mixing sarcasm and scarcely sincere ruefulness, Putin labelled Snowden 'an unwanted Christmas present'. The Russian authorities did seem to have been genuinely surprised by Snowden's eventual stranding in Russia. The normally reliable *Kommersant* newspaper, however, would claim that Snowden had secretly spent two days at the Russian consulate in Hong Kong. Snowden himself vehemently denies this.

Putin's own attitude towards whistleblowing activities was undoubtedly negative. He later described Snowden as a *stranniy paren* – a strange bloke. 'In effect, he condemned himself to a rather difficult life. I do not have the faintest idea what he will do next,' he said.

Putin was a KGB officer who served in communist East Germany in the 1980s, and was the former head of the KGB's main successor agency, the Federal Security Service or FSB. He took a dim view of traitors. In 2006 the renegade FSB officer Alexander Litvinenko died in London after drinking radioactive polonium in what the British government believes was a Russian state plot. The KGB's spy code of *omerta* was absolute.

After 13 years in power, Putin was paranoid, mistrustful, prone towards conspiratorial explanations at home and abroad, and more convinced than ever of his own unparalleled abilities. He viewed relations with the west, and the US especially, through the prism of Soviet xenophobia. Given his KGB academy training, he must have wondered whether Snowden was an American deception exercise, a classic cold war ploy.

But in reality, Snowden really was a gift. He presented a perfect opportunity for the Kremlin to highlight what it regarded as Washington's double standards when it came to human rights, state snooping and extradition. Putin must also have enjoyed the frisson of superpower parity with the United States. The idea underlay his view of a resurgent Russia, an oppositional pole to the US in global affairs. The Americans would have to beg to get Snowden back!

Within hours of Snowden touching down, pro-Kremlin voices were busily suggesting that the Russian Federation should offer him asylum.

The next day, the media circus resumed at Sheremetyevo. Several enterprising reporters had bought flight tickets and were scouring the transit zone for any sign of Snowden; some camped out there for days. Others obtained Cuban visas and booked onto the same Aeroflot flight to Havana. It was generally assumed that Snowden would be on the plane.

The *Guardian*'s Moscow correspondent Miriam Elder waited at the gate to get on. Something was afoot. The Aeroflot staff were even ruder than usual. They stopped TV crews from filming the plane through a window. Burly security guards hung around.

Elder failed to get on the flight: she didn't have a visa. Other journalists trooped on board and walked the aisles hunting for the refugee. Snowden and Harrison were booked into seats 17A and C, adjacent to the window. Jussi

Niemeläinen, a correspondent with the Finnish newspaper *Helsingen Sanomat*, was across in 17F – close enough perhaps to grab a few words with the world's most wanted man, and to secure a glorious front-page story. Minutes before take-off there was still no sign of Snowden. His seat was empty. The last four passengers were expected.

And then a whisper spread across the aircraft: '*Ne uletayet, ne uletayet!*' – Russian for 'not flying'. Snowden wasn't coming. Some of the Russian journalists broke into a chant of 'champagne trip, champagne trip'. The purser solemnly announced that the 12-hour flight to Cuba was non-alcoholic: soft drinks would be served. 'You could only laugh,' Niemeläinen said. 'During the journey I watched *The Muppets*. It felt right for the occasion.'

Snowden was in extra-territorial limbo. Over the next few weeks the Kremlin would maintain the fiction that Snowden had not entered Russian territory – he didn't have a Russian visa, after all – and that they had little to do with him. At the same time Moscow would milk his stay for all it was worth. Snowden's location was a mystery. In theory he remained in Sheremetyevo's transit zone. But no one could find him there. Probably, the authorities regarded 'transit' as an elastic concept, a sort of wiggly line that could, if necessary, be stretched across a map. Perhaps he was in the heavily guarded airport Novotel. Or somewhere else.

In the wake of Snowden's arrival, US–Russian relations plunged. One of Obama's foreign policy priorities had been to 'reset' ties with Moscow; these had grown strained under President George W Bush following the war in Iraq and Russia's 2008 invasion of US-backed Georgia. The 'reset' was already in trouble, with disagreements over a plethora of issues including Syria, the US's missile defence plans in central Europe, recriminations over NATO's military action in Libya and the imprisonment in the US of the Russian arms dealer and alleged former KGB agent Viktor Bout.

Obama had tried to cultivate President Dmitry Medvedev, Putin's temporary successor, a less hawkish figure. In fact, Medvedev was never an autonomous entity. In 2012 Putin elbowed him aside and returned as president for the third time. In a leaked cable, one US diplomat reported that Medvedev played Robin to Putin's Batman. The comparison irritated Putin. It was, he said, an example of American arrogance.

Now Obama called for Russia to hand Snowden over. Russia's veteran foreign minister, the wily Sergei Lavrov, parried by saying that Snowden wasn't actually 'in' Russia and had never crossed the border. Putin ruled out an extradition of Snowden. He pointed out that there was no bilateral treaty with the US. He also claimed – implausibly – that Russia's security services had no interest in him. Two days later Obama announced that he wouldn't expend geopolitical capital in getting Snowden back.

Behind the scenes, however, the administration was doing everything it could to close down Snowden's onward journey: pressuring allies, placing him on no-fly lists, cajoling the South Americans. Having initially been supportive of his asylum claim, Ecuador grew lukewarm. US Vice President Joe Biden called Correa, laying out what the consequences would be if Quito took him in. Correa revoked Snowden's safe-conduct pass, saying it had been issued in error. Ecuador also seemed exasperated with Assange, with its ambassador in Washington noting that WikiLeaks seemed to be 'running the show'. On 30 June, Snowden applied for asylum in 20 countries. They included France, Germany, Ireland, China and Cuba.

The following day, 1 July, Snowden issued a statement via WikiLeaks, the first of several. He said he had left Hong Kong 'after it became clear that my freedom and safety were under threat for telling the truth', and thanked 'friends new and old, family and others' for his 'continued liberty'.

Snowden then attacked Obama for using Biden to 'pressure the leaders of nations from which I have requested asylum to deny my asylum petitions'. The president had previously promised not to get involved in any diplomatic 'wheeling and dealing'. This claim now looked like something of a lie.

Snowden continued: 'This kind of deception from a world leader is not justice, and neither is the extralegal penalty of exile. These are the old, bad tools of political aggression. Their purpose is to frighten, not me, but those who would come after me.'

The White House had defended the 'human right to seek asylum' but was now denying him that option, Snowden said, complaining: 'The Obama administration has now adopted the strategy of using citizenship as a weapon … In the end [it] is not afraid of whistleblowers like me, Bradley Manning or Thomas Drake. We are stateless, imprisoned, or powerless. No, the Obama administration is afraid of you. It is afraid of an informed, angry public demanding the constitutional government it was promised – and it should be.'

The statement concluded: 'I am unbowed in my convictions and impressed at the efforts taken by so many.'

The reference to 'constitutional government' seemed to be authentic Snowden; his motive for blowing the whistle was the NSA's infringement of the US constitution. Other parts of the text, though, seemed suspiciously Assangian, especially the second-person line: 'No, the Obama administration is afraid of you.' Snowden had previously asked Greenwald to help draft his personal manifesto. Greenwald had declined, though remained Snowden's most fierce public champion. Now it appeared he had a new literary collaborator. This was J Assange.

On 2 July, the Kremlin hosted a summit of major gas exporters. One of those who flew in for the event was Evo Morales, the president of Bolivia. An indigenous Indian, who had struggled to read his inauguration speech, Morales was no fan of US power. In an interview with the Spanish-language service of RT, Morales was asked about Snowden. Speaking off the cuff, the president said he hadn't received an asylum request from the NSA whistleblower. But if he did, Bolivia would receive it favourably.

Later that day Morales and his entourage took off from Moscow for home. A couple of hours into the flight the pilot passed on some troubling news: France and

Portugal were refusing to allow the presidential plane to use their airspace. The news got worse. Spain and Italy also cancelled air permits. In desperation, the pilot got in touch with the authorities in Austria and made a forced landing in Vienna. What the hell was going on?

Someone in the US intelligence community had tipped off Washington that Morales had smuggled Snowden aboard his jet. An exemplary piece of real-time reporting! They had got him! The only problem was that Snowden was not on board. The White House had pressed the panic button with its European allies because of an intelligence blunder. This may have been the result of clever Russian disinformation. Or a classic CIA goof-up.

In Vienna, the president of Bolivia and his defence secretary Ruben Saavedra sat on an airport couch, aggrieved that the US had had the audacity to humiliate a small sovereign nation. Asked whether Snowden had been smuggled aboard, Saavedra turned white. 'This is a lie, a falsehood. It was generated by the US government,' he said. 'It is an outrage. It is an abuse. It is a violation of the conventions and agreements of international air transportation.'

From the leftist nations of Latin America there were expressions of outrage. Bolivia's vice-president Alvaro Garcia announced Morales had been 'kidnapped by imperialism'. Venezuela, Argentina, Ecuador and others issued protests. From the airport's VIP lounge Morales made telephone calls, seeking to have the airspace bans overturned. His four pilots crashed out on red leather chairs and got a few hours' sleep. Morales was marooned for 15 hours before he eventually took off again. Once home, he denounced the forced rerouting of his plane as an 'open provocation' of 'north American imperialism'.

It was an ignominious episode. In Washington, the State Department conceded that it had discussed the issue of flights by Snowden with other nations. The US's cack-handed intervention demonstrated that the caricature of the US as an aggressive playground bully prepared to trample on international norms was on this occasion perfectly correct. But it also demonstrated that Snowden's plan to get to Latin America wasn't really viable – unless, perhaps, he was prepared to travel there smuggled aboard a Russian nuclear submarine.

Three weeks after Snowden flew into Russia, Tanya Lokshina received an email. Lokshina is the deputy director of Human Rights Watch in Moscow. Her job is a tough one – defending Russian civil society from a hostile and often aggressive Kremlin. Since Putin's return to the presidency in May 2012, the job had got even tougher. The president had launched the worst crackdown on human rights since the Soviet era. This came in response to mass protests against his rule in Moscow and, to a lesser degree, in other big cities. The protests began in late 2011, following rigged Duma elections. Lokshina was feisty, fun and fluent in English and Russian. She was one of a defiant band of rights activists.

The email was scarcely believable. Signed 'Edward Joseph Snowden', it asked Lokshina to report to the arrivals hall of Sheremetyevo airport. There, 'someone from the airport staff will be waiting to receive you with a sign labelled G9'. Surely this was some kind of practical joke? 'The invitation, supposedly from one of the world's most sought-after people, had a whiff of Cold-War-era spy thriller to it,' she blogged. She fed her baby with mashed carrots, while juggling calls from the world's media.

It became clear that the invite was genuine. Airport security phoned up and asked for her passport number. Lokshina got on the airport express train; en route, the US embassy rang her up. An American diplomat wanted her to give a message to Snowden. It said that in the opinion of the US government he wasn't a human rights defender but a law-breaker who had to be held accountable for his crimes. She agreed to pass this message on.

At Sheremetyevo, Lokshina spotted the man with the 'G9' sign. At least 150 reporters had found him too, desperate for any sighting of Snowden. 'I am used to crowds, and I am used to journalists, but what I saw before me was madness: a tangle of shouting people, microphone assaults and countless cameras, national and international media alike. I feared I might be torn apart in the frenzy,' she wrote.

The G9 man was wearing a black suit. He announced: 'Invited guests come with me.' He led her down a long corridor. There were eight other guests. They included the Russian ombudsman, an MP and other representatives from human rights groups – most independent, but a handful with ties to the Kremlin and its FSB spy agency.

Lokshina was put on a bus and driven to another entrance. And there was Snowden, seemingly in good spirits, and wearing his crumpled grey shirt. With him was Sarah Harrison. 'The first thing I thought was how young he looks – like a college kid,' Lokshina wrote. There was also an interpreter.

Standing behind a desk, Snowden read from a prepared statement, his voice rather high and in places croaky. He seemed shy and nervy; this was his first public press conference. It was also a bizarre one. For years, the Kremlin had denigrated human rights organisations for being spies and lackeys of the west. Now they were being courted. The Kremlin was keen to make a political point.

Snowden began: 'Hello. My name is Ed Snowden. A little over one month ago, I had family, a home in paradise, and I lived in great comfort. I also had the capability without any warrant of law to search for, seize, and read your communications.'

He read on: 'Anyone's communications at any time. That is the power to change people's fates. It is also a serious violation of the law. The fourth and fifth amendments to the constitution of my country, article twelve of the Universal Declaration of Human Rights, and numerous statutes and treaties forbid such systems of massive, pervasive surveillance …'

At this point there was a loud *bing-bang-bong!* The airport tannoy burst into Russian and English; it announced the business lounge could be found on the third floor, next to gate 39. Snowden folded his body and smiled; his small audience laughed with him. When he resumed, another blaring message sawed him off. 'I have heard this many times over the last couple of weeks,' Snowden said croakily. Harrison joked she knew the announcements so well, she could practically sing along to them.

Snowden's substantive points were interesting. He said that secret US FISA court rulings 'somehow legitimise an illegal affair' and 'simply corrupt the most basic notion of justice – that it must be seen to be done'. He also traced his own actions back to the Nuremberg trials of 1945, quoting: 'Individuals have international duties which transcend the national obligations of obedience.' And he defended himself from criticism that he had deliberately set out to hurt, or even irreparably damage, US national security:

'Accordingly, I did what I believed right and began a campaign to correct this wrongdoing. I did not seek to enrich myself. I did not seek to sell US secrets. I did not partner with any foreign governments to guarantee my safety. Instead, I took what I knew to the public, so what affects all of us can be discussed by all of us in the light of day, and I asked the world for justice. The moral decision to tell the public about spying that affects all of us has been costly, but it was the right thing to do and I have no regrets.'

Snowden interpreted the US government's global pursuit of him as 'a warning to all others who might speak out as I have'. No-fly lists, the threat of sanctions, the 'unprecedented step of ordering military allies to ground a Latin American president's plane' – all were what he called 'dangerous escalations'. He then praised countries that had offered him support and asylum in the face of 'this historically disproportionate aggression'. Snowden cited Russia, Venezuela, Bolivia, Nicaragua and Ecuador:

'[They] have my gratitude and respect for being the first to stand against human rights violations carried out by the powerful against the powerless. By refusing to compromise their principles in the face of intimidation they have earned the respect of the world. It is my intention to travel to each of these countries to extend my personal thanks to their people and leaders.'

And then an announcement: Snowden said he was requesting asylum from Russia. He made clear this was a temporary move, forced upon him by circumstances, and until such time as he could travel to Latin America. He said he wanted the activists to petition the US and Europe not to interfere with his movements. The meeting broke up after 45 minutes.

'Mr Snowden is not a phantom: such a man exists,' Genri Reznik, a defence lawyer, said afterwards, as he and the other guests were reunited with the media scrum in Terminal F. 'I shook his hand. I could feel skin and bones,' Vladimir Lukin, Russia's human rights commissioner, told Russian TV, 'He [Snowden] said that of course he is concerned about freedom of movement, lack of it, but as for the rest, he is not complaining about living conditions. As he said: "I've seen worse situations.'"

Snowden's prolonged stay in Russia was involuntary. He got stuck. But it made his own story – his narrative of principled exile and flight – a lot more complicated. It was now easier for critics to paint him not as a political refugee but as a 21st-century Kim Philby, the British defector who sold his country and its secrets to the Soviets.

Other critics likened him to Bernon F Mitchell and William H Martin, two NSA analysts who defected in 1960 to the Soviet Union, and had a miserable time there for the rest of their lives. Martin and Mitchell flew to Cuba and then boarded a Soviet freighter, popping up in Moscow several months later at a press conference in the House of Journalists. There, they denounced their former employer, and revealed that the US spied on its allies and deliberately sent aircraft into Soviet airspace to trigger and capture Soviet radar patterns.

The analogies were unfair. Snowden was no traitor. He wasn't a Mitchell or a Martin or a Philby. But, for better or worse, the 30-year-old American was now dependent on the Kremlin and its shadowy spy agencies for protection and patronage.

For anyone who knew Russia – its brutal wars in Chechnya, its rigged elections, its relentless hounding of critics – part of Snowden's speech struck a tin note. Russia may have stood against human rights violations in Snowden's case. But this wasn't because the Russian government believed in human rights; it didn't. Putin frequently talked of human rights in disparaging terms. Rather, he saw Snowden as a pawn in a new great game, and as a golden opportunity to embarrass Washington, Moscow's then-and-now adversary.

The very day before Snowden's unlikely press briefing, one of the most surreal moments in legal history had taken place. In scenes that could have been written by Gogol, Russia had put a dead man on trial. The 37-year-old auditor Sergei Magnitsky died in prison in 2009. Magnitsky had uncovered a massive tax fraud inside Russia's interior ministry. The corrupt officials involved arrested him; in jail he was refused medical treatment and tortured. The case had become a totemic one for the Kremlin and the White House, after the US and some EU states banned the Russian officials involved and froze their overseas assets. Where the defendant should have been was an empty cage. It was a Dadaist spectacle.

A week later, Russia's vocal opposition leader Alexei Navalny also appeared in court. A lawyer and anti-corruption blogger, with a substantial middle-class following, and sometimes darkly nationalist views, Navalny was Putin's best-known opponent. (Putin was unable to bring himself to utter Navalny's name, and referred to him disparagingly as 'that gentleman'.) Navalny was jailed for five years for 'stealing' from a timber firm. Nobody really believed the charges. The sentence was later suspended in what looked like a moment of Kremlin in-fighting.

Russia's direction of travel, then, was becoming murkier; corruption, show trials and political pressure on the judiciary were everyday facts of life. In a very KGB twist, Putin had passed a new law requiring all non-governmental organisations that received western funding to register as 'foreign agents'. Ahead of the 2014 winter Olympics, to be held in the Black Sea resort of Sochi, the Duma had enacted legislation against 'gay propaganda'. These moves were part of a wider political strategy in which Putin appealed directly to his conservative base – workers, pensioners, state employees – over the heads of Moscow's educated and restive bourgeoisie.

According to the activists who met him at Sheremetyevo, Snowden had several new minders. Who were they? All of Moscow assumed they were undercover agents from the FSB.

The FSB is Moscow's pre-eminent intelligence agency. It is a prodigiously resourced organisation that operates according to its own secret rules. After the collapse of the Soviet Union the KGB was dissolved. But it didn't disappear. In 1995 most of the KGB's operations were transferred to the new FSB. Nominally it carries out the same functions as the FBI and other western law enforcement agencies – criminal prosecution, investigations into organised crime and counter-terrorism. But its most important job is counter-espionage.

One of the lawyers invited to Snowden's 12 June press conference was Anatoly Kucherena. Afterwards Snowden sent an email to Kucherena and asked for his help. Kucherena agreed. He returned to Sheremetyevo two days later and held a long meeting with Snowden. He explained Russian laws. He also suggested Snowden abandon his other asylum requests. 'I don't know why he picked me,' the lawyer says.

The following day Kucherena visited again, and put together Snowden's application to Russia's migration service for temporary asylum. Suddenly, Kucherena was taking the role of Snowden's public advocate, his channel to the world. 'Right now he wants to stay in Russia. He has options. He has friends and a lot of supporters … I think everything will be OK,' he told reporters.

It's unclear why Snowden reached out to Kucherena. But the defence lawyer had connections in all the right places. A Kremlin loyalist, he publicly supported Putin's 2011 campaign to return as president. Bulky, grey-haired, bonhomous, the 52-year-old Kucherena was used to dealing with celebrities. (He had represented several Russian stars including the Kremlin-friendly film director Nikita Mikhalkov.)

But as well as high-society contacts, Kucherena has other useful connections. He is a member of the FSB's 'public chamber', a body Putin created in 2006. The council's mission is nebulous, given that it involves a spy agency: it is to 'develop a relationship' between the security service and the public. The FSB's then director Nikolai Patrushev approved Kucherena's job; he is one of fifteen members. Fellow lawyers say he is not an FSB agent as such. Rather, they suggest, he is a 'person of the system'.

Few, then, believe Kucherena is an independent player. He was one of very few people allowed to visit Snowden. During his trips to the airport he brought gifts. They included a Lonely Planet guide to Russia, and a guide to Moscow. The lawyer also selected several classics 'to help Snowden understand the mentality of the Russian people': Fyodor Dostoyevsky's *Crime and Punishment*, a collection of stories by Anton Chekhov, and writings by the historian Nikolai Karamzin. Snowden quickly polished off *Crime and Punishment*. After reading selections from Karamzin, a 19th-century writer who penned the first comprehensive history of the Russian state, he asked for the author's complete works. Kucherena also gave him a book on the Cyrillic alphabet to help him learn Russian, and brought a change of clothes.

Snowden was not able to go outside – 'he breathes disgusting air, the air of the airport,' Kucherena said – but remained in good health. Nonetheless, the psychological pressure of the waiting game took its toll. 'It's hard for him, when he's always in a state of expectation,' Kucherena said. 'On the inside, Edward is absolutely independent; he absolutely follows his convictions. As for the reaction, he is convinced and genuinely believes he did it first of all so the Americans and all people would find out they were spying on us.'

As soon as Snowden arrived in Russia, one question began to be asked with increasing intensity: had the Russians got hold of Snowden's NSA documents? On 24 June, the *New York Times* quoted 'two western intelligence experts' who 'worked for major government spy agencies'. Without offering any evidence, the experts said they believed that the Chinese government had managed to drain the contents of the four laptops Snowden brought to Hong Kong.

Snowden categorically denies these media claims, which spread rapidly. He also insists he has not shared any NSA material with Moscow. 'I never gave any information to either government and they never took anything from my laptops,' Snowden told Greenwald in July in two interviews. Greenwald would furiously defend Snowden against the charge.

Snowden was extremely good at digital self-defence. When he was employed by the CIA and NSA one of his jobs was to teach US national security officials and CIA employees how to protect their data in high-threat digital environments. He taught classes at the Defense Intelligence Agency (DIA), which provides top-grade foreign military intelligence to the US Department of Defense. Paradoxically, Snowden now found himself in precisely the kind of hostile environment he had lectured on, surrounded by agents from a foreign intelligence agency.

Snowden corresponded about this with Gordon Humphrey, a former two-term Republican senator from New Hampshire. In a letter to 'Mr Snowden', Humphrey wrote: 'Provided you have not leaked information that would put in harm's way any intelligence agent, I believe you have done the right thing in exposing what I regard as a massive violation of the United States constitution.' (Humphrey also called Snowden a 'courageous whistle-blower' who had unearthed the 'growing arrogance of our government'.)

Snowden's reply is worth quoting in full:

Mr Humphrey

Thank you for your words of support. I only wish more of our lawmakers shared your principles – the actions I've taken would not have been necessary.

The media has distorted my actions and intentions to distract from the substance of constitutional violations and instead focus on personalities. It seems they believe every modern narrative requires a bad guy. Perhaps it does. Perhaps in such times, loving one's country means being hated by its government.

If history proves that be so, I will not shy from that hatred. I will not hesitate to wear those charges of villainy for the rest of my life as a civic duty, allowing those governing few who dared not do so themselves to use me as an excuse to right these wrongs.

My intention, which I outlined when this began, is to inform the public as to that which is done in their name and that which is done against them. I remain committed to that. Though reporters and officials may never believe it, I have not provided any information that would harm our people – agent or not – and I have no intention of doing so.

Further, no intelligence service – not even our own – has the capacity to compromise the secrets I continue to protect. While it has not been reported in the media, one of my specialisations was to teach our people at DIA how to keep such information from being compromised even in the highest-threat counter-intelligence environments (i.e. China).

You may rest easy knowing I cannot be coerced into revealing that information, even under torture.

With my thanks for your service to the nation we both love,

Edward Snowden

The letter set out cardinal Snowdon themes: love of country, civic duty, a desire to protect the constitution. Its tone was high-minded and in parts melodramatic: 'If history proves that to be so, I will not shy ... ' But it left no doubt that Snowden was aware of the peril from hostile foreign intelligence agencies, and that he had taken extreme steps to keep his material safe.

Barton Gellman of the *Washington Post*, one of Snowden's few early interlocutors, says that he believes Snowden had put the data beyond reach. 'I think he rendered himself incapable of opening the archive while he is in Russia,' Gellman told US radio network NPR. He added: 'It isn't that he doesn't have the key any more. It's that there is nothing to open any more. He rendered the encryption information impossible to open while he is in Russia.'

But none of this, of course, meant the Kremlin was uninterested in the contents of Snowden's laptops. The FSB was adept at electronic surveillance. Like its KGB predecessor, its procedures involved bugging, hidden video cameras and entrapment. Unlike the NSA, the FSB also used what might be called 'suspicion-ful' surveillance. With western intelligence agencies, the idea was to monitor a target without him or her ever knowing about it. The FSB, by contrast, also engaged in '*demon-strativnaya slezhka*', demonstrative pursuit.

Using tactics perfected by the 1970s Stasi, East Germany's secret police, the FSB would break into the homes of so-called enemies. Typically these were western diplomats and some foreign journalists. But the FSB also played a leading role in the suppression of internal dissent, and targeted Russians too, including those working for US or British embassies. A team of agents would break into a target's flat. They would leave clues that they had been there – open windows, central heating disconnected, mysterious alarms, phones taken off the hook, sex manuals by the side of the bed.

These methods of psychological intimidation became more pervasive during Putin's second 2004–2008 presidential term, as Kremlin paranoia at the prospect of a pro-reform Orange-style revolution grew. In 2009 the then US ambassador John Beyrle wrote a frank cable to the US State Department, one of several thousand written from Russia and leaked by Chelsea Manning. It read: 'Harassing activity against all embassy personnel has spiked in the past several months to a level not seen in many years. Embassy staff have suffered personally slanderous and falsely prurient attacks in the media. Family members have been the victims of psychologically terrifying assertions that their USG [United States government] employee spouses had met accidental deaths. Home intrusions have become far more common and bold, and activity against our locally engaged staff continues at a record pace. We have no doubt that this activity originates in the FSB.'

This, then, was the FSB. Ironically, the Kremlin's security services also carried out widespread NSA-style surveillance on the Russian population.

Russia's nationwide system of remote interception is called SORM. The KGB developed SORM's technical foundations in the mid-1980s; it has been updated to take account of rapid technological change. SORM-1 captures telephone and mobile phone communications, SORM-2 intercepts internet traffic, and SORM-3 collects data from all communications including content and recordings, and stores them long-term.

The oversight mechanism in the US may have been broken, but in Russia it didn't exist. Snowden's documents showed that the NSA compelled phone operators and internet service providers to give information on their customers. Secret FISA court orders made this process legal. The companies could – and would – contest these orders in court, and argued they should be allowed to reveal more detail of what the government agencies were demanding.

In Russia FSB officers also needed a court order to eavesdrop on a target. Once they had it they didn't need to show the warrant to anybody. Telecoms providers weren't informed. According to Andrei Soldatov, an expert on Russia's security services, the FSB doesn't need to contact the ISP's staff. Instead, the spy agency calls on the special controller at the FSB HQ that is connected by a protected cable directly to the SORM device installed on the ISP network. This system is copied all over the country: in every Russian town there are protected underground cables, which connect the local FSB department with all providers in the region. The result is that the FSB is able to intercept the email traffic of opposition activists and other 'enemies' without oversight.

The wheels of Russian bureaucracy turn slowly. In this case, however, the reasons for delay weren't official inertia. Putin was carefully weighing up the likely fall-out from granting Snowden asylum. On 24 July, Kucherena said Snowden's status was still unresolved. In the mean-time, Snowden would stay at the Moscow airport.

The lawyer indicated that Snowden was now thinking long-term about a life and possibly a job in Russia: that he intended to stay in the country and to 'study Russian culture'. He had apparently picked up a few words of Russian: 'Hi' and 'How are you doing?' Snowden had even tried khatchapuri, Georgian cheese bread.

On 1 August 2013 – 39 days after he flew into Moscow – Snowden strolled out of the airport. Russia had granted him one year's temporary asylum. The state channel Rossiya 24 showed a photo of Snowden's departure. He was grinning, carrying a rucksack and a large holdall, and accompanied by a delighted Harrison. Out of the transit zone at last, he exchanged a few words with Kucherena on the pavement. Snowden climbed into a grey unmarked car. The car drove off. Snowden disappeared.

Kucherena showed reporters a copy of Snowden's new temporary document, which allowed him to cross into Russia. His name, 'SNOWDEN, EDWARD JOSEPH', was printed in Cyrillic capitals. There was a fingerprint and fresh passport photo. Security officials said Snowden had left the transit zone at about 3.30pm local time. Russia had apparently not informed the US beforehand.

Kucherena said he wasn't giving any details about where Snowden was going since he was the 'most wanted man on the planet'. A statement from WikiLeaks said that he and Harrison were headed to a 'secure confidential place'. It quoted Snowden as saying: 'Over the past eight weeks we have seen the Obama administration show no respect for international or domestic law, but in the end the law is winning. I thank the Russian Federation for granting me asylum in accordance with its laws and international obligations.'

US reaction was bitter. The White House announced that Obama was cancelling his bilateral meeting with Putin scheduled to take place during September's G20 summit, which Russia was hosting in St Petersburg. The president's spokesperson Jay Carney said the White House was 'extremely disappointed'. Carney effectively accused Snowden of gifting US secrets to a rival power: 'Simply the possession of that kind of highly sensitive classified information outside of secure areas is both a huge risk and a violation. As we know he's been in Russia now for many weeks. There is a huge risk associated with … removing that information from secure areas. You shouldn't do it, you can't do it, it's wrong.'

It was left to the Republican senator John McCain to twist the knife further. McCain, whom Snowden, writing as TheTrueHOOHA, had admired, was a long-standing critic of the White House's efforts to 'reset' relations with Moscow – an accommodationist policy which in McCain's view merely encouraged Putin's more obnoxious behaviour. McCain tweeted: 'Snowden stays in the land of transparency and human rights. Time to hit that reset button again #Russia.'

Where did Snowden go? Red Square and the Kremlin are an ensemble of high ochre walls and golden orthodox towers. At the end of Red Square are the surrealistic onion domes of St Basil's cathedral.

If you walk up the hill from here past the Metropole Hotel and a statue of Karl Marx you reach a large, forbidding, classically cut building. This is the Lubyanka. Once the headquarters of the KGB, it is now the home of the FSB. Inside, the answer to that question is certainly known. Meanwhile, Russian journalists would speculate Snowden was staying at a presidential sanatorium somewhere near Moscow.

The hacker turned whistleblower had got his asylum. But the longer he stayed out of public view the more it appeared that he was, in some informal way, the FSB's prisoner.

12

DER SHITSTORM!

Stasi headquarters, Normannenstrasse,
East Berlin
October 2013

OBERSTLEUTNANT GRUBITZ: 'Dreyman's good, eh?'
WIESLER: 'I'd have him monitored.'
The Lives of Others, 2004

In the lobby is a statue of a man with a goatee beard.
He is 'Iron' Felix Dzerzhinsky, the head of Lenin's
secret police. On the wall is a map. It depicts what
used to be the German Democratic Republic (GDR),
before its dramatic collapse in 1989. The map is divided
into districts. Major cities are marked in bold: (East)
Berlin – the capital in communist times – Dresden,
Magdeburg, Leipzig.

This forbidding building in Berlin-Lichtenberg was
once the headquarters of the GDR's Ministry for State
Security, an organisation better known by its abbrevia-
tion – the Stasi. The Stasi was modelled on Dzerzhinsky's
Cheka. It was in part a criminal investigation department.
But it was also a secret intelligence agency and a political
secret police. For nearly four decades – from 1950 until
the collapse of the Berlin Wall – the Stasi conducted a
sweeping campaign against the GDR's 'enemies'. These

were, for the most part, internal. The Stasi's declared goal was 'to know everything'.

On the first floor are the offices of the man who directed this campaign, Erich Mielke, the Stasi boss from 1957 to 1989. Seen through modern eyes, his bureau seems modest. There is a comfy chair, 1960s furniture, an old-fashioned dial telephone and an electric type-writer. Next door is a day bed in case Mielke needed a snooze. Built into one of the cabinets is a concealed tape machine. There is a large conference room on the same floor. Whenever Mielke met with his fellow Stasi generals he recorded their conversations.

By the standards of the Soviet bloc, East Germany was a success. In a relatively brief period it managed to establish the most thorough surveillance state in history. The number of Stasi agents grew from 27,000 in 1950 to 91,000 in 1989. Another 180,000 worked as *Inoffizielle Mitarbeiter* (IMs), or unofficial informers. The true figure was probably higher. They spied on friends, work-mates, neighbours and family members. Husbands spied on wives. By the time of the GDR's demise, two in every 13 citizens were informers.

The Stasi's favoured method of keeping a lid on dissent was eavesdropping. There was bugging, wire-tapping, observation. The Stasi monitored 2,800 postal addresses; the agency steamed 90,000 letters a day. This was laborious stuff. Most of the voluminous information gathered was banal, of little intelligence value. The Stasi's version of the Puzzle Palace came crashing down on 15 January 1990, when angry protesters stormed Mielke's compound in Normannenstrasse and ransacked his files.

Given Germany's totalitarian backstory – the Nazis then communists – it was hardly surprising that Snowden's revelations caused outrage. In fact, a newish noun was used to capture German indignation at US spying: *der Shitstorm*. The Anglicism entered the German dictionary *Duden* in July 2013, as the NSA affair blew around the world. *Der Shitstorm* refers to widespread and vociferous outrage expressed on the internet, especially on social media platforms.

The ghosts of the Gestapo helped define the West German state, which existed next door to the Stasi. The cultural memory of state snooping still haunts its unified successor. Many of the most successful recent German films and books, such as *The Lives of Others* – a telling fantasy set in the GDR of 1984 – or Hans Fallada's Nazi-era *Alone in Berlin*, dramatise the traumatic experience of being spied on.

For these reasons, the right to privacy is hardwired into the German constitution. Writing in the *Guardian*, John Lanchester noted that Germany's legal history focused on carving out human rights: 'In Europe and the US, the lines between the citizen and the state are based on an abstract conception of the individual's rights, which is then framed in terms of what the state needs to do.' (Britain's common law, by contrast, is different and focused not on the existence of abstract rights but on remedying concrete 'wrongs'.)

Germans have a visceral dislike of Big Brother-style surveillance; even today there are few CCTV cameras on the streets, unlike in the heavily monitored UK. Google met widespread resistance in 2010 to its Street View project; click yourself through a map of Germany and you'll still find large areas pixelated. Germany published its first post-reunification census only in the summer of 2013 – previous ones in the 1980s were widely boycotted because people felt uncomfortable with giving the state their data.

The days of Adolf and the Erichs – Erich Mielke and Erich Honecker, the GDR's communist boss – were over. Or that's what most Germans thought. The NSA's post-9/11 practices made the German constitution look like something of a bad joke. Snowden's documents, dripped out in 2013, revealed that the NSA spies intensively on Germany, in many respects out-Stasi-ing the Stasi. For 10 years the agency even bugged the phone of German chancellor Angela Merkel, Europe's most powerful politician. Merkel grew up in the GDR and had personal experience of living in a pervasive surveillance state. Of the agency's many poor judgements this was perhaps the crassest: an act of spectacular folly.

The story began when the Hamburg-based news magazine *Der Spiegel* revealed that the NSA routinely harvests the communications of millions of Germans. In an average month it collects around half a billion phone calls, emails and text messages. On a normal day this includes 20 million telephone calls and 10 million internet exchanges. On Christmas Eve 2012 it collected about 13 million phone calls, the magazine reported. Sometimes the figures are higher. On 7 January 2013, the NSA had nearly 60 million communication connections under surveillance. This data was stored at Fort Meade.

In addition, the NSA carried out a sophisticated campaign of state-on-state espionage against foreign diplomatic missions in the US. Bugging the Chinese and the Russians was explicable. They were ideological adversaries. But the NSA also spied on friendly embassies – 38 of them, according to a leaked September 2010 file. Targets included the EU missions and the French, Italian and Greek embassies, as well as several other American allies, including Japan, Mexico, South Korea, India and Turkey.

The agency's spying methods were extraordinary. It placed bugs in electronic communications gear, tapped cables, and collected transmissions using specialised antennae. Under a program codenamed DROPMIRE, the NSA put a bug in the fax machine at the EU's office in Washington. It also targeted the EU's Justus Lipsius building in the Belgian capital Brussels, a venue for top-level summits and ministerial get-togethers.

Germany and France were close US allies and NATO members. Their governments shared values, interests, strategic obligations. German and American soldiers had fought and died together in Afghanistan. As far as the NSA was concerned, however, France and Germany were fair game. Neither country was a member of Five Eyes, the exclusive Anglophone spy club. Instead they were 'third-party foreign partners'. An internal NSA power point says bluntly: 'We can, and often do, target the signals of most third-party foreign partners.' According to BOUNDLESS INFORMANT, Germany is in the same top category in terms of level of US snooping as China, Iraq and Saudi Arabia.

By the time Barack Obama visited Berlin in June 2013 the NSA row was straining US–German ties. In the wake of the revelations, German commentators likened the NSA to the Gestapo. The comparison was overblown. But the disquiet in Germany triggered by Snowden's disclosures was real enough.

Obama and Merkel held a press conference in the chancellor's washing machine-shaped office in Berlin. It was a short but historically resonant walk to the Reichstag, with its transparent Norman Foster dome, and to the Brandenburg Gate. The NSA revelations dominated the agenda.

Obama sought to reassure. He described himself as a critic of his predecessor. He said he came in with a 'healthy scepticism' towards the US intelligence community. After closer inspection, however, he felt its surveillance programs struck the 'appropriate balance' between security and civil rights. The NSA focused 'very narrowly' on terrorism and weapons of mass destruction: 'This is not a situation in which we are rifling through the ordinary emails of German citizens or American citizens or French citizens, or anyone else.' Obama insisted the system was 'narrowly circumscribed'. It had saved lives, including German ones.

Merkel was unconvinced. She acknowledged that intelligence-sharing with the US had helped prevent an Islamist terrorist plot in Germany's Sauerland region in 2007. Nonetheless, Germans were worried: 'People have concerns precisely about there having possibly been some kind of across-the-board gathering of information.'

In an interview with the *Guardian* and other European newspapers, Merkel was scathing. She described the spying scandal as 'extremely serious': 'Using bugs to listen in on friends in our embassies and EU representatives is not on. The cold war is over. There is no doubt whatsoever that the fight against terrorism is essential ... but nor is there any doubt that things have to be kept proportionate.'

Still, it appeared that Merkel was keen to avoid a full-scale confrontation, her legendary pragmatism once more to the fore. Meanwhile, *Der Shitstorm* billowed across Germany's media, in print and online. Generally, the tone was alarmed. The German sage Hans-Magnus Enzensberger referred to the 'transition to a post-democratic society'. Hans-Peter Uhl, a staunch conservative, called the scandal a 'wake-up call'. Even the right-wing *Frankfurter Allgemeine Zeitung* was worried. Publishing the Snowden files was crucial if freedom were 'to exist in the future', it said.

Nevertheless Merkel chose to downplay the topic in the run-up to Germany's September 2013 general election, while the opposition Social Democrats (SPD) tried to big it up. The SPD's strategy backfired when it emerged Gerhard Schröder, the party's former chancellor, had approved a wide-ranging intelligence-sharing agreement with the US back in 2002.

It was left to ordinary Germans to make a noise. Hundreds took to the streets and waved placards with anti-surveillance slogans; others heckled Merkel's election rallies and blew vuvuzelas. In Berlin, one group wearing Snowden masks gathered in the Tiergarten, next to the classical victory column, where presidential hopeful Obama had made a memorable foreign policy speech in 2008. Participants held banners which read 'Nobama', '1984 is Now' and 'Those who sacrifice freedom and security deserve neither'. Down the road, along Unter den Linden, diggers were busy rebuilding a neo-classical palace on the spot where the communist Palace of the Republic once stood, an emblem of communist dictatorship.

By the time of the election most of the earlier indignation had ebbed away. Ronald Pofalla, Merkel's chief of staff, declared the NSA affair 'over'. Merkel breezed to a third straight victory with an increased majority. The new and insurgent Pirate Party – which had done well in regional elections and campaigned on data protection – slumped to 2.2 per cent in the polls. It failed to enter parliament. *Der Spiegel* captured this debacle with the headline 'Calm instead of Shitstorm'.

And then suddenly in October 2013 came a new and extraordinary claim: the NSA had bugged Frau Merkel's phone!

Der Spiegel found Merkel's mobile number on an NSA document provided by Snowden. Her number featured next to the words: 'GE Chancellor Merkel'. The document, S2C32, came from the 'European States branch' of the NSA's Special Collection Service (SCS). It was marked top-secret. Discovery would lead to 'serious damage' in the relations between the US and a 'foreign government', the document warned.

The magazine rang the chancellery. German officials launched an investigation. Their findings were explosive: officials concluded that it was highly likely the chancellor had been the victim of a US eavesdropping operation. German sources said Merkel was livid. Her spokesman Steffen Seibert said that such practices, if proved, were 'completely unacceptable', a 'serious breach'.

Ironically enough, Merkel picked up the phone, called Obama and asked him what the hell was going on. The president's reply was a piece of lawyerly evasion; Obama assured her that the US wasn't bugging her phone and wouldn't do so in the future. Or as White House spokesman Jay Carney put it: 'The president assured the chancellor that the United States is not monitoring and will not monitor the communications of the chancellor.'

It didn't take an Einstein to work out that the White House was saying nothing about what had happened in the past. It emerged the NSA had bugged Merkel's phone since 2002, beginning during George W Bush's first term. Merkel had a personal and an office phone; the agency bugged the personal one, which she used mostly in her capacity as Christian Democrat (CDU) party chief. The eavesdropping continued until a few weeks before Obama's Berlin visit in June 2013. According to Susan Rice, Obama's national security adviser, the president had been in the dark about this.

It was well known the German chancellor was a fan of the 'Handy', as Germans call their mobiles. Indeed, Merkel ruled by Handy. Her mobile phone was her control centre. At a 2008 EU summit in Brussels she had used it to speak to French president Nicolas Sarkozy; the pair had swapped text messages. In 2009 Merkel got a new encrypted smartphone. It seems the NSA found a way round the encryption. But if the president didn't know about the bugging, who did?

This unedifying snooping may have given the US an edge in diplomatic summits and an insight into the thinking of friends and foes. But, as the revelations piled up, sparking diplomatic crises in Europe, Mexico and Brazil, it was reasonable to ask whether such practices were really worth the candle.

Certainly, they were causing enormous damage to the US's global reputation. Obama appeared increasingly isolated on the world stage, and strangely oblivious to the anger from his allies. The man who had charmed the Nobel committee simply by not being President Bush was no longer popular. Europeans didn't like him. 'Barack Obama is not a Nobel peace prize winner. He is a troublemaker,' Robert Rossman wrote in the *Süddeutsche Zeitung*. On its cover, *Stern* magazine called Obama *Der Spitzel* – the informer.

Excruciatingly, Obama's fellow Nobel Laureates turned on him as well. More than 500 of the world's leading authors warned that the scale of mass surveillance revealed by Snowden had undermined democracy and fundamental human rights around the globe. 'In their thoughts and in their personal environments and communications, all humans have the right to remain unobserved and unmolested,' the statement read. Snooping by states and corporations had rendered this basic right 'null and void', it added.

Ouch! For Obama, a president and an intellectual, this must have hurt. The statement's signatories amounted to a who's who from the world of letters, among them five winners of the Nobel Prize for Literature, Günter Grass, Orhan Pamuk, JM Coetzee, Elfriede Jelinek and Tomas Tranströmer – and numerous other grandees of countries from Albania to Zimbabwe.

The NSA affair was turning into a foreign-policy disaster for an administration that already seemed semi-detached. The *Guardian*'s diplomatic editor Julian Borger wrote: 'With each leak, American soft power haemorrhages, and hard power threatens to seep away with it ... Nothing could be more personal for a foreign leader than to find their own mobile phones tapped by a nation they considered an essential friend and ally.'

The storm unleashed by Merkel's bugged mobile reached France the same week, when *Le Monde* published further embarrassing claims of NSA spying. *Der Shitstorm* became *la tempête de merde*. Using material fed by Greenwald, the paper revealed the US was also spying in France on a massive scale. The numbers were astonishing. Over a 30-day period, from 10 December 2012 to 8 January 2013, the NSA intercepted data from 70.3 million French telephone calls.

According to the paper, the NSA carries out around 3 million data intercepts a day in France, with 7 million on 24 December 2012 and 7 January 2013. Between 28 and 31 December no interception took place. Were the NSA's spies having a festive rest? The documents don't say.

There were intriguing clues as to how NSA operations work. Spying against France is listed under a secret codename, US-985D. Germany gets its own espionage codes, US-987LA and US-987LB. The programs include DRTBOX – used for data collection – and WHITEBOX, for recording content. Further clandestine acronyms are used to describe spying on French diplomats in the US. In Italy it was the same picture. The Special Collection Service that spied on Merkel was bugging the Italian leadership too, from embassy 'sites' in Rome and Milan. Italian metadata was ingested by the millions.

The French government's response to this was double-layered. In what by now was a much-repeated ritual, the US ambassador to Paris, Charles Rivkin, was summoned to explain himself. François Hollande, the country's struggling president, called Obama to remonstrate, while his foreign minister Laurent Fabius dubbed the affair 'totally unacceptable'. 'Rules are obviously needed when it comes to new communication technologies,' France's interior minister Manuel Valls said.

But French reaction was milder than in Germany, and more *outrage* than outrage. In June, Hollande had threatened to suspend transatlantic trade talks but overall his response was half-hearted, with his rhetoric aimed at domestic voters. One paper, *Le Parisien*, characterised it as 'gentlemanly'. Everyone knew that France had its own spying operation, and was a leader in industrial snooping. More importantly, Paris was clearly keen to preserve good relations with Washington. That said, French politicians did seem genuinely stunned by the sheer scale of NSA trawling.

By this point the US was giving the same stock response to anxious allies around the world. The White House said that questions raised by France and other disgruntled Europeans were 'legitimate', adding that Washington was reviewing 'the way that we gather intelligence' so that 'we properly balance' security and privacy. On the other hand, Caitlin Hayden, the National Security Council spokesperson, said: 'The US gathers foreign intelligence of the type gathered by all nations.' In other words, 'We spy on you and you spy on us. Get over it, dude.'

Director of national intelligence James Clapper – the man who misled Congress – said *Le Monde* had got its facts wrong. Clapper denied that the NSA *recorded* 70.3 million French phone calls. He gave no further details but seemed to imply that the NSA only scooped up the metadata. He suggested that western intelligence agencies were themselves behind much of this European spying.

In effect, the Europeans were hypocrites. Was Clapper right?

The answer – up to a point – was yes. European intelligence agencies also spied, albeit with fewer resources than the NSA. They worked closely with the US intelligence community, and had done so for decades. Germany's external intelligence body, the BND, for example, shared information with Fort Meade including metadata and had even handed over copies of its two digital spy systems, Mira4 and Veras. Snowden himself flagged these close connections, telling the journalist and internet freedom activist Jacob Appelbaum that the NSA was 'under the same roof' as the Germans, and 'most other western states'.

The extent of this collaboration could be confusing. One BOUNDLESS INFORMANT slide, shared by Greenwald with the Norwegian tabloid *Dagbladet*, suggests the NSA is hoovering up 1.2 million Norwegian telephone calls daily. Norway's military intelligence service, however, said the slide had been misread. It said Norway itself collected the calls from Afghanistan, and passed them on to Fort Meade. This claim, however, is difficult to reconcile with NSA's own PowerPoint, subtitled: 'The mission never sleeps.' It makes clear that collection of metadata under the program is *against* a country rather than from it. There is a separate slide for each country, including Norway and Afghanistan.

The big picture was obvious. And troubling. With or without help, the NSA was sucking in everyone's communications. One document seen by *Le Monde* said that between 8 February and 8 March 2013 the NSA collected 124.8 billion telephone data items and 97.1 billion computer data items. These figures were for the entire world. In an editorial the paper noted that new technology had made possible a 'Big Brother' planet. There were no prizes for guessing which nation played the role of Winston Smith's nemesis.

The NSA's core mission was national security. At least that was the idea. But by the end of 2013 it appeared that the agency's intelligence-gathering operations were about something much simpler – global power.

Merkel, it transpired, wasn't the only foreign luminary whose phone the NSA had hacked. An NSA memo from 2006, published by the *Guardian*, showed it was bugging at least 35 world leaders. The agency had appealed to other 'customer' departments such as the White House, State and the Pentagon to share their 'Rolodexes' so it could add the phone numbers of leading foreign politicians to the NSA's surveillance system. One eager official came up with 200 numbers, including the 35 world leaders. The NSA immediately 'tasked' them for monitoring.

The NSA subsequently targeted other leaders as well, including the president of Brazil, Dilma Rousseff, and her Mexican counterpart Enrique Peña Nieto. On the face of things this tasking was bizarre, since both countries enjoyed positive relations with the US. Rousseff's predecessor, the leftist populist Luiz Inácio Lula da Silva, had annoyed Washington by inviting Iran's then president Mahmoud Ahmadinejad for a visit. After taking office in 2011, however, Rousseff sought to improve ties with the White House. She distanced herself from Tehran and hosted Obama, who had previously cancelled his Brazil trip.

The NSA wasn't interested in these good vibrations; what interested US spies was Rousseff's private thinking. An NSA slide obtained by *Der Spiegel* shows that analysts managed to get access to Rousseff's messages. Fort Meade investigated 'the communication methods and associated selectors of Brazilian president Dilma Rousseff and her key advisers', *Spiegel* reported. It also discovered other 'high-value targets' inside her inner circle.

As well as bugging democratically elected leaders, the NSA was secretly targeting the country's most important company, the state-run oil firm Petrobras. Petrobras is one of the 30 largest businesses in the world. Majority-owned by the state, it is a major source of revenue for the Brazilian government. It is developing several massive new oilfields, which are in a region deep under the Atlantic.

Files given by Greenwald to Brazil's news programme *Fantástico* show the NSA managed to crack Petrobras's virtual private network. It did this using a secret program codenamed BLACKPEARL. Other targets identified by BLACKPEARL include the Swift network for global bank transfers, the French foreign ministry and Google. A separate GCHQ document, titled 'network exploitation', suggests that UK–USA routinely targets the private network traffic of energy companies, financial organisations, airlines and foreign governments.

Unsurprisingly, Rousseff took a dim view of the NSA's snooping, seeing it as an outrageous violation of Brazil's sovereignty. The White House responded to her protests with generalities; it used the same template with the Germans and the French. In September, Rousseff announced she was cancelling her official visit to Washington, due to take place on 23 October. Obama called Rousseff in a vain attempt to get her to change her mind. In the absence of a 'timely investigation ... there aren't conditions for this trip to be made,' the Brazilian government said.

At best, the NSA's activities in Brazil looked distinctly un-fraternal. At worst, they appeared to be a clear-cut example of industrial espionage, and precisely the kind of economic spying the US heartily condemned when the Chinese or the Russians did it. The NSA said it was doing something different, telling the *Washington Post*: 'The department does *not* engage in economic espionage in any domain including cyber.' In a somewhat pained statement, Clapper insisted that the US didn't steal trade secrets from foreign entities and pass them to US companies, so as to give them a competitive advantage.

But Clapper's vague defence of the NSA's goals did little to assuage Rousseff. In a blistering speech to the UN in September, the president said the US's now exposed 'global network of electronic spying' had caused worldwide anger. Not only was this 'meddling' an affront to relations between friendly states, it was a breach of international law, she said. Rousseff stamped on the idea that the NSA was somehow fighting terrorism. 'Brazil knows how to protect itself,' she said.

If anything, the US's southern neighbour Mexico was the subject of even greater intrusion. According to *Der Spiegel*, the NSA mounted a sophisticated spying campaign against President Nieto, and his pro-US predecessor Felipe Calderón. A special NSA division, Tailored Access Operations (TAO), carried out this delicate mission.

In May 2010, TAO managed to hack into the mail server hosting President Calderón's public email account. Other members of Mexico's cabinet used the same domain. The NSA was delighted. It could now read 'diplomatic, economic and leadership communications' which provided 'insight into Mexico's political system and internal stability'. The operation was called FLAT-LIQUID. Two years later the NSA was at it again; it managed to read Peña Nieto's private emails, when he was a presidential candidate, according to Brazil's TV Globo.

The US's main clandestine objective in Mexico was to keep tabs on the country's drug cartels. A secret April 2013 document seen by *Der Spiegel* lists Washington's priorities from 1 (high) to 5 (low). Mexico's drug trade is 1; its leadership, military capabilities and foreign trade relations 3; with counter-espionage at 4. In another August 2009 operation the NSA successfully hacked the email accounts of top officials from Mexico's public security secretariat, yielding useful information on drug gangs and 'diplomatic talking points'.

How is this spying done? The NSA, it appears, monitors Mexico's mobile phone network under an operation called EVENINGEASEL. The NSA's facility in San Antonio, Texas, is involved, together with US listening stations in Mexico City and Brasilia. The agency's resources are formidable. In the early summer of 2012, alarmed that Nieto might shift resources away from fighting the drug cartels, the NSA zoned in on Nieto's mobile phone as well as the phones of 'nine of his close associates'. Software sifted out Nieto's most important contacts; they too were then placed under surveillance, *Der Spiegel* said.

By early 2014 it was clear that the ramifications from Snowden's revelations were far greater than those caused by WikiLeaks. The publication of secret US diplomatic cables from around the world in late 2010 did have consequences. A handful of US ambassadors were forced to depart; others shifted posts; the cables fed into the Arab Spring, crystallising popular resentment against corrupt regimes in Tunisia, Libya and Egypt. Not all of the consequences were negative. Paradoxically, the reputation of the US foreign service went up. American diplomats, broadly speaking, emerged as intelligent, principled and hard-working. A few had genuine literary talent.

With the Snowden files, however, the consequences were more profound. It felt, slowly and not always coherently, as if the world was re-ordering itself – coming to terms with the fact that the US was spying not just on foreign leaders but on entire civilian populations. The question – for European allies, and for rival authoritarian powers – was how to react? The NSA seemed to view close US allies with shared values and history not really as allies at all. Rather, they were 'frenemies', part friend and part enemy.

There were several trends. In the aftermath of the 'Handy crisis', Merkel called for a new framework to regulate spying between partners. In the early stages of the Snowden affair the NSA and BND had been trying to patch things up. Now Merkel and Hollande said they wanted a new transatlantic no-spy accord negotiated by the end of 2013. Britain and other EU states were free to sign up to this code of conduct, which would regulate the behaviour of the security and intelligence services.

In the meantime Merkel was keen to get answers – something the Obama administration had been frugal about. In particular she wanted to know the scope of the NSA's surveillance operations against Germans. There were also lingering questions about her personal situation. Just who had signed off on this? What was the justification?

Documents suggested that the US and its British GCHQ partner were using their embassies abroad as rooftop listening stations to spy on host governments. In Berlin this was especially brazen: the US embassy in Pariser Platz is only a few hundred metres away from the parliament building and Merkel's office. From here, the NSA and CIA can spy on the entire government quarter. *Spiegel* branded the antennae bristling from the top of the embassy '*Das Nest*'.

It was the same story elsewhere. In 2010 the NSA operated 80 embassy spy stations worldwide. Nineteen of them were in European cities, including Paris, Madrid, Rome, Prague and Geneva – where Snowden worked for the CIA. The Americans also had a station in Frankfurt.

Other Five Eyes partners were doing snooping of their own. A Snowden document, published jointly by *Guardian* Australia and the Australian Broadcasting Corporation, revealed that Australia's spy agency had eavesdropped on Indonesia's president Susilo Bambang Yudhoyono, plus his wife, Ani, senior minsters and confidants. The top-secret slide presentation is from Australia's Department of Defence and the Defence Signals Directorate. It dates from November 2009. Another leak, meanwhile, shows that the NSA spied on 25 heads of state attending a 2010

G20 summit in Toronto. The covert operation was carried out from the US embassy in Ottawa. Canada's own spy agency, the Communications Security Establishment Canada (CSEC), was closely involved.

Like his German, Mexican and Brazilian counterparts, Indonesia's president was furious at Australia's un-neighbourly behaviour. He downgraded diplomatic relations with Canberra, and stopped co-operation on issues such as people-smuggling and boat-people. Australia's prime minister Tony Abbott refused to apologise. Nor would he confirm if the snooping had taken place. Instead, the debate in Australia was a depressing echo of the one in Britain, with some politicians and Murdoch-owned newspapers attacking the media that broke the story.

In Europe, displeased politicians were trying to formulate a response to the Snowden revelations. The topic dominated an EU summit in Brussels. Merkel told fellow European leaders the issue at stake wasn't her mobile but what it represented – 'the phones of millions of European citizens'. German politicians called for talks on a trade agreement with the US to be suspended until the White House responded fully. There were calls to take witness evidence from Snowden in Moscow. And to offer him asylum, something Merkel had declined.

The summit put Britain in a tricky position. David Cameron found himself the target of veiled criticism. He declined to say whether GCHQ had been involved in top-level bugging, or if he had seen a readout from Chancellor Merkel's mobile. It is highly likely that any information gleaned by the NSA would have been shared with GCHQ. It's even possible that the eavesdropping was conducted through Menwith Hill, the NSA's European hub in North Yorkshire. Cameron merely defended Britain's 'brave spies'.

European parliamentarians voted for tough new rules on data privacy. Their aim was to stop EU data collected by firms like Google, Yahoo or Microsoft from ending up in the NSA's servers. The proposal, an explicit push-back against PRISM, envisaged restricting the sharing of EU information with non-EU countries. It also proposed the right of EU citizens to erase their digital records from the internet, as well as big fines for firms that broke the rules.

The measure had dropped out of the original proposal made by the European Commission in 2012, following US lobbying. The US argued these new regulations were bad for business. Silicon Valley agreed. But the accusations of NSA spying hardened the mood in the European camp, giving impetus to those who wanted reform. (In the end Britain came to the US's rescue, with Cameron persuading EU allies to postpone any new rules until 2015.)

The EU's response was part of a wider post-Snowden trend to 'de-Americanise' the internet. Already, in 2012, countries including Russia, China and several Middle Eastern states had made moves to bring cyberspace under greater domestic control. Now, the Europeans and Latin Americans were going in the same direction. Brazil and Germany began work on a resolution in the UN's general assembly to place boundaries on NSA spying.

The new buzzword was 'cyber-sovereignty'. The shared goal among the US's disgruntled allies was to make it harder for the NSA to get access to national data. For authoritarian countries such as Russia, there was an added bonus. Greater state control of the internet made it easier to snoop on their own citizens and keep a lid on dissent.

The most vociferous reaction came from Brazil. In October, Rousseff announced plans to build a new undersea cable linking South America with Europe. This would, in theory, shut out the US and make it harder for the NSA to siphon off Brazilian information. The president also mulled over legislation that would force Google and other US tech giants to store the data for Brazilian users on local servers. Thousands of federal workers, meanwhile, were ordered to adopt a form of highly encrypted email. The policy was accelerated after Snowden's disclosures.

Some experts doubted the effectiveness of Brazil's fight-back. They pointed out that, unless Brazil came up with a rival to Google, the NSA would still be able to get hold of its data – if necessary by court order. Either way, Snowden's disclosures seemed to have triggered what Google's CEO Eric Schmidt dubbed the 'Balkanization' of the internet. What was supposed to be a universal tool was in danger of becoming fragmented and 'country-specific', he warned.

In Germany, state-backed Deutsche Telekom floated plans for a new national internet network. Its slogan, 'Email made in Germany', suggested consumers could have the same confidence in their email as they would expect to have in a German dishwasher. Emails between German users would no longer go via US servers. Traffic, mostly, would be kept within the EU's Schengen area (which, helpfully, excluded Britain). The aspiration was to keep out the nosy Anglophone spies.

Perhaps the most unexpected corollary of the Snowden affair was the return of the typewriter. After discovering that the NSA bugged its diplomats, the Indian government turned to old technology. From the summer of 2013 the Indian High Commission in London began using typewriters again. Nothing top secret was stored in electronic form, high commissioner Jaimini Bhagwati told the *Times of India*. Diplomats had taken to strolling outside: 'No highly classified information is discussed inside the embassy building. And it's very tedious to step out into the garden every time something sensitive has to be discussed.'

The Russians had reached the same conclusion. The Kremlin's super-secret Federal Protection Service (FSO) – a branch of the FSB, that some believe is guarding Snowden – put in a large order for typewriters.

The personal computer revolution that transformed communications had crashed to a halt. Those who cared about privacy were reverting to the pre-internet age. Typewriters, handwritten notes and the surreptitious rendezvous were back in fashion. Surely it was only a matter of time before the return of the carrier pigeon.

The NSA's clumsy international spying operation generated much heat and light. One document revealed the agency was even spying on the pornographic viewing habits of six Muslim 'radicalisers', in an attempt to discredit them. None of the radicalisers were actually terrorists. The snooping – on individuals' private browsing activities – was redolent of the kind of unjustified surveillance that led to the original Church committee.

There was a distinct sense of history repeating itself. Some old hands suggested that the US had been engaged in similar activities for decades.

Claus Arndt, a former German deputy responsible for overseeing Germany's security services, saw echoes of previous scandals in the current Snowden one. Arndt told *Der Spiegel* that up until 1968 the US had behaved in West Germany like the occupying power they once had been – bugging whomever they wanted. After that, the Americans had to ask permission from German officials to conduct surveillance. In West Berlin, however, the US behaved 'as if it had just marched in' up until 1990, Arndt said. He recalled how one US major had a row with his girlfriend and gave an order for her phone to be tapped and her letters read. Arndt said he had had no choice but to agree the request.

What about the US's modern methods? Arndt said indiscriminate collection was ineffective, and that evaluating a vast 'data-heap' was virtually impossible. Nevertheless, the Americans had always been 'crazy about information', he said, and were still 'hegemons' in his own country.

He summed up the impact of the Snowden revelations in a single phrase: 'Theoretically we are sovereign. In practice we are not.'

13

THE BROOM CUPBOARD

New York Times office,
Eighth Avenue, New York
Summer to Winter 2013

'You come here often. #nsapickuplines'
JOKE ON TWITTER

The room is a glorified broom cupboard. A few paintings
belonging to the late Arthur Sulzberger, Snr, are stacked
against a wall. One print shows a newspaper man puffing
on a cigar; above him are the words: 'Big Brother is
watching you'. (A note says Arthur will review the paintings 'when he returns'. He died in 2012.) There are strip
lights, a small table, a couple of chairs. No windows. On
a metal shelf, boxes of cream-coloured envelopes. They
belong to Arthur Sulzberger, Jr, – Arthur senior's heir –
and the current publisher of the *New York Times*. On the
corridor outside are photos of the *Times*'s Pulitzer Prize
winners. They are a distinguished bunch. From the staff
cafeteria comes the hum of intelligent chatter.

The offices of the *New York Times* are on Eighth
Avenue, in midtown New York. The paper's executive
stationery cupboard was to play an unlikely role in the
Snowden story. It was from here that the *Guardian*
carried on its reporting of the NSA files, in partnership

with the *Times*, after its London operation was shut down. The cupboard was pokey. It was also extremely secure. Access was highly restricted; there were guards, video cameras and other measures. Its location on US soil meant that the journalists who worked there felt they enjoyed something they didn't have in London: the protection of the US constitution.

In the US, the Obama administration distanced itself from the destruction of the *Guardian*'s hard drives – an act widely condemned by EU organisations, the rest of the world, and the UN's special rapporteur on freedom of expression. Evidently, the White House wasn't delighted by the Snowden revelations. But it understood the first amendment guaranteed press freedom. No such smashing up could happen in America, White House officials said.

Two days after the GCHQ hobbits supervised the destruction, the British government followed up Rusbridger's offer. It asked the *Guardian* to identify the paper's US media partners. The editor told them it was working with the *New York Times* and the non-profit ProPublica.

But it was another three and a half weeks before the UK's foreign office did anything about the intelligence. On 15 August, Philip Barton, Britain's deputy ambassador in the US, finally put in a call to Jill Abramson, the *Times*'s executive editor. He requested a meeting. Abramson had been planning to travel to DC anyway. She had arranged to see James Clapper, the embattled director of national intelligence. Not about Snowden but about the alarming frequency with which the administration was exerting pressure on the *Times*'s reporters, particularly those covering intelligence matters.

'We have decades of experience publishing sensitive stories dealing with national security,' Abramson says. In 1972 the *Times* published the Pentagon Papers, during the Arthur Sulzberger era. 'We're never cavalier. We take them [senior administration officials] seriously. But if a war is being waged against terrorism, people need to know the dimensions of that war.'

The deputy ambassador invited Abramson to drop into the British embassy. Rusbridger advised against doing so, on grounds of spycraft. So Abramson eventually agreed to meet at the ambassador's residence, rather than at the embassy itself, which was technically on UK soil: who knew what British spooks might get up to there? At the meeting, Barton requested the return of the Snowden documents or their destruction. The UK-related leaks made his government uneasy, he said. Abramson neither confirmed nor denied that the *Times* possessed Snowden material. She promised to go away and think about it.

Two days later she called Barton back to say that the *Times* was declining his request. According to Abramson, 'The meeting was a non-event. I never heard from them again.' The British foreign office, it seemed, was merely going through the formal motions. Rusbridger had made clear that the material existed in many jurisdictions. ProPublica in New York had also been working with the *Guardian* for several months, as Number 10 knew. The British made no attempt to approach them.

That summer and autumn, *Guardian* US published several notable scoops. It revealed that the NSA was snooping on 35 world leaders, had subverted encryption, and was working with GCHQ to spy on British citizens – an apparent farewell present to the US from Tony Blair during his final days in office. The NSA also drafted procedures to spy on the British behind GCHQ's back, if they felt US interests required it. This was most ungentlemanly: under the Five Eyes agreement, it was understood that the Brits and the Americans were not supposed to spy on each other. It was unclear whether the NSA had, accidentally or otherwise, eavesdropped on Cameron himself. He wasn't on the list of 35, but some of his interlocutors were.

All these disclosures crossed the planet. Greenwald's video talk had already set viewing records for the *Guardian*'s website. Snowden then performed a live question and answer session on the site, while still in hiding in Hong Kong. Gabriel Dance, the paper's interactive editor in the US, produced a novel interactive guide to mass surveillance, 'The NSA Decoded', which combined conventional text and graphics with video inserts. The Snowden saga demonstrated that modern technology could generate global traction for such a story at a very high speed.

Not least in the US, of course, because there it was having a transforming effect on the political landscape. When the first revelations were published, reaction on Capitol Hill was negative. There was condemnation of both the leaks and Snowden himself. Members of Congress instinctively sided with the security services.

Some independent-minded individuals, though, supported Snowden from the outset. One was Snowden's hero Ron Paul. Paul said the US should be grateful to the young whistleblower for the service he had done in speaking out about the 'injustice' carried out by the government. Paul's son Rand, the Republican senator from Kentucky, echoed this. He described NSA surveillance of Americans as an 'all-out assault on the constitution'.

Figures as diverse as the right-wing commentator Glenn Beck and the liberal Michael Moore praised Snowden, as did the *New Yorker*'s John Cassidy. Al Gore sent a supportive tweet. Elsewhere in the mainstream media there was striking hostility, usually expressed in *ad hominem* terms. For example, Jeffrey Toobin, also at the *New Yorker*, described Snowden as 'a grandiose narcissist who deserves to be in prison'.

In public, most members of Congress delivered a similar anti-Snowden message. But not so much in private. The members of the House and the Senate may not have liked the leaks or even Snowden personally, holed up as he was in Russia. But among some of them there was a niggling concern about the scale of surveillance he had revealed. As the disclosures mounted, so too did unease in Congress.

Just how much disquiet there was on Capitol Hill became apparent in late July, almost two months after the first Snowden stories had appeared. A young and relatively new congressman, Justin Amash, tabled an amendment to the annual Defense Department authorisation bill. His goal seemed extravagant: to put an end to the NSA's bulk collection of Americans' phone records. As Amash put it, he wanted to 'defend the fourth amendment ... and the privacy of each and every American'.

Amash didn't stem from the liberal wing of the Democrats, as one might expect. He was a Republican. A second-generation Arab-American of Palestinian Christian and Syrian Greek Orthodox descent, Amash came from the libertarian wing of the party. He, too, was a supporter of Ron Paul. Paul was the leading advocate of small government and deference to the constitution. He was an opponent of military adventurism and a fierce critic of government intrusion into privacy. Amash donated to Paul's presidential run in 2008 – as did Snowden in 2012.

Nobody had expected Amash's amendment to get very far. However, it made it past the House rules committee. The Obama administration, the intelligence agencies and their allies in Congress then waged an all-out effort to crush it. In a marathon series of closed-door meetings in the Capitol basement General Alexander warned of dire consequences for national security; Clapper said the NSA might lose a vital intelligence tool. The White House took the unusual step of publicly objecting to a proposed amendment to a bill.

On the evening of Wednesday 24 July 2013, the *Guardian*'s Spencer Ackerman was one of only a few reporters who bothered to turn up to watch the vote in the House of Representatives. Suddenly, something was in the air. Since 9/11, the US security state had moved in one direction only: it had got bigger. Now, for the first time, there was a push-back. 'It was electric, the outcome uncertain until the end,' Ackerman says.

In a Congress normally wracked by deep partisan division, two wings of the Republican and Democratic party were coming together. Since the early days of Obama's presidency the feuding parties had been unable to agree on pretty much anything. From outside, Washington looked tribal and dysfunctional; the only topic on which there was bipartisan consensus was Iran. On domestic issues the politicians were fractious and unreconciled.

On this occasion a Democrat, John Conyers, co-sponsored Amash's amendment. The Republican and Democratic leaderships in the House, as well as the White House, bitterly rejected it. Civil liberties Democrats and libertarian Republicans formed a pro-Amash alliance. The divisions in Congress weren't the usual ones. Rather, the divide was Washington insiders versus libertarians. Institutionally, it was between intelligence committees, which oversee secret operations, and the judiciary committees, which oversee fidelity to the law and constitution.

The debate turned into one of the most impassioned for years; speakers for and against the amendment were applauded from the aisles. Leading against Amash was Mike Rogers, a former FBI agent, the chair of the House intelligence committee and a straight-talking NSA defender. 'Have we forgotten what happened on September 11th?' he asked. He mocked an online campaign backing Amash, and said: 'Are we so small we can only look at how many Facebook likes we have?'

Republican Tom Cotton, speaking against the Amash proposal, declared: 'Folks, we are at war.'

But some members opposed to warrantless surveillance invoked comparisons with colonial days. They likened the NSA's programs to the general warrants that allowed British customs officers to search private property. This was about the most emotive charge that could be laid by an American politician. (The lawyer for Snowden's father, Bruce Fein, made the same resonant comparison in a TV interview to those British 'writs of assistance'.)

The debate found strange bedfellows. Ted Poe, a leading member of the Tea Party, united with liberal Zoe Lofgren, something that nearly never happens in Washington. But Nancy Pelosi, the top Democrat, whipped against the Amash amendment. Feelings were high. During the debate Rogers scowled and smacked his rolled-up papers into his empty hand like a truncheon, pacing the rows of desks. Amash was laughing – this was a career-making moment for him – and joking with colleagues.

When it came, the vote was a shock. The amendment was defeated, but only just – by a margin of 217 to 205. Few had anticipated that dissatisfaction in Congress had reached this level. It reflected a polarisation across America. The country was engaged in full-on debate. For some, it was security versus privacy. For others, it was whether Snowden was a whistleblower or a traitor. There were those who thought it mattered and those who didn't.

For the White House, the NSA and the Office of the Director of National Intelligence the vote was a near-death experience. It was clear that something had to change. The absolutist mantra that Snowden was a 'little traitor from Hawaii', as Alexander put it, was no longer enough. The White House began to hint at compromise. Congressional hearings were pencilled in for the autumn; there were calls for legislative change to curb the NSA; work began to frame new bills.

In his press conference before the summer break, on 9 August, Obama made his first substantial remarks on the crisis. He laid out a strategy of greater transparency. But, crucially, he didn't announce any restrictions on the surveillance.

Obama proposed a new panel to review intelligence policies. He also announced greater oversight of FISC, the foreign intelligence surveillance court, and the declassification of the legal rationale that underpinned the collection of phone records under section 215 of the Patriot Act.

The president acknowledged the US had 'significant' spying capabilities. But he said that unlike other, repressive regimes it behaved with restraint, and didn't throw its 'own citizens in prison for what they say online'. His reforms, he said, were designed to ensure Americans could trust US intelligence efforts and have confidence they were 'in line with our interests and our values'.

He had a message, too, for non-Americans, a subspecies under US surveillance laws with no apparent privacy rights whatsoever. 'To others around the world, I want to make clear once again that America is not interested in spying on ordinary people.'

All of this sounded reasonable. But sceptics wondered whether Obama meant reform or 'reform'. In other words, a simulacrum of reform in which the NSA's more egregious bulk surveillance practices would be allowed to carry on unhindered. In late August the new review panel was unveiled. Obama had promised a 'high-level group of outside experts'. These 'independent' experts, it turned out, were virtually all former intelligence officials with close links to the Obama administration.

Civil libertarians sniffed a large rodent. The panel's chair was Michael Morell, Obama's former deputy CIA director; two other members included Richard Clarke, a former counter-terrorism co-ordinator under Clinton and George W Bush, and Peter Swire, Clinton's privacy director. The panel enjoyed the lugubrious name, 'Director of National Intelligence Review Group on Intelligence and Communications Technologies'. In it was a clue: the advisers were working out of the offices of the DNI, headed by James Clapper. The committee's report – to be written by the end of 2013 – went to the White House.

Critics dismissed the panel as pretend transparency, and its members as White House stooges. This may have been unfair. But it was hard to tell, since the panel's meetings were conducted in secrecy. In September it held an inaugural session with civil liberties groups including the ACLU. Another hearing followed with representatives from Facebook and other tech giants, still reeling from the PRISM disclosures.

Silicon Valley lashed out at the White House. Executives from Facebook, Google, Microsoft, Apple and Yahoo

all said the Snowden revelations had been a disaster for
their businesses, with their Europe- and Asia-based operations distinctly harmed. Billions of dollars had been lost.
The administration needed to get a handle on the situation and do something expeditiously, the tech giants said.
This conversation took place before it emerged that the
NSA had hacked into Google and Yahoo's data centres –
in effect, a state cyber-raid on two major US firms.

Throughout the summer the tech companies had
pumped out the same message: that the NSA was coercing
them, legally, to co-operate. Any data they handed over
wasn't done voluntarily, but in response to a court-
approved stick-up. A few days before their appearance at
the review panel, Silicon Valley CEOs had gathered at
the TechCrunch Disrupt Conference in San Francisco.
The mood was mutinous. Yahoo's Marissa Mayer said her
company had to obey FISA court orders, even though it
didn't like them: 'When you lose and don't comply, it's
treason.' Facebook's Mark Zuckerberg put it succinctly.
The 'government blew it,' he said.

During meetings with the review panel, however, the
tech companies didn't say anything about restricting
NSA surveillance. Instead, some attendees suggest, the
companies' chief aim was to tell the customers a good
story about how they were all protecting their data.

The news that the NSA had hacked Google and
Yahoo's data centres, however, proved a game changer.
In their most concerted deed yet, the tech giants united
to demand sweeping changes to US surveillance laws. In
an open letter to Obama and Congress, they called for a
ban on bulk data collection by spy agencies.

They wrote: 'The balance in many countries has tipped too far in favour of the state and away from the rights of the individual – rights that are enshrined in our constitution. This undermines the freedoms we all cherish. It's time for a change.'

The signatories were Apple, Google, Facebook, Microsoft, Yahoo, LinkedIn, Twitter and AOL. They were, naturally, acting in their own economic interests. But the firms also set out a series of five 'reform principles'. Chief among them was that governments – the US, UK and the rest – should end suspicion-less surveillance. Instead of spying on everybody they should focus on 'specific known users for lawful purposes'.

The Snowden revelations, Google added, were in danger of turning the internet into the 'splinternet'. 'The ability of data to flow or be accessed across borders is essential to a robust, 21st-century global economy,' they argued.

In this new post-Snowden world, the NSA faced a full-blown public relations calamity. Since it was founded – appropriately enough in total secrecy – the agency had experienced four distinct epochs. The first was creation. It lasted from 1952 until 1978. The era ended with a series of reports by the Senate committee, led by Frank Church, into unforgivable domestic abuses: the FBI's harassment of Martin Luther King, CIA assassination programs and the watch-listing of 75,000 Americans. The Church committee ushered in wide-ranging reforms. Among them was an FISA Act, which established there must be court approval for foreign intelligence surveillance inside the US.

The NSA's second era from 1978 to 2001 was one of restriction, with the agency operating within Church committee parameters. What followed after 9/11 was a second unleashing: a decade in which the intelligence agencies enjoyed popular support and a boom in White House funding. This came crashing to a stop with Snowden, and the beginning of a new, uncertain fourth era. The NSA was now under the heaviest and most uncomfortable scrutiny since the 1970s.

It was also the target of some rather amusing jokes.

LOVEINT was a pun on SIGINT. This was when NSA employees used the agency's powerful snooping tools to spy on a partner or girlfriend. NSA officials insisted the number of LOVEINT cases was small, that all the individuals involved had been fired or punished, and that most violations were self-reported. Senator Dianne Feinstein, chair of the Senate intelligence committee and the NSA's loyal friend, said LOVEINT only happened once a year.

Still, the story was a gift to Twitter. Within hours, the hashtag '#NSApickuplines' trended. The New York University media pundit Jay Rosen opened with: 'You're free Friday. Would you like to have dinner?'

@sickjew essayed: 'You come here often.'

@Adonish_P continued in the same vein with: 'I know exactly where you have been all my life.'

Perhaps the most imaginative joke came from @benwizner, who riffed off the NSA's bulk-collection habits. He tweeted: 'NSA walks into a bar and says,

"Give me all your drinks. I need to figure out which one
to order."'

For General Alexander this was humiliating stuff. In
his eight years in charge of the world's biggest intelligence agency, Alexander had amassed more power than
any previous spy chief. His imperium included three
mighty domains: the NSA, the Central Security Service
and US Cyber Command – set up by the Department
of Defense in 2009 to spearhead the nation's cyber-war
efforts. Officially, Alexander was known by the acronym
DirNSA. His subordinates came up with other names:
Emperor Alexander, or Alexander the Geek.

On first impression Alexander seems nerdy. He is
diminutive, has a slight lisp, and appears preoccupied with
hyper-technical detail. But he is a polished political operator, his success underpinned by targeted schmoozing.
Before anyone had ever heard the name Snowden, Alexander took influential congressmen on recreational tours
of the NSA. He would show them his command centre
at Fort Meade, a replica of the bridge of the *Starship
Enterprise*. Those who know him say he has a strong
sense of history and his own role in it. It is a place where
Great Men Do Great Deeds Against Evil.

But if Alexander and his senior leadership team had
hoped for White House support in their hour of need,
they were to be badly disappointed. In his August speech
Obama did pay tribute to the 'men and women of our
intelligence community'. He described them as 'patriots'
who love their country and its values. But there was no
presidential visit to Fort Meade, no noisy show of soli-
darity before the cameras.

It was left to the NSA to defend its own surveillance activities, and to make the case that the agency's controversial dragnet programs were actually legal. It did so against a backdrop of rising public antagonism. (One YouTube video in which Alexander features has more than 16,000 'dislikes'.) In the wake of Snowden, attitudes towards the intelligence community were changing for the first time since 9/11. In July a *Washington Post*/ABC poll showed that 39 per cent believed it was more important to preserve privacy than to investigate terrorism; in 2002 the figure was just 18 per cent.

With the surveillance issue now so obviously toxic the Obama administration did something it was good at: it sat on the fence. Inside a defensive Puzzle Palace there was incredulity at this, mixed with peevishness. The agency, an inward-looking institution, was used to getting its own way. Serving officials were unable to speak out. But former NSA staff made no secret of the fact they felt the White House had chucked them under the bus.

'There has been no support for the agency from the president or his staff or senior administration officials, and this has not gone unnoticed by both senior officials and the rank and file at the Fort,' Joel Brenner, the NSA's former inspector general, moaned in the pages of *Foreign Policy*, referring to the view from Fort Meade. The magazine quoted former intelligence officials who said morale inside the NSA was low. The scrutiny following Snowden's leaks, coupled with budget cutbacks, meant that the spies were 'hurting', one said.

An official White House photo captures this administration–agency estrangement. In November

Obama and Vice President Biden met with senior military leaders. The venue was the White House cabinet room. Obama sits in the middle, facing towards the camera, his right hand raised to make a point. At the far end of the oval table is a lonely General Alexander, framed by two oil paintings, in the seating equivalent of Siberia. The president and NSA chief may have chatted later over dinner. But if they did, no photo was ever released.

In large part, the NSA had itself to blame for this lack of a political embrace. Alexander's early response to the Snowden leaks was bungled. He initially claimed that the NSA's controversial domestic bulk-collection programs had stopped an impressive 54 terrorist plots, implying that these took place in the US.

Alexander's deputy Chris Inglis subsequently conceded that only about a dozen of these plots had any connection to the US homeland. Then he said that just one of them might have been disrupted as a result of mass surveillance of Americans. (He was also ambiguous as to whether the plots were real 'plots'; some of the citations he gave had more to do with financial transactions.)

But the biggest damage to the NSA's case on Capitol Hill came not from Alexander but from Clapper, the overall head of the spy agencies. Clapper had given a false answer to Ron Wyden back at the Senate hearing in March. Asked if the NSA collected 'any type of data at all on millions or hundreds of millions of Americans', he gave an unqualified and emphatic reply: 'No, sir. Not wittingly.'

This answer came back and bit him. Lying to Congress would be serious. After the Snowden revelations Clapper sought to finesse his reply, describing it as 'the least untruthful answer' possible in a public hearing. But this didn't work: Wyden's office had given him 24 hours' notice of the question and an opportunity to correct the record shortly afterwards. Clapper changed his account to say he had simply forgotten about collection of domestic phone records. This erroneous testimony sparked calls for his dismissal or resignation. Clapper publicly apologised to the Senate panel – notably not to Wyden specifically – after the outcry over his prevarication spread.

Still, there were loyal supporters who defended the NSA with gusto. One was Feinstein, in charge of the agency's oversight. On the day after Snowden revealed himself as the leaker her response was uncompromising. 'I don't look at this being a whistleblower. I think it's an act of treason,' she said. 'He violated the oath. He violated the law.' Feinstein denied that collecting phone records and internet communications amounted to any kind of surveillance, saying the NSA merely scooped up the kind of information found on a telephone bill.

After news that the agency had hacked Merkel's personal mobile, however, Feinstein did a volte-face. She called for a 'total review' of all intelligence programs, and grumbled that her Senate intelligence committee had not been 'satisfactorily informed'. Spying on friendly nations and prime ministers wasn't on, she said: 'With respect to NSA collection of intelligence on leaders of US allies – including France, Spain, Mexico and Germany – let me state unequivocally: I am totally opposed.'

Feinstein's position was confusing, both for supporters and for critics of the NSA. On the one hand, she seemed to have flipped on an activity that had always been a part of the agency's key mission: the collection of foreign signals intelligence. On the other, she remained an advocate of its extraordinary and novel bulk-collection programs, the very programs that had prompted Snowden to blow the whistle. It was deeply odd.

Despite this wobble Feinsten's loyalty to the agency was never seriously in question. In the autumn of 2013 she proposed a bill to 'reform' the NSA, one of several legislative initiatives. Hers was by far the most sympathetic to the agency. It suggested limited changes while basically maintaining the status quo, and in some cases even expanding its already formidable powers.

This wasn't immediately apparent. On 31 October a dozen reporters gathered outside the closed-door session of the Senate select committee on intelligence on the second floor of the Hart Senate Office building. The suspicion was that Feinstein would deliver a whitewash – but the senator had gone rogue days before, when she criticised the NSA's targeting of allied leaders. Nobody had seen the secret text of her proposed bill.

Half an hour after the session started, Feinstein's press team announced her bill, the FISA Improvements Act, had been approved 11–4. It increased 'transparency of critical intelligence programs' and prohibited the 'bulk collection of records'. Within minutes, however, this news unravelled. On closer examination it turned out the bill stopped the mass collection of content, something the NSA had never done in the first place. The press release was misleading. The reality was that Feinstein's proposal amounted to an entrenchment, and even an expansion, of the NSA's bulk surveillance powers.

Specifically, it codified that the NSA could sieve foreign phone and email communications for information on Americans. Speaking afterwards, Feinstein was unrepentant. She said that the threat from terrorist attacks had never been greater, and added: 'I think there's a huge misunderstanding about this NSA database program and how vital I think it is to protecting this country.'

Other senators, however, came up with tougher proposals to rein in the agency. One was Jim Sensenbrenner, chair of the House judiciary committee. Sensenbrenner was the primary author of the Patriot Act, which he devised to ensure American spooks could fight terrorism in the post-9/11 world. Now he said that the Bush and Obama administrations had misinterpreted his legislation – using it to spy on innocent Americans. It was a classic Dr Frankenstein moment, when the scientist realises his creation isn't the beautiful thing he had wished for, but an out-of-control monster.

By way of corrective, Sensenbrenner introduced a 'USA Freedom Act'. The act, proposed with Senator Patrick Leahy, envisages major reforms. Among them an end to bulk-collection programs and a new 'special advocate' who could represent civil liberties and challenge secret government requests in the FISA court. In essence, Sensenbrenner proposed a return to the targeted model of spying. He asserted: 'Intelligence professionals should pursue actual leads – not dig through haystacks of our private data.'

Meanwhile, Senators Wyden and Udall, the two critics of the NSA in pre-Snowden times, introduced their own draft legislation to stop warrantless snooping on Americans. Wyden suggested that the Senate should have the power to confirm the NSA's new director.

In Kremlinological fashion, the White House had let it be known that it favoured a clear-out at the top. Alexander – a four-star general – confirmed his departure from the NSA in March 2014. (The *Wall Street Journal*, citing a senior US official, said Alexander offered his resignation in June. The White House declined it.) Other officials whispered that it would be a good idea if Clapper moved on at the same time. In theory Clapper was supposed to be conducting the government's intelligence review. In practice he was a dead man walking, fatally damaged by his false statement before Congress.

The NSA used every opportunity to remind Americans of 9/11 and of its role in keeping America safe. The NSA's critics pointed out that Angela Merkel wasn't exactly al-Qaida. In an interview with *Der Spiegel*, Senator John McCain called for a 'wholesale housecleaning' in the US intelligence community, starting from the top. Asked why US spooks had bugged Chancellor Merkel, he offered a concise reply: 'The reason I think they did it is because they could do it.'

New faces, then, but by 2014 it seemed that most of the programs exposed by Snowden would carry on. The White House had promised transparency but seemed unwilling to pull the plug on mass surveillance, and its electronic equivalent of Bentham's panopticon.

According to the *New York Times*, Obama had reluctantly concluded there was no workable alternative to the bulk collection of metadata, including metadata from Americans. The administration hinted that it might reduce the number of years it keeps this information – from five to three. But this was hardly a concession.

The judiciary, however, took a different view. In December 2013, Richard Leon, a federal judge, delivered a massive legal blow to the NSA. He ruled that the agency's bulk collection of Americans' phone records probably violated the US constitution. The program was 'almost Orwellian' in its scope, he said, adding 'The government does not cite a single case in which analysis of the NSA's bulk metadata collection actually stopped an imminent terrorist attack.' Leon said the constitutional challenge – brought by two plaintiffs – was likely to succeed. There was one crumb of comfort for the government: it was allowed to appeal.

Snowden had achieved the debate he had always wanted, and then some. But in terms of legislative reform it was too early to say whether meaningful change would happen.

In the meantime, hostility towards the leaker from the administration was undimmed. Neither Obama nor Secretary of State John Kerry showed any backtracking in their attitude towards a man whom Kerry dubbed a 'traitor to his country'. Presidential pardon? Nope. The espionage charges against him still stood. These were unauthorised communication of government property and wilful communication of classified intelligence to an unauthorised person.

Were he to return from Moscow he would face a total of 30 years in jail. Further charges could be added. The death penalty is also available under a section of the act. Despite changing the course of political history by his extraordinary disclosures, it would be a long time before Snowden saw home again.

14

SHOOT THE MESSENGER

Custody suite, Heathrow airport, London
Sunday 18 August 2013

'Please do not make any reference to
espionage activity. It is vital that MIRANDA
is not aware of the reason for this ports stop.'

MESSAGE FROM BRITISH SECURITY SERVICE, MI5

It was a Sunday morning in the English countryside,
and two middle-aged men were blowing up an inflatable
canoe. One was 59-year-old Alan Rusbridger, the editor
of the *Guardian*. The *New Yorker* magazine describes
him thus: 'He wears square, black-framed glasses and
has a mop of dark hair that sprawls across his head and
over his ears. He could pass for a librarian.' Rusbridger's companion was his friend Henry Porter. Porter, aged
60, writes for *Vanity Fair* and the *Observer*; he publishes
thrillers and campaigns for civil liberties.

The two journalists were acting out a mildly eccentric
boyhood dream – to paddle up the Avon in Warwickshire,
savouring the tranquil sights of the riverbank. They set off
from Stratford-on-Avon, home of the Bard. They hoped
for moorhen, ducks and maybe even a vole. This trip could
have come straight from the pages of *Scoop*, a delicious
novel about the press by the English satirist Evelyn Waugh.

Scoop's journalist hero William Boot pens nature columns for a living. '*Feather-footed through the plashy fen passes the questing vole*' was one of his more famously memorable lines. When Boot is sent to cover a war in far-off Africa he takes with him an inflatable canoe. (Boot was modelled loosely on Bill Deedes, legendary editor of the *Daily Telegraph*, who in 1935 arrived to cover the war in Abyssinia with a quarter of a ton of baggage.)

Rusbridger's canoeing weekend was intended to be a break from the gruelling demands of editorship. It didn't last. Still on the riverbank, he answered his mobile phone. Police had arrested David Miranda, the 28-year-old partner of Glenn Greenwald, at Heathrow airport! They were holding him under schedule 7 of the UK's Terrorism Act! They had confiscated his rucksack!

The terrorism law, enacted in 2000, is aimed at killers. It is designed to allow police to stop possible jihadists or IRA members planning bombings, as they enter Britain. It is a draconian piece of legislation: no 'probable cause' or specific suspicion is needed. The purpose of the stop is a grave one: to assess whether someone may be involved in the 'commission, instigation or preparation of acts of terrorism'.

Miranda wasn't a terrorist. The British authorities knew that perfectly well. He was the partner of a journalist. They suspected he was in fact carrying copies of Edward Snowden's NSA and GCHQ files, which Greenwald was engaged in researching and publishing. Their prime purpose, as they were later to admit, was simply to get hold of the files, and find out how much Greenwald knew.

On 11 August, Miranda had set off from their home in Rio de Janeiro to Berlin, flying via Heathrow. He spent several days with Greenwald's fellow journalist Laura Poitras in the German capital. They discussed film projects. He did some sightseeing. He spent a couple of nights in a hotel. He was now flying home, again via the UK. The British and Americans had him under surveillance – possibly even the same spooks who had bugged Angela Merkel's phone.

The heavily encrypted Snowden files Miranda was carrying formed the basis of Greenwald and Poitras's numerous articles for the *Guardian* and for other international publications, including France's *Le Monde*, Germany's *Der Spiegel*, the *Washington Post* and the *New York Times*. One of the files was an index, compiled by a piece of specialised software, to Greenwald's 58,000 GCHQ documents. There was also further encrypted material. A passphrase to the index was scribbled down and carried in Miranda's wallet.

Rusbridger knew nothing about the details of Miranda's journey. Greenwald had booked Miranda's flight through the paper's New York office, as part of the steady stream of research the paper was financing. It was one of the perils of working with freelancers: the *Guardian* was picking up the bills, but it wasn't always calling the shots.

In moments of crisis Rusbridger radiates calm. The *New Yorker*'s Ken Auletta calls him 'unflappable'. Profiling him, Auletta wrote that Rusbridger's mild-mannered appearance is deceiving; underneath he is steely. One of his tasks as an editor is to apply himself in a calm manner to multi-dimensional problems.

The Snowden story was certainly one of those. On his iPad, Rusbridger carried a sprawling spider diagram linking the diverse issues around the Snowden material. They were legal and editorial. And physical – the need to keep the material safe. There were multiple actors in different jurisdictions; precarious alliances between the Fourth and Fifth Estates. Seemingly the spy agencies were now actively bugging *Guardian* contributors. This made communication difficult.

During his 18 years as *Guardian* editor, Rusbridger had run numerous big stories. He had presided over its transformation from a left-leaning British niche print title to a global digital brand. In 2009 the *Guardian* had uncovered rampant phone hacking in Rupert Murdoch's newspaper empire, and brought about the closure of his tabloid *News of the World* followed by a dramatic series of arrests. In 2010 Rusbridger published the pioneering WikiLeaks documents. But the Snowden story was the biggest of all.

The editor's immediate problem was how to help Miranda. Police had held him at Heathrow airport since 8.05am. Under the Terrorism Act they could detain him for nine hours. Rusbridger phoned Gill Phillips, the *Guardian*'s in-house head of legal. She was in a village in Wiltshire. Too far from Heathrow. Phillips called Bindmans, prominent solicitors specialising in civil liberties. One of them, Gavin Kendall, scrambled to the airport.

In the meantime, Rusbridger and Porter spent the next four hours paddling along the Avon. They were heading downstream from Stratford to Bidford, a village where William Shakespeare is said to have crashed out under a crab-apple tree after a drinking competition. The editor kept his phone in a waterproof bag; every so often he would unzip it, to get updates.

Miranda describes his ordeal in detention as 'intimidating, stressful and deeply frightening'. Police had demanded passports of all passengers as they came off the BA plane; when they reached Miranda, they led him in silence to a custody suite. There, they told him he was being examined under anti-terrorism legislation. 'This made me very afraid,' Miranda says. 'When I heard "terrorism" I was really shocked and told them I had nothing to do with terrorism.'

The two examining officers told him that if he didn't answer their questions he would go to prison. They rifled through his backpack. They seized his possessions – a Samsung laptop, personal photos, DVDs. They also took two highly encrypted thumb drives and a hard drive.

Miranda wanted Greenwald to be phoned, as his lawyer. Police refused on the grounds that Greenwald was not a UK-registered lawyer. They offered him a call to a duty solicitor, which Miranda refused, suspicious of an unknown person. He had no interpreter. Eventually, the police did call Greenwald in Brazil – waking him at 6.30am Rio time, 10.30am in the UK – and told him Miranda was being held as a terrorist. 'I was deeply upset, shocked and worried for him,' Greenwald says.

The two police asked virtually nothing about terrorism. They didn't inquire if Miranda were a member of a terrorist group. Miranda says the questions he was asked 'seemed random and unfocused ... They gave me the impression that they were questioning me just to give themselves time to examine the material.'

Documents obtained in the subsequent legal proceedings from MI5, the British security service, explain this lack of curiosity. MI5 and the NSA decided several days earlier to have Miranda stopped at Heathrow and his documents seized. They knew for certain he was carrying the data – either through intercepts or an informant – and were desperate to find out how much Snowden had leaked. For the spies, it was an extraordinarily lucky opportunity. But they seem to have been anxious not to let Miranda and his friends realise they had been betrayed.

On 15 August – three days before the stop – MI5 contacted the Metropolitan Police's counter-terrorism command, SO15. The agency requested detective super-intendent James Stokley to have Miranda grabbed. The agency filled in what is known as a 'ports circulation sheet' (PCS) with the official request. In a box which asked the author to confirm that possible terrorism was involved, MI5 wrote: 'Not applicable.'

Unfortunately, the police had only one power to search and seize passengers' baggage without the need to give any sort of a reason. This was schedule 7 of the act. A controversial clause, regularly the subject of complaints that it was being abused, schedule 7 nevertheless had certain technical requirements. It could only be used to assess whether someone was involved in 'acts of terrorism'.

The police pointed out the problem. MI5 redrafted the PCS form. Twice. In its final version MI5 claimed: 'Intelligence indicates that MIRANDA is likely to be involved in espionage activity which has the potential to act against the interests of UK national security ... We assess that MIRANDA is knowingly carrying material, the release of which would endanger people's lives. Additionally the disclosure, or threat of the disclosure, is designed to influence a government, and is made for the purpose of promoting a political or ideological cause. This therefore falls within the definition of terrorism and as such we request that the subject is examined under schedule 7.'

It was an absurd account. It was written to mimic the wording of the language in the act defining 'terrorism'. But of course, the authors knew it was not Miranda's intention to make threats to endanger anyone's life, least of all to achieve some 'ideological objective'. The definition in the act was supposedly aimed at a fanatic who threatened to blow up a plane.

MI5 explained their anxiety: 'Please do not make any reference to espionage activity. It is vital that MIRANDA is not aware of the reason for this ports stop. We would be grateful if this stop could be made to seem as routine as possible, and that it appears that this stop is not at the request of the Security Service.'

The use of schedule 7 against someone who was known not to be a terrorist was a blatant abuse – and an alarming precedent in which a government matched journalism with terrorism. This was the first time the much-criticised section of the act had been used against a journalist carrying source material. Coming on top of the forced destruction of the *Guardian*'s computer on 20 July, it looked like a chilling attack on press freedom.

During its dealings with the *Guardian* over the summer, Downing Street had never once suggested that the newspaper was engaged in terrorism. 'If there had been a real risk of a terrorism-related offence, one would have expected a prompt application for an injunction,' Rusbridger says. Under the UK's 1984 Police and Criminal Evidence Act, journalistic material enjoys protection. MI5 should have got a judge to approve Miranda's detention. Instead it circumvented court procedures by using anti-terror laws.

Miranda was eventually released without charge at 5pm, and encouraged to board a flight – minus his stuff – back to Rio. His lawyer only managed to see him an hour before the nine hours were up. (Only one in 2,000 people stopped under schedule 7 are held for more than six hours. He was one of them.) News of his detention set off an international firestorm. The Brazilian government expressed 'grave concern'. It said the use of schedule 7 in this case was 'without justification'.

Back in Rio, Greenwald met an exhausted Miranda at the airport, with cameras looking on. Greenwald characterised his partner's ordeal as a 'failed attempt at intimidation … This is obviously a rather profound escalation of their [the US and UK's] attacks on the newsgathering process and journalism,' he wrote. He added emotionally, in terms that were perhaps somewhat over the top: 'Even the mafia had ethical rules against targeting the family members of people they feel threatened by.'

The allegation that Greenwald and co were pushing a 'political or ideological cause', in much the same way as al-Qaida, caused civil liberties campaigners to express outrage. If true, this was an alarming threat to democracy, the group Liberty said. In Brussels there was astonishment. The Council of Europe, which polices human rights, wrote to home secretary Theresa May. It asked May to explain how Miranda's treatment was compatible with article 10 of the European convention on human rights, guaranteeing freedom of expression.

A telling commentary came from Lord Falconer, the Labour minister who had helped introduce the Terrorism Act. 'The state has exceeded its powers in this case,' he said. 'I am very clear that this does not apply, either on its terms or in its spirit, to Mr Miranda.'

May, however, was unapologetic. So was Oliver Robbins, the deputy national security adviser who had forced the *Guardian* to bash up its own laptops. Lawyers acting for Miranda challenged his detention in the High Court. In a blistering affidavit, Robbins said the Snowden disclosures had hurt national security. He offered no proof but accused Greenwald of 'very poor information security practice'.

This was ironic: it was the British agency GCHQ that had lost control of sensitive information, not the

Guardian. Robbins made no mention of the UK's dysfunctional intelligence-sharing deal with the NSA, which apparently meant thousands of American officials – and passing private contractors – could read top-secret GCHQ files.

Two days after police scooped up Miranda, Rusbridger reacted by telling the story for the first time of what had happened in the *Guardian*'s basement – the hot, messy work of pulverising hard drives. The paper's Simon Jenkins described the episode as the 'most bizarre act of state censorship of the internet age'; the two GCHQ boffins who supervised the destruction were 'like so many book burners sent by the Spanish inquisition'.

Wherever he went the *Guardian* editor carried a small piece of destroyed computer in his inside pocket, rather as a medieval pilgrim would cherish a saint's bone. 'It's a sort of artefact, a symbol of the role of the state versus the journalist,' he says.

Rusbridger's revelations and the absurdity of the Miranda affair had had a galvanic effect on British politicians. It was as if a jolt of electricity at last stirred a body that had previously been in a state of comfortable slumber. Since the *Guardian* published its first NSA article on 5 June, the story had ignited a debate across the world. In Germany, there was uproar; in the US, Congress was reviewing oversight; in Britain … torpor. Most MPs and newspapers ignored it. A handful of Conservatives batted the news away with the phrase 'spies' spy'. Downing Street said: nothing to see here.

Why this silence? There was one immediate explanation. When the Snowden revelations began, the secretary of Britain's unique DA notice organisation, retired Air Vice-Marshal Andrew Vallance, secretly circulated a letter among the BBC and the newspapers, on 7 June 2013, reminding them to be mindful of national security issues. He was issuing the notice on GCHQ's behalf.

His 'Private and Confidential' letter said: 'There have been a number of articles recently in connection with some of the ways in which the UK intelligence services obtain information from foreign sources ... The intelligence services are concerned that further developments of this same theme may begin to jeopardise both national security and possibly UK personnel.'

The DA notices, a rusty hangover from the cold war, are supposed to be voluntary advice; and they are supposed to protect patriotic media organisations from inadvertently publishing sensitive military information. In practice, the notices, with their hint of menace should they be defied, serve as a good way of closing down, or at least dampening, public debate. Those media who reported the Snowden disclosures at all, therefore, initially did so in a subdued fashion, particularly the state-funded BBC. The DA notice kept down the British public temperature.

There were further, cultural, reasons. Britain did not endure the same 20th-century totalitarian nightmare as Germany, or Nazi- or Soviet-occupied countries. The British took freedoms for granted. There hadn't been a revolution since 1688, and that bloodless one didn't really count. Moreover, spies in British popular culture were always the good guys: James Bond in the racy fantasies of Ian Fleming, or the dedicated professionals from the BBC TV drama *Spooks*.

The *Guardian*'s Jonathan Freedland observes that Britain 'has a fundamentally different conception of power to, say, the United States'. It doesn't have a Bill of Rights or a written constitution, or the American idea that 'we the people' are sovereign. Rather, the British system still bears the 'imprint of its origins in monarchy', with power emanating from the top and flowing downwards. Britons remain subjects rather than citizens. Hence their lack of response towards government intrusion.

'It's not the old stiff upper lip of stoicism that you're seeing, but a shrug of resignation and a habit of deference so deeply ingrained we hardly notice it,' Freedland argues.

In Aldous Huxley's dystopian novel *Brave New World*, the citizens are happy to chew *soma*, a drug that confers bliss and forgetfulness. Apart from a few troubled intellectuals – alpha specimens such as Bernhard Marx – the inhabitants of Huxley's London of the future are content playing Obstacle Golf, engaging in promiscuous sex or watching Feeling Pictures. The summer of 2013 in Britain felt a bit like that to those writing about Snowden's disclosures.

As more alarming details emerged of GCHQ's mass capture of data, however, some stirred and opened their eyes. They began to wonder if the system that was supposed to oversee the UK's spy agencies might be in need of reform. The system wasn't working. The former cabinet minister Chris Huhne revealed that the cabinet hadn't been told about TEMPORA, which was tested in 2008 and fully implemented in 2011. Huhne sat in on the National Security Council. But even he and other members were in the dark. So who signed off on it?

Apparently, the spy agencies had briefed no politician other than foreign secretary William Hague about their new, aggressive powers. They effectively misled a parliamentary committee that was busy scrutinising the government's communications data bill. The Home Office proposed it. The bill would have allowed the police, the security services and other national agencies to get access to all British metadata and emails on a massive scale. And the companies would have to keep data available for their trawling for 12 months. The bill was killed off in spring 2013 following a revolt by Nick Clegg, the Liberal Democrat leader and David Cameron's coalition partner.

The political wrangling over the bill – dubbed the snoopers' charter – was largely a sham exercise, it now emerged. Secretly, GCHQ was already doing a version of what the bill envisaged. The agency had kept quiet. A joint memo from MI5, MI6 and GCHQ made no mention of mass data collection. Legislators felt duped.

'I think we would have regarded this as highly, highly relevant,' the Tory peer Lord Blencathra – David Maclean when he was an MP – said. He added: 'Some people were very economical with the actualité.'

With a few exceptions, the opposition Labour party was surprisingly silent on the issue. The Labour leader Ed Miliband said nothing of substance. Labour was in government when GCHQ trialled TEMPORA. Miliband's brother David was foreign secretary between June 2007 and May 2010 under both Tony Blair and Gordon Brown. According to the documents, David Miliband signed the secret certificates in 2009 giving GCHQ legal cover for their bulk fibre-optic cable hacking.

Another watchdog that failed to bark, or even growl, was the Commons intelligence and security committee (ISC), the parliamentary body that oversees the UK's three spy agencies. Its chair, Sir Malcom Rifkind, hadn't heard the name TEMPORA before the Snowden revelations – though he does maintain he knew of GCHQ's broad surveillance powers. He also sniffs at disclosures of cable-tapping, and says this practice has gone on since the second world war.

Rifkind personifies the problem with the ISC: that it is a tame creature of the executive, and not the public. Rifkind is a former Conservative party foreign secretary and defence minister. When in government he received briefs from MI6, the agency he is now supposed to drag to account. The prime minister hand-picked the ISC's members, vetting anyone likely to cause trouble. In the words of Huhne, 'All its MPs are paid-up members of the security establishment.'

From the outside the ISC looks weak, too close to government, and reluctant to grill Britain's securocrats. It has a small team of part-time staff and only nine cross-party members. This lack of clout raises the question of how it can provide credible oversight. (The three agencies have a £2 billion budget and 10,000-plus staff.) Rifkind shrugs this off. He says the ISC got new powers in early 2013, reports to parliament, and can now force the spooks to hand over material. Its budget also went up from £700,000 to £1.3 million, he says.

Arguably, the ISC's biggest weakness is that its members are not ... well, getting any younger. Most are in the twilight of their political careers. Like Dianne Feinstein, the 80-year-old chair of the Senate intelligence committee, Rifkind isn't exactly a child of the internet age. As supposed regulators, can they really decipher highly complex and technical documents? Rusbridger cites the example of a very senior member of the British cabinet who had followed the Snowden stories only hazily and whose main experience of intelligence seemed to date back to the 1970s. 'The trouble with MPs,' this senior politician admitted, 'is most of us don't really understand the internet.'

In the Snowden files, GCHQ types boast of Britain's flexible surveillance laws and comparatively weak regulatory regime – a 'selling point' for the Americans. (The other two advantages, according to a top-secret 2013 GCHQ document, are the UK's 'geography' and 'partnerships'.) The UK's legal regime isn't merely open to elastic interpretation. It was drafted in an analogue age, well before the explosion in technology and Big Data.

Under the outdated 2000 Regulation of Investigatory Powers Act (RIPA), the only legal control on what GCHQ can do with their vast pool of purloined data is a secret certificate, signed by the foreign secretary of the day. This lists the categories under which GCHQ can run searches of their own database. The NSA's access to the British data, however, seems only limited by a 'gentleman's agreement'. And, as everyone knows, spies are not gentlemen.

In the year 2000, when RIPA was enacted, the massive global shift in telecommunications to a network of submarine fibre-optic cables was just starting to take place: but no ordinary civilian could have envisaged that the obscure RIPA regulations would allow GCHQ to break in to the swirling internet. Buffering, to provide a holding pool for the flowing streams of global data, wasn't even possible until 2008–9. The idea of 'collecting all of the signals all of the time' would have seemed meaningless. Online communication and social media were in their infancy. As the technologies raced ahead, Britain's spying law remained silent – and permissive.

The former director of public prosecutions, Ken Macdonald, says that these 'blinding transformations' have rendered RIPA and other intelligence legislation 'anti-modern'.

As far as the spooks were concerned, however, no changes were wanted. David Cameron, William Hague and other government ministers asserted – somewhat childishly – that Britain had the best oversight regime in the world. They insisted there was nothing to debate. The only thing to talk about was the perfidious behaviour of the *Guardian* which – no concrete examples were ever given – had helped the bad guys.

One senior Whitehall figure called Snowden a 'shit-head'. Dame Stella Rimington, the former head of MI5, branded him and Julian Assange 'self-seeking twerps'. (Dame Stella was at a literary festival, promoting her new career as a writer of spy novels.) Snowden hadn't acted out of patriotic reasons. He was a narcissist, a traitor and quite probably a Chinese agent, the officials fumed. A more subtle critique, expressed by one neo-con, said Snowden had acted from a sense of 'millennial generational entitlement'.

In October 2013, Andrew Parker, MI5's new boss, used his first public appearance to berate the media for publishing Snowden's leaks. He didn't need to mention the *Guardian* by name, but said the disclosures had handed 'the advantage to terrorists … We are facing an international threat and GCHQ provides many of the intelligence leads upon which we rely. It causes enormous damage to make public the reach and limits of GCHQ techniques,' he said. Another unhappy insider claimed 'our targets are going dark'. He argued: 'If you talk about your SIGINT capabilities you don't have any SIGINT capabilities.'

Did these claims stack up?

Nobody was disputing that Britain and the US had plenty of enemies – terrorists, hostile states, organised criminals, rogue nuclear powers and foreign hackers intent on stealing secrets and making mischief. Nor did anybody object to individual targeting: this was what the spy agencies did. The problem was with strategic surveillance, the non-specific ingestion of billions of civilian communications, which Snowden laid bare.

The government's claims of damage were always un-particularised. Without any accompanying detail they were impossible to prove, or disprove.

The novelist John Lanchester – who spent a week trawling through GCHQ's secret files – cast doubt on whether publishing information on broad surveillance powers really helped al-Qaida. He noted that Osama bin Laden's compound in Abbottabad didn't even have a telephone line running into it, let alone email, computers or mobile phones. Clearly the bad guys have known for some time that electronic communications might be intercepted. As Lanchester writes, bin Laden's lack of electronic footprint was itself dodgy: a sign to the spies that Something Was Up.

Nigel Inkster, the former deputy head of MI6, came to a similar conclusion. 'I sense that those most interested in the activities of the NSA and GCHQ have not been told much they didn't already know or could have inferred,' he said.

But for Britain's right-wing newspapers the claims by the security agencies were hallowed fact. And an opportunity to smite the *Guardian*, a paper deeply unpopular on Fleet Street since its revelations of phone hacking. The scandal had brought the prospect of state-backed regulation of the newspaper industry much nearer, something the *Sun*, *Daily Mail* and *Telegraph* bitterly oppose. All ignored the Snowden leaks. It could be charitably argued that it was difficult for rival newspapers without access to the documents to cover the story.

In the wake of Parker's speech, the *Daily Mail* led a furious patriotic assault on the *Guardian*, calling it 'The paper that helps Britain's enemies.' It was, the *Mail* said, guilty of 'lethal irresponsibility'. Journalists were incapable of deciding questions of national security, it added, raising the question of what the *Mail* would have done if it had got hold of the Snowden files. All in all it was a curious abnegation of journalism from a newspaper that in other contexts vigorously asserts the principles of independence and press freedom.

The rest of the world, however, took a different view. Some two dozen respected editors from a range of international titles defended the *Guardian*, and the role of the press in informing the public and holding those in power to account. Some of the titles – the *New York Times*, the *Washington Post*, *Der Spiegel* – had done their own reporting on the Snowden leaks. Others – such as *Haaretz*, the *Hindu*, *El Pais* – hadn't. But all acknowledged that the disclosures had stimulated legitimate debate – over the role of spy organisations and the 'proper perimeters for eavesdropping', as the *Times*'s Jill Abramson put it.

For the Germans there were echoes of the '*Spiegel* affair' of 1963, when the *Spiegel*'s legendary editor Rudolf Augstein was arrested and jailed for publishing defence leaks. It was a key test for West Germany's postwar democracy: Augstein was freed and the Bavarian defence minister who imprisoned him, Franz Josef Strauss, resigned. The smashing up of the *Guardian*'s laptops was front-page news all across Germany.

Siddharth Varadarajan, the editor of the *Hindu*, meanwhile remarked that the details of snooping exposed by newspapers are 'not even remotely related to fighting terrorism'.

He wrote: 'Osama bin Laden did not need Edward Snowden's revelations about PRISM to realise the US was listening to every bit of electronic communication: he had already seceded from the world of telephony and reverted to couriers. But millions of people in the US, UK, Brazil, India and elsewhere, including national leaders, energy companies and others who are being spied upon for base reasons, were unaware of the fact that their privacy was being compromised.'

None of this permeated to Downing Street. The prime minister instead chose to shoot the messenger. He dropped ominous hints that charges could follow if the *Guardian* carried on publishing. In a speech in Brussels, Cameron said that he couldn't afford to take a 'la-di-da, airy-fairy' view of the work of the intelligence services, a dangerous choice of words for an old Etonian. Cameron dodged awkward questions about whether Britain was complicit in the bugging of Angela Merkel's phone.

A previously obscure Tory MP, Julian Smith, suggested the paper had compromised the identities of British agents (it hadn't) and 'stands guilty potentially of treasonous behaviour'. Smith's campaign would have had more credibility were it not for a gaffe of his own. He hosted a visit to parliament by staff from Menwith Hill, the NSA's super-secret facility in North Yorkshire in his constituency. Afterwards, Smith, MP for Skipton and Ripon, posed with intelligence staff outside the Gothic building. Smith put the photo on his website. The identities of NSA and

GCHQ employees were there for all to see. Smith said they had consented to the picture.

The British strategy was to talk tough on security, while ignoring the more embarrassing revelations of GCHQ spying on friends and allies. In November, the affair spilled from parliamentary committee rooms, bowled along the Thames, and reached the neo-Gothic portals of the Royal Courts of Justice. Court 28, next to the cafe, was the venue for a two-day judicial review. Outside fell a fine London drizzle. Inside the courtroom bewigged barristers leafed through their files. One QC had a book titled *Blackstone's Guide to the Anti-terrorism Legislation*; a British flag above a balustraded building adorned its cover.

Lawyers acting for Miranda were challenging the use of schedule 7 powers to detain him over the summer. A coalition of 10 media and free speech organisations supported Miranda. The Brazilian was the claimant; the Home Office and police defendants. Three judges, led by Lord Justice Laws, were hearing the divisional court case.

Matthew Ryder QC set out the facts: Miranda was in transit between Berlin and Rio when counter-terrorism police stopped him at Heathrow. He had been carrying journalistic material. Articles based on this material had revealed previously unknown US–UK government mass surveillance, and had started an 'international debate'. The authorities had abused Miranda's right to freedom of expression. Their actions had been disproportionate, wrongly purposed, and incompatible with counter-terrorism law.

The three judges, however, seemed unimpressed with Ryder's reasoning. Lord Justice Laws interrupted repeatedly. His courteous interventions showed a twinkling intelligence. But it was clear the judge didn't know a great deal about the internet. The three judges were in their mid or late sixties. When Miranda's barrister mentioned the NSA's PRISM program, Laws interjected: 'It means they [the security services] can't read the terrorists' emails!'

Laws also took a dim view of investigative journalism. 'I don't really know what is meant by the term "responsible journalist",' he mused at one point. 'It doesn't make a journalist omniscient in security matters … It's just rhetoric really.'

The other judges, fellow members of the establishment, had little sympathy with Snowden, or his situation. 'There must be a quid pro quo about Snowden sitting in Russia. It's an obvious thought,' Mr Justice Ouseley chipped in.

'Why is Russia allowing Snowden to stay? Snowden is in Russia with encrypted stuff. Does it not cross Snowden's mind that the Russians might want to decrypt it?' Judge Openshaw said.

It looked an uphill struggle to persuade the judges of the key point behind the case. Greenwald put in a statement saying: 'The most serious and problematic aspect of the defendants' response to this claim is their equating of publishing articles based on national security material with acts of terrorism.'

The authorities were having none of this. The Home Office said it had acted in the interests of national security.

The authorities had wanted to know 'where Mr Miranda fitted in the broader Edward Snowden network'. The journalists involved weren't motivated by public interest but were 'advancing a political or ideological cause'.

The day after the review finished – with Laws and co retiring for some time to consider their judgement – the action moved back to Westminster, and to a committee room of parliament. The 2013 James Bond movie *Skyfall* features M – the head of MI6, played by Judi Dench – giving evidence at a public inquiry. A group of MPs from the ISC lob hostile questions at her. (They are fed up because MI6 has lost a hard drive containing the names of undercover agents ...)

Dench's/M's public grilling gets worse. The film's bad guy is a renegade MI6 officer, Raoul Silva, played by Javier Bardem with psychopathic glee. Bardem/Silva bursts into the room, dressed as a policeman. He opens fire. Fortunately James Bond (Daniel Craig) arrives to rescue his boss. The ISC's chairman, Gareth Mallory (the British actor Ralph Fiennes), proves useful in a tight spot. He shoots several bad guys.

The real-life ISC's first public hearing on 7 November was a more sedate affair. Seated around a horse-shoe-shaped table were Sir Malcom Rifkind and nine MPs and peers. There was no Bond villain. Instead, a flunkey in a gold chain opened the door for the committee's star witnesses. The three heads of MI5, MI6 and GCHQ – Andrew Parker, Sir John Sawers and Sir Iain Lobban – sat in a row. Behind them were other officials from Whitehall's twilight world (and a huge bodyguard, no doubt armed with an exploding pen).

Previously the ISC's meetings with UK intelligence chiefs had been held in private. This one was televised live – or almost live. There was a two-minute delay on the TV feed in the unlikely event someone blurted out a secret. Opening the 90-minute session, Sir Malcolm hailed the hearing as a 'significant step forward in the transparency of our intelligence agencies'. He omitted to mention that the chiefs had secretly got the questions in advance. Inevitably journalists went with the same tired intro. The spies were coming out of the shadows!

Anyone who had hoped Lobban and co might shed light on the Snowden revelations was to be disappointed. In broad terms, the service chiefs defended their mission – its legality, appropriateness, targets and methods. For much of the session, it appeared that Snowden didn't exist. Asked how a 'junior clerk' had managed to gain access to GCHQ's secrets, Parker said British agencies had 'stringent security arrangements'.

Rifkind inquired: 'Can we assume that you are having discussions with your American colleagues about the hundreds of thousands of people who appear to have access to your information?'

Parker replied: 'All three of us are involved in those discussions.'

If anyone had been fired over GCHQ's debacle we never found out. Nor was there any explanation of how the NSA allowed the biggest leak in the history of western intelligence to take place.

Rifkind asked another question. It was the equivalent of a friendly tennis player lobbing the ball up in the air so his partner could smash it. 'Why do you think it is necessary to collect information on the majority of the public in order to protect us from the minority of potential evil-doers?'

Lobban replied with his favourite analogy – the haystack. He said: 'We don't use our time listening to the telephone calls or reading the emails of the vast majority.' Instead, GCHQ was engaged in 'detective work'. It needed access to 'an enormous haystack' – the communications on the internet – in 'order to draw out the needles'. The GCHQ boss offered a defence of his staff. They were, he said, patriotic and motivated by finding terrorists and serious criminals.

'If they were asked to snoop, I wouldn't have the workforce. They would leave the building,' Lobban said.

There would be a gradual but inexorable darkening of GCHQ's knowledge of its targets, Lobban added. Over the previous five months potential terrorists had chatted on an almost daily basis about how to adapt their methods of communication, he said. (Clearly, though, GCHQ could still listen in on them.)

It was left to Sawers, the real M, to attack the evil-doers of the moment: the global media. In a confident and suave performance, Sawers said the Snowden revelations had been 'very damaging … They have put our operations at risk. It is clear our adversaries are rubbing their hands with glee. Al-Qaida is lapping it up.' He offered no details.

Some ISC members did gently press the three chiefs. Lord Butler, the former cabinet secretary, asked if it were credible that legislation passed in 2000 was 'fit for purpose in the modern world', given that the agencies' capabilities had 'developed so hugely' in the meantime. Sawers and Lobban said they were prepared to accept changes to their legal framework, but that it was up to politicians to propose them.

Overall, the hearing was cosy.

An American or European visitor would have been struck by what the committee didn't ask. It barely touched on the substantive issues raised by the Snowden documents, and skated over any serious questioning about mass surveillance, civil liberties and privacy. There were no questions about GCHQ's reported role in tapping British traffic between Google's own data servers. There was nothing on the bugging of Chancellor Merkel's phone, or spying on friendly world leaders. Nothing either on the reliance on corporate telecoms partners who offered help 'well beyond' what they were compelled to do.

The previous week Sir Tim Berners-Lee – the man who invented the internet – had described the UK–USA's secret efforts to weaken internet encryption as 'appalling and foolish'. Nobody asked about this either.

It was left to Rusbridger to point out the obvious to his critics. Snowden – luckily – had entrusted his files to journalists. They had worked conscientiously (in consultation with governments and agencies), disclosing only a small proportion of what he had leaked. It was the media that had, paradoxically, saved the intelligence agencies from a much greater catastrophe.

If governments, officials and spy chiefs wanted to kick newspapers, that was their prerogative. But they should consider what the next leaker might do in the absence of professional journalist outlets. He or she might just dump everything out on the uncensorable worldwide web. 'Be careful what you wish for,' the editor warned.

There was a coda to all this. In early December 2013, the action shifted back to parliament. The home affairs select committee – chaired by a plummy-voiced Labour MP, Keith Vaz – summoned Rusbridger to explain himself. This, in itself, was an odd request: in mature democracies newspaper editors didn't usually have to account for editorial decision-making before legislators; that was, after all, what freedom of the press meant.

Nonetheless, Vaz suddenly asked Rusbridger: 'Do you love this country?' The chair's intention may have been helpful rather than hostile. But the question had an unmistakably McCarthyite hue about it. Rusbridger replied in the affirmative, saying that he was 'slightly surprised to be asked this question', then adding: 'But yes, we are patriots and one of the things we are patriotic about is the nature of democracy, the nature of a free press.'

The editor gave a calm account of the *Guardian*'s journalistic processes over the previous six months – the responsible way it had handled Snowden's files, its 100-plus interactions with government, and the enormous public-interest dimension that drove publication. The Tory MPs on the committee had another angry agenda, however. It was to toss Rusbridger in jail.

The most bizarre line of questioning came from Conservative MP Michael Ellis. As part of its coverage, the *Guardian* had reported that GCHQ had a branch of the gay pride organisation Stonewall; this information was on Stonewall's website. Evidently furious, Ellis accused Rusbridger of transmitting stolen material and revealing the 'sexual orientation' of persons working at GCHQ.

'You've completely lost me, Mr Ellis. There are gay members of GCHQ. Is that a surprise?' Rusbridger said. Ellis replied: 'It's not amusing, Mr Rusbridger.' He bafflingly accused the paper of betraying further secrets by reporting that GCHQ staff with their families had visited Disneyland Paris.

These contributions from the *Guardian*'s political enemies may have been wild and not a little silly. But the British criminal investigation into the Snowden affair was real enough. Speaking to the same committee, Cressida Dick, assistant commissioner at Scotland Yard, confirmed that detectives were investigating whether 'some people' had broken the law. Specifically section 58a of the Terrorism Act. This said it was an offence to communicate any information about intelligence staff 'likely to be of use to terrorists'. Not just secret info but anything at all: photos, addresses, even the name of their cat.

Dick said: 'We need to establish whether they [some people] have or haven't. That involves a huge amount of scoping of material.'

The journalists who published the Snowden revelations had been involved in the most thrilling story of their careers. It was in the public interest. Now, it seemed, they were suspects.

Epilogue: Exile

Somewhere near Moscow
2014–?

'Even in Siberia there is happiness.'

ANTON CHEKHOV,
In Exile

For nine weeks Edward Snowden was mostly invisible. There was the odd photo – of a young man pushing a shopping trolley across a Moscow street. (Surely a fake? The man looked nothing like him!) Another leaked image was more convincing. It showed Snowden on a tourist boat cruising along the Moscow River. It's summer. He's wearing a cap, and has a beard. In the distance, a bridge and the golden domes of Christ the Saviour cathedral, blown up by Stalin and rebuilt by Yeltsin. Just out of shot are the high walls of the Kremlin.

These leaks to the Russian media were designed to give the impression Snowden was leading a 'normal' life. Given his circumstances, that seemed unlikely. Clues pointed in the opposite direction. The news agency that got the Snowden picture, Lifenews.ru, is known for its ties to Russia's security agencies. Snowden's lawyer, Anatoly Kucherena, meanwhile, said his client was settling in, learning Russian and had got a new job with a large internet firm. But VKontakte, Russia's equivalent of Facebook, and others said this wasn't so.

It was in October that Snowden definitively re-emerged. Four Americans travelled to Moscow to meet him. All were fellow whistleblowers who had spent their careers in US national security and intelligence. They were Thomas Drake, the former NSA executive whose case Snowden had followed, one-time CIA analyst Ray McGovern, Jesselyn Radack, who worked in the Justice Department, and Coleen Rowley, ex-FBI.

It was an unusual trip. Before setting off from Washington DC the four hired a lawyer in case they had problems re-entering the US. They also left behind their electronics. As Radack noted, the US might geolocate their whereabouts from mobile phones or laptops, and thus find out Snowden's hiding place. The authorities could search and confiscate their devices when they flew back.

In Moscow, the four were driven in a van with darkened windows to a secret location. There was Snowden. WikiLeaks released a video. The oil paintings, chandelier and pastel colours in the background suggest an upmarket hotel, of which Moscow has plenty. More probably, though, this was a government guesthouse. The Americans found him well, relaxed, good-humoured and – as McGovern put it afterwards – at peace with himself and his decision to speak out. Snowden joked darkly that he could not have been a Russian spy: he said Russia treats its spies much better than to leave them trapped in the Sheremetyevo transit zone for over a month.

The group presented him with the Sam Adams Award for Integrity in Intelligence. They also delivered a message: that in contrast to official US vitriol, many Americans back home warmly supported him, including inside the intelligence community. According to Radack, Snowden – brilliant and humble, in her words – was concerned not about himself but what might happen to Greenwald, Poitras and the young WikiLeaks activist Sarah Harrison, who had stuck with him since Hong Kong.

Snowden had been following events. Over dinner, he explained why he had done what he did. The relationship between the governing and the governed in America had come 'increasingly into conflict with what we expect as a free and democratic people', he told his guests. He contrasted his fate for telling the truth – exile and vilification – with that of Clapper, who had received no punishment whatsoever.

And he returned to his chief theme: that the programs of NSA mass surveillance he exposed 'don't make us safe'. In his words: 'They hurt our economy. They hurt our country. They limit our ability to speak and think and to live and be creative, to have relationships, to associate freely … There's a far cry between legal programs, legitimate spying, legitimate law enforcement where it's targeted, based on reasonable, individualised suspicion and warranted action, and a sort of dragnet mass surveillance that puts entire populations under a sort of an eye that sees everything, even when it's not needed.'

His father Lon Snowden flew to Moscow at the same time. They had a private reunion.

Three weeks later Snowden had another public visitor. This time it was Hans-Christian Ströbele, a flamboyant Green member of Germany's parliament and radical lawyer, now aged 74. Over in Germany, the Merkel bugging affair had shaken the political class. Ströbele bore an invitation: for Snowden to testify before a parliamentary committee of the Bundestag investigating US spying. Ströbele sat with Snowden and Harrison around a table; there was discussion, moments of laughter, and a group photo.

Snowden gave Ströbele a typed letter to deliver to Frau Merkel and the German parliament. In it he said he felt 'a moral duty to act' after witnessing 'systematic violations of law by my government'. As a result of reporting these concerns, he had faced 'a severe and sustained campaign of persecution'. Snowden also wrote that 'my act of political expression', as he termed it, had led to a heartening response around the world, including 'many new laws' and a growing knowledge for society.

In Snowden's view, the White House's campaign to criminalise his behaviour and pile on felony charges was an injustice. He was prepared to say as much before the US Congress – if it would let him. 'Speaking the truth is not a crime.'

One paragraph caught the eye. Though he didn't say so explicitly, it seemed Snowden hoped to leave Russia at some future point. He signed off: 'I look forward to speaking with you in your country when the situation is resolved and thank you for your efforts in upholding the international laws that protect us.

'With my best regards

'Edward Snowden'

Days later, Harrison said goodbye to Snowden and flew to Berlin. She had been with him in Moscow for four months. On what was said to be legal advice, she declined to return to the UK. The German capital and East Berlin in particular was now a hub for a growing number of Snowden exiles: Poitras, journalist Jacob Appelbaum and Harrison. For anyone with a sense of history this was ironic. Stasiland had become an island of media freedom.

Greenwald, meanwhile, announced his resignation from the *Guardian* to join a new media venture backed by the eBay billionaire Pierre Omidyar.

What were Snowden's prospects of exiting Moscow for a new life in western Europe? Left-leaning politicians, intellectuals and writers called on the German government to grant him asylum. There was even a campaign to rename a Berlin street next to the US embassy 'Snowden Strasse'. (An artist erected a new street sign, and posted the video on Facebook.) But Germany's strategic relationship with America was more important than the fate of one individual, at least in the probable view of Merkel, now chancellor for a third time.

So it was in Moscow that Snowden remained. The lawyer Kucherena gently reminded the world that if he did try and leave he would forfeit his asylum status. He was a guest of the Russian Federation, whether he liked it or not. And in some sense its captive. No one quite knew how long his exile might last. Months? Years? Decades?

A Year On

Golden Apple Hotel,
11 Malaya Dmitrovka Street, Moscow
10 July 2014

'Do we want to live in a controlled society
or do we want to live in a free society?
That's the fundamental question
we're being faced with.'

EDWARD SNOWDEN

The eight-storey building at number 11 Malaya Dmitrovka
Street in Moscow was once home to Anton Chekhov. In
spring 1899 the writer moved in for four months; the
Moscow Art Theatre was staging his play *The Seagull*
nearby. The next year Chekhov returned. He wrote some
of *The Three Sisters* there, in a modestly furnished apartment. Chekhov's home was always crowded. One of his
visitors included Tolstoy.

Over a century later and the building is now a
boutique hotel – the Golden Apple. There are no hints of
Moscow's gloomy communist past: it has gleaming walls,
leather chairs, and a lime-green bar area. Red Square is a
ten-minute walk away. The route passes Pushkin Square,
a green enclave amid the traffic of Tverskaya Street.

It passes the Bolshoi Theatre and skirts along the head-quarters of the Duma, Russia's federal parliament.

At midday on 10 July 2014, a year after the *Guardian* published the first story from the NSA files, Ewen MacAskill and Alan Rusbridger were in Moscow to meet Edward Snowden at the Golden Apple Hotel. Snowden usually chatted online late into the Moscow night with friends on the US east coast, on three computers. He had always led something of a night-owl existence. Exile and the dramatic events of the previous twelve months hadn't changed that.

MacAskill was keen to see Snowden for various reasons. Journalistically, obviously: it was good to get an interview one year on, and while Rusbridger had been very involved in the story he hadn't actually met the American. But more than that, MacAskill had heard rumours that Snowden was depressed and wanted to check on him – as well as thank him in person for the debate he had started, and for what he had done for the journalists who had worked with him.

Snowden called MacAskill's phone to confirm he was on his way to the hotel. MacAskill chatted to two *Guardian* colleagues while he waited. Then, through the room's open door, the journalist saw a pale figure materi-alise at the end of the corridor. The figure hung back. It was Snowden. 'It was typical of him that he just stayed in the corridor, not pushing into the room and announcing himself,' MacAskill says.

The two hadn't seen each other since Hong Kong. Back then, Snowden had been on the run, somewhat dishevelled. Now he was smartly dressed in black trousers and a grey jacket, his hair tidily cut. 'He was bright-eyed,' MacAskill says.

But if anything Snowden was even thinner than during their previous stress-fuelled encounters. 'Probably three steps away from death,' Snowden said, amused, of his jockey-like appearance. He explained: 'I mean, I don't eat a whole lot. I keep a weird schedule. I used to be very active, but just in the recent period I've had too much work to focus on.'

The pair talked for about 30 minutes – relaxed chit-chat. This conversation was important because it showed, contrary to reports, that Snowden was far from depressed. 'He was alert, engaged, all the nervous tension that had existed in the Mira Hotel was gone,' MacAskill says. He thought Snowden might suggest a change of venue, to throw any would-be pursuers off the trail. Instead, Snowden agreed to do the interview in another suite, where Rusbridger would join them. He also ordered room service: chicken curry and a Pepsi.

In Hong Kong Snowden, then a fugitive, had expected the CIA to come for him at any moment. He had reacted with near hysteria when MacAskill had produced his iPhone, viewing it as tantamount to a microphone for the NSA. Now, he appeared to be taking a more relaxed view of his personal security. When they moved to the new suite, which was upstairs, on this occasion MacAskill took his iPhone with him in a backpack. Halfway through the interview, it started ringing. 'That's an iPhone,' Snowden said. But there were no demands to get rid of it, or questions about why it had been brought into the room. 'I just switched it off and the interview continued,' MacAskill says.

This didn't mean that he thought the Russians and the Americans weren't surveilling him. They were, Snowden said, though not demonstrably. 'I think it's reasonable to assume that I am under surveillance,' he admitted. 'Anyone in my position is subject to some surveillance, but you take the precautions you can to make sure that even if you are under surveillance there's no sensitive information for you to expose.'

The interview at the Golden Apple lasted for seven hours. Most of it was on the record, some off. Snowden gave some details of his life. 'I don't live in absolute secrecy. I live a pretty open life. But at the same time I don't want to be a celebrity,' he said. In fact his Russian lawyer, Anatoly Kucherena, had written a novel called *Time of the Octopus*, which was a thinly fictionalised account of his meetings with Snowden (the book's American hero, Joshua Cold, fights against the BLISM program). Snowden declined to comment on whether he'd read it.

His Russian, he said, was basic – enough to order groceries in a supermarket. Rusbridger asked if Snowden might say a few words; Snowden, laughing, turned the invitation down. 'I think I'm going to avoid that because the last thing I want is for clips of me speaking Russian floating around the internet.' And, yes, he got recognised. 'It's a little awkward at times, because my Russian is not as good as it should be. I'm still learning.' Snowden said he had been belatedly catching up with *The Wire*, reading a memoir by Daniel Ellsberg, and picking his way through Dostoyevsky – *The Brothers Karamazov* was next on his list. He mostly cooked for himself – usually Japanese noodles.

Snowden's enemies had sketched his first year in Russia as one of misery – a descent into booze and unhappiness. Michael Hayden, the former NSA director, predicted that Snowden would be stuck in Moscow for the rest of his life, 'isolated, bored, lonely, depressed … and alcoholic.' But if Snowden were miserable, it didn't show. And he turned down the offer of a beer, saying: 'I actually don't drink.' Of Hayden's gloomy forecast, he added: 'I was like, wow, their intelligence is worse than I thought.'

What about the rare sightings of him? The photo taken on a Moscow boat trip was him ('Right, I didn't look happy in the picture'); the shot of an American pushing a shopping trolley was anyone's guess ('I actually don't know, because it was so far away and it was blurry'). Snowden humorously denied claims he wandered around Moscow in an elaborate disguise. 'Before I go to the grocery store, I make sure to put on, you know, my Groucho Marx glasses and nose and moustache.' The only props in evidence were an ACLU baseball cap and dark glasses – not exactly secret agent stuff.

But some details remained hazy. Snowden wouldn't say where he was living, merely acknowledging that getting home – he'd been dropped off by a driver – involved 'a massive logistics chain'. He paid his own rent and bills. With what money? He had savings from his career in intelligence, he said. He received fees from speaking engagements across the world. He wasn't employed by a Russian company. He was working on a new project to create tools to allow journalists to communicate securely with their sources – an important assignment, given the implications of the NSA spying on investigations.

One of the most significant revelations of the previous year, Snowden believed, was that 'unencrypted communications on the internet are no longer safe'. Journalists, lawyers, doctors, accountants – anyone, in fact, who was obliged to protect the privacy interests of their clients – hadn't fully grasped this fact.

What about his own digital habits? Snowden said he didn't use Google and Skype. Or Dropbox ('They just put Condoleezza Rice on their board!' he exclaimed). Instead, he recommended SpiderOak, a fully encrypted Dropbox alternative.

Snowden felt the world had got some things wrong about him, though he was reluctant to correct the record publicly. He was exasperated at being marked down as a conservative libertarian – he says his views are more centrist. But, again, he wouldn't discuss specifics. Journalists, he felt, had devoted too much time to speculating about his family – his father Lon's visit to Moscow; the absence of a visit from either his mother or his sister. They had misunderstood his relationship with Lindsay Mills, his (ex?) girlfriend, whose silence – she had given no interviews – hinted at loyalty.

Snowden's vagueness about his new life in Russia was understandable. But it fed into an awkward question: was

Snowden a Russian spy – or simply a 'useful idiot' whose extended stay in Moscow was helping an undemocratic regime in a propaganda battle with the west?

In April 2014 Snowden had popped up on a TV phone-in with Putin, an annual event at which Russia's boss answers a series of softball questions from a hand-picked audience on everything from geo-politics to gardening. Snowden asked Putin if Russia conducted sweeping surveillance in the manner of the NSA. Putin's reply was warm. Too warm, perhaps. 'Dear Mr Snowden. You are a former intelligence agent, and in the past I have had something to do with intelligence. So we will talk between ourselves as professionals.'

The president denied that Russia engaged in 'out-of-control surveillance'. Its agencies merely go after terrorists and criminals, he said. But as ever, Putin's answer was half-true. Yes, FSB agents have to get a warrant. But they don't have to show it to anybody. In effect, Russia conducts remote interception, with internet service providers and telecoms companies completely in the dark about what is going on within their own networks.

The episode was a PR catastrophe for Snowden. Michael McFaul, the former US ambassador to Russia, brutally tweeted: 'Why did he [Snowden] ask that silly question of Putin? Why did he agree to do it? Stunt was great for Putin, bad for HR [human rights] in Russia.' Snowden defended himself in a piece the next day for the *Guardian*. He pointed out that the question had been a 'rare opportunity' to lift Russia's taboo on state spying. Putin's answer had been 'evasive', he wrote.

Speaking to Rusbridger in the hotel suite, Snowden tacitly conceded the phone-in had been a mistake. He insisted, however, that he hadn't shared secret files with the Russians, as some of his more lurid critics had claimed. 'I didn't bring any classified material with me to Russia … Even if this is a Gulag state, my fingers are being broken every night and I'm being beaten with chains, there's nothing for them to gain,' he said. He described such fears as 'overblown'.

Reviewing his extraordinary year, Snowden said that he had ended up in Russia 'entirely by accident'. If he were a traitor, he pointed out, he would have flown directly from Hawaii to Moscow. Instead, he'd gone to Hong Kong. 'The purpose of my mission was to get this information to journalists.' Reaching Ecuador 'would have been a bonus'. It hadn't happened, and when the US annulled his passport he was stuck. 'If we have anybody to thank [for this] it's the State Department,' he said dryly.

Snowden dismissed the various internet conspiracy theories about him – that, for example, he had met Russian handlers during a training course in India; or that the FSB had recruited him in Hawaii or back in Geneva. The former theory was 'bullshit' (he had attended a six-day programming course there, he said). 'If the government had the tiniest shred of evidence, not even that [I was an agent], but associating with the Russian government, it would be on the front page of the *New York Times* by lunchtime.'

In fact, by summer 2014 the NSA had reached the same conclusion. Admiral Mike Rogers, the NSA's new head, admitted that Snowden was 'probably not' working for a foreign intelligence agency. Speaking at a conference on cyber-security, he distanced himself from claims by the other Mike Rogers – chair of the House intelligence committee – that Snowden had given secrets to the Russians. 'Could he have? Possibly. Do I believe that's the case? Probably not,' the NSA chief said.

The Snowden of 2013 had been largely invisible. By contrast, 2014 Snowden had emerged under the public gaze. He gave evidence to the Council of Europe. He delivered a video message to a technology festival in Austin, Texas, against the backdrop of a copy of the US constitution. He was selectively available to journalists via Ben Wizner, his New York attorney and the director of the ACLU. There was a notable interview with NBC, his first given to a major US network. (In it, Snowden revealed that he had been outside the NSA building in Fort Meade when the 9/11 attacks happened.)

These appearances were deliberate. The White House had not forgiven Snowden, of course, but the Wizner–Snowden strategy was still to win hearts and minds back home. Snowden's goal – medium-term, long-term – was to create a sympathetic political climate in the US. There was no naivety here: Snowden knew US opinion towards him was bitterly divided, with the security establishment implacably hostile. Growing public support might allow Snowden to fly back at some point.

There were some successes. In January the *New York Times* published an important editorial, which stated that Snowden was a whistleblower who should not have to remain in Russia. It called for the US government to offer him clemency or a plea bargain, observing: 'Mr Snowden deserves better than a life of permanent exile, fear and flight.'

But there were setbacks, too. Relations between Moscow and Washington dramatically worsened. Putin annexed a chunk of Ukraine – Crimea. He also fuelled a separatist uprising in the east of the country and supplied heavy weaponry to pro-Russian rebels. In July these rebels were strongly suspected of shooting down a civilian plane that had set off from Amsterdam – flight MH17 – killing all 298 people on board. Increasingly, Moscow was looking like a terrible place for Snowden to be.

But, for better or worse, Russia was becoming Snowden's home. In August the Kremlin extended his residency permit for a further three years, with the possibility of three more after that. This meant he could remain in Moscow until 2020. Now 31, he would be 37 when the permit expires. In theory, the permit allows him to travel abroad – though the risk of arrest remains.

Kucherena announced the news of the extension at a press conference in Moscow. The same day, the Russian government banned food imports from the EU and US in retaliation for the latest round of western sanctions. Snowden, his lawyer said, had got used to Russian food. 'He won't starve.'

The obstacle to Snowden's return was the US Espionage Act. Under this, Snowden wouldn't be able to make his case before a jury in an open court; the information it got would be constrained. Nor would Snowden be able to argue that his disclosures had served the public interest; his motives for leaking were irrelevant. The act upheld strict liability – there was no whistleblower defence. The likelihood was that he would spend the rest of his life in prison.

But might the US drop the espionage charges, and accuse him of lesser or ordinary crimes? If so, Snowden would probably go home.

For some months, negotiations on this theme had carried on with the US Justice Department and the Department of Defense. In spring 2014 they fizzled out. Perhaps the NSA concluded Snowden had nothing to trade. Rick Ledgett, the NSA's deputy director, intimated that a deal was unlikely. 'As time goes on, the utility for us of having that conversation [with Snowden] becomes less,' he said, adding that it had been 'over a year' since Snowden had had access to the NSA's networks.

And while Europe may have been outraged by NSA spying, it was no more willing than before to offer Snowden asylum. Snowden said he found the EU's attitude 'tremendously surprising'. But despite this lack of progress, Snowden was remarkably sanguine about his situation.

His personal fate, he told the *Guardian*, was unimportant; his mission had been accomplished once he'd handed the NSA files to the journalists in Hong Kong. 'That's why I was so peaceful afterwards, because it didn't matter what happened,' he explained. In the meantime, the reporters involved had been showered in glory – in April the *Guardian* US and the *Washington Post* were awarded the Pulitzer Prize for Public Service; Glenn Greenwald and Laura Poitras were famous. Snowden, by contrast, had been banished. 'I didn't do this seeking reward. I did this because it was the right thing to do,' he insisted.

Snowden appeared to have few regrets. He described the public response to his disclosures as 'encouraging' and 'energising'.

Outside, in central Moscow, the skies were darkening. Snowden ordered a bowl of chocolate and vanilla ice cream and strawberry sorbet. Why had he decided to become a whistleblower? What had driven him? He recounted his disillusionment with government spying. It had happened, he said, 'very gradually'. He'd begun to have doubts about the ethics of what he was doing as he moved from 'merely overseeing' powerful tools such as PRISM and XKeyscore to working as an analyst and 'actively directing their use ... I designated individuals and groups for targeting.'

Slowly, he came to realise that the 'majority of the communications in our databases are not the communications of targets' but the 'deep, intense and intimate communications' of ordinary people. Inevitably, Snowden said, this led to abuse:

'Many of the people searching through the haystacks were young enlisted guys, 18 to 22 years old. They've suddenly been thrust into a period of extraordinary responsibility, where they now have access to all your private records. In the course of their daily work, they stumble across something

that is completely unrelated in any sort of necessary sense – for example an intimate nude photo
of someone in a sexually compromising situation.
But they're extremely attractive. So what do they
do? They turn around in their chair and show a
co-worker. And their co-worker says, "Oh, hey,
that's great. Send it to Bill down the way," and
then Bill sends it to George, George sends it to
Tom, and sooner or later this person's whole life
has been seen by all of these people.'

Snowden said that he had personally witnessed such
incidents. They took place 'probably every two months',
he estimated. Within the NSA, the passing around of
nude photographs was seen as 'sort of the fringe benefits
of surveillance positions'. The abuses were never reported
because the 'auditing of these systems is incredibly weak'.
After all, he added, nobody had even noticed when he'd
walked out of the NSA with tens of thousands of its most
precious secrets.

Snowden said he had frequently raised concerns about
some programs with ten colleagues. (The NSA denies
this.) He'd wanted to know if the NSA's practices broke
the constitution or violated human rights. And why did
NSA intercept more US communications than Russian
ones? His co-workers were sympathetic, he said. They
were not 'moustache-twirling villains', they were 'people
like you and me'. Even so, they counselled him to shut
up, since taking the matter further would inevitably 'end
his career'.

MacAskill asked Snowden about TEMPORA. Snowden said it was true that GCHQ has fewer legal restraints than other western spy agencies, as its internal documents showed. As a consequence, Britain had become a 'testing ground' for new intelligence plat-forms, later rolled out across Five Eyes. One of these was TEMPORA. It was 'the world's largest internet buffer', where 'all of your communications are intercepted without any criminal suspicion,' Snowden said.

In his view, indiscriminate surveillance isn't merely wrong – it is ineffective. It doesn't stop terrorist plots. He cited the 2013 Boston bombings, when two Chechen-Americans, Dzhokhar and Tamerlan Tsarnaev, detonated two bombs near the finish line of the city's marathon. Three people were killed, and more than 260 were wounded, many grievously. The FSB had previously tipped off the FBI that the men were linked to Islamist terror groups, Snowden said. 'We didn't actually fully investigate them. We just made a cursory visit and went back to all of our keyboards looking at everybody's emails and text messages.'

Listening to Snowden speak, his sentences perfectly crafted, MacAskill was struck by how comfortable he had grown in dealing with the media. Snowden described himself as he'd been in Hong Kong as a 'virgin source' who had never met a journalist before. Now he was a global figure, which meant he was some-times constrained in what he said and had to weigh up the possible consequences.

In his anniversary *Guardian* interview Snowden was coming across as sane and rational. Lawyerly, even. This was good. But it was clear Snowden had also acquired something of the skills of a politician, and his audience was US public opinion. His intonation and bearing were those of a statesman, and well beyond his years. 'He's a smart guy. He's much smarter than I realised at the time [in Hong Kong],' MacAskill says.

When asked how he was coping with the demands of professional life, Snowden replied that sometimes he was busy, sometimes not. He wasn't writing a book, but he might do so in the future. His schedule, he said, was unpredictable – dead periods followed by frantic moments where 'everything happens'. 'I really wish the universe divided its resources more equitably,' he remarked.

He may have been stuck in a foreign land, but technological innovations were helping to overcome his isolation. In April 2014 Glasgow University had elected him as its rector, a ceremonial post that would normally require him to take an active part in campus life. As part of his duties Snowden was supposed to conduct rector's surgeries in order to talk to students about their concerns. The student council was considering installing a moving robot on site. 'You've got the keyboard, and you literally drive it like a [remote-controlled] car,' Snowden explained. It was a different experience from a Skype session 'because of the fact that you can move' and talk to people at eye level, he said.

One year after the first NSA stories were published, causing outrage in all corners of the earth – and apathy, too – what exactly had changed?

There were several answers to this. In January 2014 Obama had given his most significant response to the Snowden revelations. It came in the form of a thoughtful speech, crafted to confront the crisis that had engulfed America's most secret agency.

The president mentioned the useful role intelligence had played throughout the ages. He talked of the reconnaissance balloons used during the American civil war to track the size of Confederate armies (they counted the campfires); the US codebreakers who gave insights into Japan's plans in the second world war; the importance of intelligence during the post-1945 stand-off with the Soviet Union.

Then there was the 9/11 – the 'horror' that transformed America's intelligence community. Clues were missed. The agencies were subsequently called upon to do far more 'to identify and target plotters in some of the most remote parts of the world' before these plotters carried out attacks. In the rush to fulfil this new mission the previous US government – Obama didn't actually name George W Bush – had sometimes engaged in practices that contradicted 'core liberties'. Practices such as enhanced interrogation techniques and warrantless wiretapping.

The president said that he himself had called for robust public discussion about security versus liberty, a month before Snowden's leaks. Snowden himself got scant mention. 'Given the fact of an open investigation, I'm not going to dwell on Mr Snowden's actions or his motivations; I will say that our nation's defense depends in part on the fidelity of those entrusted with our nation's secrets," Obama said.

Finally, he got to the point. He announced that the NSA would no longer collect the phone records of millions of Americans. The reform concerned section 215 of the Patriot Act, which allowed bulk collection. The NSA's own database was to cease. In future, the agency would have to go to the phone companies to obtain customer data, pursuant to a judicial order. (The companies don't have a discrete database as such; they merely hold the data.)

This wasn't quite the triumph for which civil liberties campaigners had hoped. But it was still a significant concession. The state keeping private data was different from the state having to go to phone companies and ask for information.

Obama also announced that the US would no longer listen in on the phones of friendly heads of state, unless there were compelling national security grounds to do so. No more bugging of Angela Merkel. The NSA would continue to collect information of a kind that other spy agencies sought – in other words, spying on foreign governments would go on. And the secret FISA court would be reformed. In future, independent advocates would be allowed to address judges in 'significant cases', Obama said.

The president asked Congress to act. But by the time the House passed a reform bill in May – the USA Freedom Act – many of its key provisions had been watered down. It wasn't entirely clear if bulk-data collection had actually been banned. The US government was still able to acquire call records on the basis of a 'reasonable articulable suspicion' of wrongdoing. Not just of a suspect but also his or her friends and acquaintances – and their friends and acquaintances, potentially representing hundreds of thousands of people with a single judicial order.

Worse, the act had apparently been revised in a series of back-room hearings. Intelligence veterans and congressional leaders had made changes. The NSA may have gone through global embarrassment, but the agency had powerful allies on Capitol Hill, willing to dig in against surveillance reform. 'This is not how American democracy is supposed to work,' Zoe Lofgren, the Californian Democrat, said. She had supported the bill, but went on to vote against it.

Technology groups and civil libertarians felt cheated too. In summer 2014 Patrick Leahy, a Vermont Democrat, brought an enhanced version of the bill before the Senate. The *New York Times* hailed Leahy's proposed legislation as a 'significant improvement' on the 'half-hearted measure' passed by the House. Leahy's proposed bill ended bulk collection of US phone records. Significantly, it also imposed new restrictions on how much data the NSA could request. It required the agency to ask for the records of a specific entity or account, rather than a dragnet of an entire area code or city. The Obama administration supported the senator's bill. So did privacy groups.

As the *New York Times* recognised, the NSA's abusive spying programs had 'tarnished the nation's reputation'. But Leahy's bill did nothing to enhance the privacy rights of non-Americans. Indeed, Washington's appetite for global information seemed as big as ever.

In early 2014 the US and Germany had tried to move on from the bugging scandal of Merkel's 'Handy'. But, by summer, a new spying affair destroyed any rapprochement. The BND, Germany's domestic spy agency, discovered that one of its employees, the 31-year-old Markus R, had been selling secret information to the CIA. For two years.

The CIA's operation seemed rather old-fashioned – amateurish, even. According to the German press, Markus R worked as a technical assistant at the BND's headquarters in Pullach, near Munich. He had offered his services by sending an email – using Gmail, apparently – to the US embassy in Berlin. Instead of alerting its German partners, the CIA station decided to recruit him.

Markus R then downloaded secret documents onto USB sticks. He met US agents in the baroque Austrian city of Salzburg. They gave him cash – 25,000 euros in total – and he gave them information. From late 2012, some 218 files were handed over to the Americans against a picturesque Alpine backdrop. The US spies also installed an unusual weather app on his laptop. When you asked for the weather in New York, a cryptography program automatically launched.

What made the case embarrassing for Washington is that some of the filched documents concerned an investigation by the German parliament into US spying. A parliamentary committee was examining the Snowden disclosures of mass surveillance against Germans.

It had considered inviting Snowden to testify in person in Berlin – later cooling on the idea. So the Americans were secretly spying on the committee examining US spying, an extraordinary state of affairs.

Markus R was caught after firing off another email offering his services, this time to the Russian embassy in Berlin. He was arrested in Bavaria, on his way home from meeting his CIA handlers in Austria. Investigators asked him if he'd been in contact with the Russians. His alleged reply stunned them: 'Yes, this is true. But for the last two years I've been passing stuff to the Americans.'

Germany's political class was dumbfounded. Outrage grew when a second American mole was allegedly uncovered, working in the political department of Germany's defence ministry. Merkel told German TV that she regretted the breakdown in trust between Berlin and Washington, and what seemed to be a return to the thinking of the 'Cold War era where everyone is suspicious of everyone'.

This was the worst US–German row since the dark days of 2003, when Gerhard Schröder had refused to support the invasion of Iraq. The Germans expressed their displeasure in crisp terms. They asked the CIA's station chief in Germany to leave the country. He quietly exited on a commercial flight from Frankfurt in July. There were whispers that Germany would now resume its own spying operations against the US for the first time in decades.

Over in Britain, meanwhile, the securocrats were battling to keep GCHQ's spying powers intact. In April

2014 the European Court of Justice – an EU body – declared that some of the existing surveillance measures in the UK were invalid. The court struck out the EU-wide data-retention directive, which required internet service providers to store everyone's data for a year, ruling that this was a breach of fundamental rights. It said the state could ask providers to track the data of bad guys – paedophiles or terrorists, for example – but couldn't ask for everyone's data to be automatically stored.

GCHQ faced a second challenge from human rights groups, including Privacy International, Liberty, Amnesty International and the ACLU. These groups complained that GCHQ may have monitored their communications using TEMPORA – and that the NSA might have passed GCHQ similar information obtained via PRISM, deliberately bypassing UK legal protections.

In early summer 2014 Britain's most secretive court, the Investigatory Powers Tribunal (IPT), heard the case, with a verdict due later in the year. The court's track record wasn't encouraging: over 14 years it had found against the intelligence agencies … well, never. Internet providers from around the world brought complaints before this same body. They suspected that GCHQ had used malicious software to break into their networks – citing the agency's attack, reported by *Der Spiegel*, on the Belgian telecoms group Belgacom.

Another Snowden document published by the *Guardian* seemed to confirm GCHQ's cavalier tactics. It revealed that the UK monitoring agency was intercepting private Yahoo video chats as part of a secret program called Optic Nerve that allowed analysts to collect still images from webcams. The images were recorded every five minutes.

And not just a few images, it turned out – in 2008, for example, 1.8 million were harvested over just six months. In theory, Optic Nerve was used to monitor GCHQ's existing targets, as well as any new ones, using automated facial recognition techniques. In practice, the agency hacked the webcams of millions of users, regardless of whether they were a target or not. These weren't conversations between terrorists. They were 'unselected' chats between ordinary people.

British spies found … a lot of nudity. Between 3 and 11 per cent of all Yahoo webcam imagery involved one or both of the parties showing bits of themselves on camera, sometimes to a large audience. It must have left those watching in Cheltenham squirming. But GCHQ seemed unconcerned about the ethics of peeking into intimate chats. It merely noted that its attempts to screen out 'undesirable' porn weren't entirely successful. And in a briefing note added: 'Users who may feel uncomfortable about such material are advised not to open them.'

With so many legal challenges, you might have thought that in post-Snowden Britain the surveillance state was crumbling. Far from it. After the European Court of Justice ruling there was silence. Then, in July, the Home Office rushed an emergency surveillance bill through parliament. Its name was the Data Retention and Investigatory Powers Bill – or Drip, as its opponents called it. The bill's aim was to force internet service providers to keep data, in effect negating the court's recent ruling. Downing Street, it appeared, wanted no debate or broader public discussion.

The prime minister insisted that Drip did nothing more than confirm existing surveillance powers, and put them beyond legal question. Critics, however, said it did a lot more than that. The government now had new power to impose sanctions on overseas internet and phone companies, should they refuse to comply with a UK interception warrant. Moreover, the bill didn't comply with the European court ruling – or the European convention on human rights. Rusbridger, not a fan, described it as 'a piece of Elastoplast' to dress up the security services' existing practices.

Speaking to Rusbridger and MacAskill in Moscow, Snowden said that it was unusual for a public body to pass emergency laws in circumstances other than total war. 'I mean we don't have bombs falling. We don't have U-boats in the harbour,' he said, adding: 'It defies belief.' For Snowden, Drip was a throwback to similarly regressive legislation passed in haste by the Bush administration – the Protect America Act of 2007. This act had indemnified the telecoms companies that had cooperated with Bush's warrantless wiretapping program.

Head of the Liberal Democrats Nick Clegg and Labour leader of the opposition Ed Miliband both gave Drip their support. Their previous concern for civil liberties had apparently evaporated. Nevertheless, it seemed clear that whichever party won the UK's 2015 general election would have to introduce new surveillance laws.

The situation was a mess. GCHQ's dragnet practice was at odds with European law, and arguably illegal. Oversight wasn't working; the intelligence and security committee was a national joke.

One problem, Snowden noted, was that the people in charge of overseeing the intelligence community were old. Typically, they were experienced and trusted. But they were rarely technically literate. For oversight to work, experts are needed to advise politicians and senior civil servants: 'I mean they [senior figures] are not going to try and understand a Bulgarian manuscript – why are they going to understand a program that's written in a program language that they don't understand anything about?'

For the moment, the spooks still had the upper hand. But one year after Snowden had first fled to Hawaii, something had changed. For 15 years the US–UK intelligence community had had the playing field to itself. It was able to act entirely in secret. Now there was contestation; the need for political debate over surveillance, the need for accountability – these ideas had become culturally entrenched. From now on, spies were going to have to work harder to justify their methods, at home and abroad.

What of Snowden's plans? 'I have a pretty normal life,' he said. 'I would absolutely like to be able to continue to travel as I have in the past. I'd love to be able to visit western Europe again.' Including the UK, which Snowden had visited during his time in the CIA. He said he'd been surprised to discover that the Brits use butter on sandwiches – growing up in the US he was used to mayonnaise.

The interview was drawing to a close. As a parting gift, Rusbridger gave Snowden a fragment of the *Guardian*'s smashed-up hard drive, destroyed exactly a year previously under the gaze of 'Ian' and 'Chris'. It was a memento of the paper's tussles with GCHQ. 'Wow, this is the real deal,' Snowden muttered as he examined the scarred circuit board. And then – still very much a spy – he speculated that the fragment might have a tracking device on it.

When it was time to say goodbye, Snowden wondered if the journalists would even want to shake hands with him – after all, they might regret it later should he turn out to be an undercover Russian agent, as the critics were fervently suggesting. 'Right, exactly, if you guys are running for office, then you'd be in trouble,' he joked.

They posed for photos. They shook hands. Snowden picked up his backpack and slipped out of the room. Then he disappeared back into his twilight life – half in shadow, half in light.

ACKNOWLEDGEMENTS

The author would like to thank:

Spencer Ackerman, Richard Adams, James Ball,
Douglas Birch, Jane Birch, David Blishen,
Julian Borger, Rory Carroll, Sarah Churchwell,
Kate Connolly, Nick Davies, Lindsay Davies,
Martin Dewhirst, Miriam Elder, Peter Finn,
Sheila Fitzsimons, Nora FitzGerald, Kemlin Furley,
Janine Gibson, Glenn Greenwald, Laura Hassan,
Bernhard Haubold, Henning Hoff, Nick Hopkins,
Paul Johnson, Jeff Larson, David Leigh, Paul Lewis,
Ewen MacAskill, Justin McCurry, Stuart Millar,
Sara Montgomery, Richard Norton-Taylor,
Philip Oltermann, Anna Pallai, Gill Phillips,
Laura Poitras, Mark Rice-Oxley, Alan Rusbridger,
Phoebe Taplin and Jon Watts

INDEX

(the initials ES in subentries refer to Edward Snowden)

INDEX

INDEX